BATTLE
CASTLES

BY THE SAME AUTHOR
Battlefield Britain
Death or Victory: The Battle of Quebec and the Birth of Empire
The World's Greatest Twentieth-Century Battlefields

BATTLE CASTLES

500 YEARS OF KNIGHTS & SIEGE WARFARE

DAN SNOW

Harper
Press

To Zia,
There is no castle you cannot take

HarperPress
An imprint of HarperCollinsPublishers
77–85 Fulham Palace Road
Hammersmith, London W6 8JB

Published in Great Britain by HarperPress in 2012

1

Maps: mediahouse
CGI: The Sequence Group/Nicole Hogan

A catalogue record for this book
is available from the British Library

ISBN 978-0-00-745558-4

Typeset in Granjon, Mason Sans and Gill Sans
Printed and bound in China

Note that although the spelling of 'Krak des Chevaliers'
has been adopted for the book, the spelling
'Crac des Chevaliers' is also commonly used.

introduction: the rise and fall of the medieval castle

I grew up in a landscape marked by violence. We all did. I spent my childhood in Britain where, even before the bombs which fell during the Second World War, hilltop after hilltop and every town in between bore the scars of war. The memories of these older wars have long been fading. It has been centuries since hostile armies criss-crossed the English landscape, since villages were torched, and since desperate men, women and children sought refuge behind strong walls. Nevertheless, the country's towns, cities and wider landscape were shaped – are still shaped – by a brutal past.

Family car journeys when I was a boy took us past the jagged outlines of ancient buildings. They were mostly ruins, but even in a dilapidated state, with uneven walls and collapsed towers, they captured the imagination of everyone who saw them, especially children like me. They were castles: a type of fortification so widespread and so iconic that they have come to symbolize an entire period in our history.

This is not only true of England: thousands of castles remain in every corner of Europe, North Africa, the Middle East and beyond. From the mouth of Lough Foyle in the north of Ireland, to the Alborz Mountains of Iran, castles or their ruins still dominate the landscape and our imaginations. Their massive walls have survived the assaults of both the human and natural worlds, from trebuchets to earthquakes. They are a constant reminder to us today of a time when violence, or the threat of it, was the norm.

As an adult I have continued to be enthralled by these massive skeletons, or

EVEN BEFORE THE SECOND WORLD WAR, HILLTOP AFTER HILLTOP AND EVERY TOWN IN BETWEEN BORE THE SCARS OF WAR

ghosts, which stand in our landscape, speaking of very different times. What are they? And what do they tell us? I recently made a television series about some of the greatest surviving castles. I travelled across Europe and the Middle East to walk their battlements, crawl through tunnels, and climb the hills on which they often stand. Built during a period of over two hundred years, from the late twelfth to the early fifteenth centuries, they have helped me to understand how the medieval castle developed during its period of greatest dominance. In different fields of conflict – from the English struggles to subdue the rebellious Welsh to the efforts by Christian kingdoms in Spain to conquer territory held by Muslims; from the Crusades by European knights in the Holy Land to the lesser-known Northern Crusade of the Teutonic Knights in Poland – an arms race took place between the builders of fortifications and the designers of attack weaponry. It oscillated one way then the other, at times evenly poised, until finally it favoured the well-equipped besieging army whose arsenal was too powerful for even the strongest castle. The age of the castle was over; but their influence continued long after in the ways we built. Many of these castles still stand, demanding to be understood.

RIGHT *Maiden Castle in Dorset, England, is one of Europe's biggest Iron Age hill forts*

What, then, is a castle? And how did this type of building come to exist and to play such an important role for centuries? To some extent, of course, castles speak of a universal human desire for security. Like other animals, humans have always sought to protect themselves. Even today we use bricks and mortar, wood, metal and stone to give ourselves some measure of protection from both the elements and other people. The earliest humans used the natural defences of the landscape: caves, mountain passes, rivers and swamps. Nearly 12,000 years ago Neolithic man built a massive stone wall to protect Jericho. Iron Age defensive structures – ramparts and ditches – remain clearly visible, particularly from the air. The Romans built walls, forts and camps right across their vast domain: an attempt to secure themselves against the incursions of barbarian tribes like the Saxons and the Franks.

ABOVE *Hadrian's Wall was built by the Romans across a 70-mile stretch of northern Britain in the second century AD*

TO SOME EXTENT, CASTLES SPEAK OF A UNIVERSAL HUMAN DESIRE FOR SECURITY

In Britain it was the Anglo-Saxons who were the principal successors to the Romans, but they in turn came under pressure from without. Their response to the seafaring, warlike Vikings was to put their faith in fortifications. They built walls round important towns, creating defended settlements called 'Burhs' (Wareham and Wallingford are well-preserved examples).

In France, meanwhile, the Viking onslaught prompted people to build subtly different defences. It was here that a new kind of fortress appeared on the scene: the castle.

The word 'castle' came from the Latin *castellum*, a term which simply meant any kind of fortified building or town. In English the word has come to describe the grand fortified residences of kings and lords. Most people agree that a castle was a combination of a fort, the residence of a lord and a centre of authority. However, in his excellent recent history book, *The English Castle*, John Goodall remarks that, 'a castle is the residence of a lord made imposing through the architectural trappings of fortifications'. This gets round the tricky problem that many buildings that look like massive castles are actually lavish palaces; they look imposing, but are in fact militarily indefensible and not really forts at all.

Castles spread fast through a fragmented, violent Europe. In the 840s, Charles the Bald had just succeeded as King of the West Franks (a kingdom that was to morph roughly into modern France). He and his brothers were at each other's throats as they wrestled with the problem of governing their grandfather Charlemagne's vast legacy, which stretched from the north of modern Spain through France, Germany and Northern Italy. They faced external threats: the spread of Islam in the Iberian Peninsula; the Vikings who raided deep inland, as far as Paris several times in the ninth century. Within, they faced the perpetual aggravation of a restless and independent-minded aristocracy, eager to bolster their position by building. It was in the midst of all this, in 846, that King Charles issued a historic order: 'We will and expressly command that whoever at this time has made castles and fortifications and enclosures without our permission shall have them demolished.'

Charles was referring to strongly-fortified residences of the aristocracy. Initially they were simply strong houses, such as Doue-la-Fontaine in Anjou which was given much thicker walls and an easily defensible entrance on the first floor. In the region which would become the kingdom of England, homes of lords were not designed to withstand a determined onslaught – the main fortifications were the burhs, communal defensive structures built by royal command. In France, by contrast, the local magnates responded to collapsing central authority by taking matters into their own hands. Government came to be exercized by the local lords. They issued coins, collected the taxes, defined and enforced the law. Every local warlord became a king, and kings needed grand fortified residences. Political authority was becoming fragmented and the architecture of the castle was the physical manifestation. The Italian word describing this breakdown of authority is *incastellamento*, explicitly linking the rise of castles with the decline of central control. Castles conferred autonomy, which is exactly why rulers like Charles the Bald, desperate to re-establish royal control, wanted them destroyed.

Ultimately the attempt to destroy them was, of course, in vain. (Often, in the course of my travels round Europe, I mused on the futility of Charles the Bald's command.) Castles were here to stay. Once Charles' vassals had seen the strength of castle walls and felt the independence they gave them, they were loath to give them up. Too many of them had developed a taste for power. To the south-west of Paris, near Tours, the Count of Anjou Fulk III, for instance, built one of the earliest stone towers in Europe: the Château de Langeais. The tower was called a *donjon,* from the Latin *dominium* or lordship. In Spain they would become known as *torre del homenaje*, meaning place of homage. Both terms emphasize that these buildings were the physical demonstration of power.

ABOVE *Neuschwanstein is a nineteenth-century palace in southern Germany with a castle-like appearance, built by King Ludwig II of Bavaria*

In one region of modern France, meanwhile, a further change took place which saw these fortified houses evolve into what we would now recognize as castles. In the north-west corner of the country, a particular group had taken local autonomy to the point of outright independence. The Normans were the descendants of Vikings – Norsemen who had arrived as raiders and stayed as settlers. They were tolerated by the French kings as long as the Normans paid lip service to their royal authority. But while the Normans swore fealty to the Crown, they also built castles.

By the mid-tenth century strange mounds were appearing across France, and particularly in Normandy. Known as 'mottes', meaning turf in Norman French, they were artificial hillocks to bolster defensive structures. They would often be surrounded by a wooden stockade or 'bailey' with animal hides hung on them to combat the effects of fire. On the motte it was customary to find a wooden or even a stone donjon. In the first half of the eleventh century, Normandy became thick with castles. The Duke's palace at Rouen had a mighty donjon, and another twenty-six castles –

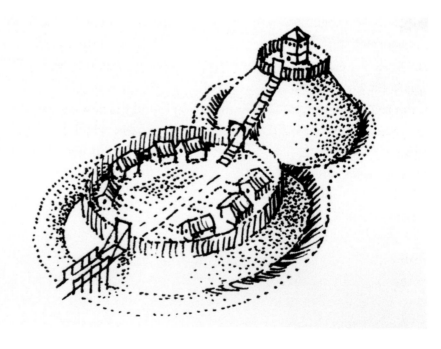

RIGHT *A drawing of a wooden motte-and-bailey castle. This design became commonplace in England with the arrival of the Normans*

mostly built in the first half of the century – sprang up between the towns of Falaise and Caen alone. The process was described by a French chronicler:

> *The richest and noblest men … have a practice, in order to protect themselves from their enemies and … to subdue those weaker, of raising … an earthen mound of the greatest possible height, cutting a wide ditch around it, fortifying its upper edge with square timbers tied together as in a wall, creating towers around it and building inside a house or citadel that dominates the whole structure.*

In Normandy, when Duke Robert the Magnificent died on the way to the Holy Land, his seven-year-old son, William, succeeded him. Chaos ensued. As always when political authority fragmented, castles appeared. Normandy was deeply unstable. Three of William's guardians were killed by usurpers, one in William's bedchamber. A Norman chronicler, William of Jumièges, wrote that at this time, 'many of the Normans, renouncing their fealty to him, raised earthworks in many places and constructed the safest castles'. In his late teens, however, William crushed the rebels at the battle of Val-ès-Dunes in 1047. Another biographer wrote that this was 'a happy battle indeed which in a single day brought about the collapse of so many castles'. William exploited his new power. He issued the so-called *Consuetudines et Justicie* in which he banned the building of castles in his domain without his consent. Importantly, he defined a castle as any building which had a motte and bailey, plus ditching, earth ramparts and palisading.

The Bayeux Tapestry – a 70-metre-long embroidered cloth record of Anglo-Norman relations in the eleventh century, culminating with the Battle of Hastings and the crowning of William the Conqueror in Westminster Abbey – gives useful depictions of several

BELOW A penny struck during the reign of William the Conqueror, King of England (1066–87)

The eleventh-century Bayeux Tapestry tells the story of the Norman Conquest. In this section, the process of layering soil to build a motte is depicted by the different colours in the embroidery

castles, particularly where it portrays William on campaign in Brittany. Three castles are shown: Dol, Rennes and Dinan. All have mottes, and they are strengthened with towers and walls. These defences seem to be made out of wood, since the soldiers are trying to set fire to them. It is clear that by the second half of the eleventh century, castles were becoming a common sight across the French landscape; and in fact they were beginning to spread abroad.

Even before the Norman Conquest, kings of England like Edward the Confessor spent time in Normandy, had a Norman family and Norman advisers. In 1051 an English chronicler wrote that these Norman supporters, granted land by the King, were making themselves unpopular – and one way they did this was by building castles. In Herefordshire, he recorded, these 'foreigners' had built a castle, from which they 'inflicted every possible injury and insult upon the King's men in those parts'. The site of this castle was probably Ewyas Harold, halfway between Hereford and Abergavenny. I have stood here on a spur looking west towards the higher hills of the Welsh border. You would not think it had much significance now. No walls or battlements survive to inspire daydreams of medieval knights; there is only a tell-tale mound or 'motte', and the age-old tussle between goats and undergrowth.

But here at Ewyas Harold the story of the English castle began: for this was probably the site of the first French-style castle built in England. Others quickly followed, and a century later there would be few corners of England without one.

Even at this early stage their purpose and impact was clear. A castle was what you built if the locals really didn't want you there. The snippet of the *Anglo-Saxon Chronicle* is illuminating despite its brevity. Castles allowed lords to behave with impunity. From a secure base they could inflict 'every possible injury and insult', without fear of retaliation. They might look like defensive structures, but castles were not for cowering. They were springboards from which owners were able to dominate the surroundings, and they made the most striking claim possible about lordship in the domain.

When Edward the Confessor died childless in 1066, three men claimed to be his rightful heir. The English magnate and warlord Harold Godwinson seized the throne, and near York he annihilated the army of King Harald Sigurdsson of Norway ('Hardrada', as he was known: 'hard ruler'). Then William, Duke of Normandy, landed on the south coast, and his first act, tellingly, was to build a castle.

He appears to have brought the necessary materials with him from Normandy. In the ruins of the Roman fort at Pevensey, William's first castle quickly took shape. Days later, he marched along the coast to Hastings where he immediately set to work on a second, whose motte still stands: part of a stunning castle site which man, weather and sea have left a beautiful ruin. Standing in the ruins it is easy to imagine the trepidation that William's men must have felt, looking down at the thin strip of ground beneath the walls: their only toehold in a hostile and warlike land.

THE BAYEUX TAPESTRY SHOWS THE BUILDING OF HASTINGS, AND GIVES US A VITAL PIECE OF EVIDENCE FOR THE CONSTRUCTION PROCESS

The Bayeux Tapestry shows the building of Hastings, and gives us a vital piece of evidence for the construction process. Mottes were built in layers – a band of soil, then a band of stone or shingle, followed by another layer of soil. Baileys would have been built around the motte, while on top would have been a timber tower probably with a fighting platform or walkway. Although, unsurprisingly, none of these wooden structures survive, at Abinger in Surrey archaeologists have discovered post-holes in a motte built within a few decades of 1066. Labour would almost certainly have been provided by the unfortunate natives, forced to build buildings that were both the means and symbol of Norman imperialism. It all became too much for two workers, depicted in the tapestry having a fight with their shovels behind the supervisor's back.

William's two new castles were not to be tested during that late summer. King Harold of England marched south to meet this new invader, hoping that the same lightning tactics that had surprised and defeated Hardrada would also beat William. It was a mistake, but only just. In one of the longest and hardest-fought battles of medieval history, William won an attritional, bloody contest. The best guess is that the English army broke just before sunset after Harold was terribly wounded or killed by an arrow in the eye. The corpses of Harold, his brothers and the cream of the Anglo-Saxon warrior class lay mutilated on the battlefield. The throne was William's, but he harboured few illusions that he would be widely welcomed. From Sussex he marched to Kent and took possession of the strategic fortress at Dover, the important site which guarded the narrows between Britain and mainland Europe. Its defences would be improved by William and his successors until it stood as one of the mightiest castles in the world (see Chapter 1). From here, William moved slowly towards London and briefly visited Westminster for his coronation, before heading east into Essex while a suitable castle could be built 'against', writes his biographer, 'the inconstancy of the huge and savage population'.

Faced with inhospitable locals, the invaders built castles. To control London the Normans built two, one in the west and one in the east. Soon there were three: Montfichet, near the present-day Ludgate Circus, Baynard's Tower on the site of the modern Blackfriars, and a castle that would be forever synonymous with English kingship and royal authority, referred to simply as The Tower.

William ordered his engineers to build a castle which reflected his new-found status as king, in the south-eastern corner of the old Roman wall that surrounded the city. They started constructing a vast stone tower, one of the largest in Christendom. Nothing like it had been seen in Britain since the Romans left, over 600 years before. At the same time he began a castle in the old Roman capital at Colchester; this had a donjon which sadly has not survived as completely as the tower. The ground plan of Colchester was the largest of any great tower in Europe. Not for

ABOVE *The White Tower is the keep at the heart of the Tower of London. Built by William the Conqueror, its basic design provided a model for Henry II's keep at Dover*

the last time, a king of England would build castles to claim the mantel of the Romans.

The Tower of London was a rectangle. It had extremely thick walls and turrets at the four corners. There were four storeys with the entrance on the first floor, accessed by a wooden walkway that could be removed in war. It was divided in two by a spine so that even if half of the donjon fell, the other half could still act as a final stronghold. The rooms inside were palatial. It appears to have been heavily influenced by castles on the continent. Ivry-la-Bataille in Normandy took the same general form, and it is tempting to think that the blueprint for all these eleventh-century great towers might have been the massive ducal palace in Rouen, demolished in the thirteenth century. Much of the facing stone for The Tower comes from quarries in Normandy, the rubble fill is ultra-hard Kentish ragstone. It was a huge project and William would not live to see it completed.

William's attitude to his new subjects only hardened as he grew to know them. Initially he seems to have hoped he could rule through the existing elite. But this uncharacteristic compassion was not rewarded by loyalty. Rebellions broke out with infuriating regularity in the years after the Conquest. From the south-west to the north-eastern tip of his new kingdom he was forced to fight vicious campaigns to secure his new domain. In addition, opportunist neighbours – Irish, Welsh, Scots and Vikings – could be relied upon to raid and harry frontier lands.

Typically, William would crush the rebellion in person and then build castles to ensure a strong Norman presence right across the kingdom. These would be garrisoned by reliable allies, often relatives, who were expected to keep the peace and were allowed to enrich themselves in return. William's biographer tells how, 'in castles he placed capable custodians, brought over from France, in whose loyalty no less than ability he trusted, together with large numbers of horse and foot. He distributed fiefs (or landholdings) among them, in return for which they would willingly undertake hardships and dangers.'

BELOW *Clifford's Tower, York. The remains we see today are thirteenth century, but the site was once topped by an earlier fortification built by William the Conqueror*

First William had to march south-west to Exeter, where he erected a castle in the remains of the Anglo-Saxon burh. The following year he marched north through the east Midlands and East Anglia, planting castles at Warwick, Cambridge and York, among other places. Perhaps the most serious challenge came in 1069 when Edgar, the Anglo-Saxon with the best claim to the throne, invaded northern England, killed William's lieutenant in the north and captured York, England's second city. William sent an army north which defeated the rebels, forced Edgar into exile and punished the region heavily, salting the land to make it infertile and slaughtering inhabitants. As land and power was stripped from the English lords and churchmen who William could not trust, a small group of foreigners took over almost the entire national wealth.

Such a heist would have been impossible without castles. William continued building them at strategic points in the kingdom. He created an entire system of land ownership and obligation aimed at supporting the castle, seen as the bedrock of his regime. Land was given to knights, who in return had to serve as garrison for the nearby castle. Even tradesmen like cooks and carpenters were given places to live in return for service. On the south coast, six castles – Hastings, Pevensey, Lewes, Bramber, Arundel and Chichester – were established with a vast hinterland geared up to support them. The Welsh borders were parcelled out, as was the far north of England. Just as the Romans had fortified the coast, so too did the Normans. Whereas the Romans paid for their forts with a sophisticated central treasury and a standing army that served from province to province, Norman castles were designed to be self-sufficient. The local lord and his warriors were rooted to the

WILLIAM WOULD CRUSH THE REBELLION AND THEN BUILD CASTLES TO ENSURE A STRONG NORMAN PRESENCE RIGHT ACROSS THE KINGDOM

land, paid not by a distant exchequer, but by the proceeds of what they could grow or acquire locally.

The power of local Norman lords meant William was not alone in building castles. An explosion in castle building followed his accession. Almost one hundred are referred to in sources before 1100, but there were many more. Across England and parts of Wales numerous surviving earthworks date from this time: 85 in Shropshire, another 36 in what used to be Montgomeryshire. John Goodall estimates that as many as 500 could have been founded in the decade after 1066 alone – some built by the king, others by the great magnates who now dominated England, and others still by relatively minor gentry, given parcels of land in reward for loyal service, their names now lost to history. This was a militarized landscape. In the words of the *Anglo-Saxon Chronicle*, the king and his warlords built castles 'far and wide throughout the country, and distressed the wretched folk, and always after that it grew worse'. Often mottes were sited in positions of mutual visibility, no more than a day's march apart, so one garrison could reinforce another that found itself under attack. Visiting these ghostly mounds today, their size much-reduced by 900 years of erosion, one should imagine the three- or four-storey towers which stood on top of them, dwarfing the small dwellings nearby, and think of the wood, earth and stone with which the Normans locked down the country.

The most powerful castle builder in the kingdom, apart from William, was his relative and childhood friend William FitzOsbern, who was given a huge swathe of land from the south coast of England up to the Welsh borders. The various Welsh peoples had maintained an ancient enmity with the Anglo-Saxons which their Norman successors now inherited. Using the river network as modern humans would use roads and rail, FitzOsbern built castles, large and small, across the shifting frontier zone at places like Berkeley, Wigmore, Clifford and Monmouth. He is remembered for the stunning castle at Chepstow, sitting proud on towering cliffs, dominating the sweeping bend of the River Wye. To visit it

today is to feel like you are entering a royal palace, and it may in fact have been just that. When FitzOsbern was killed on campaign in Flanders in 1071, the site reverted to King William, and it may have been William who built a palatial fortress on his Welsh border. Tellingly, it is built on the Welsh side, sending the lords of Gwent an unambiguous signal. As in Colchester or London, further clues into the Norman mindset are built into the fabric of the castle. A crumbling Roman fort nearby was looted for bricks, which were incorporated into the walls. William was embracing physically and symbolically the Roman imperial legacy. He was a new Caesar, locking barbaric Britain into a civilized empire. A new imperial project was born, and castles were its symbol.

What these castles did was make it possible for around 7,000 men to pacify a country of two million people: they were the most efficient 'force multiplier' available in this period. This, it has always struck me, was the true reason behind their sudden supremacy. Castles burst onto the scene in medieval Europe not as expressions of strength but of weakness. They were the tool of small-scale imperial powers, such as William's Normans, who commanded only relatively minor forces. When the Romans invaded Britain 1,000 years earlier, they did so with some 20,000 legionaries and a similar number of auxiliary troops – a massive army which was much larger than the numbers at William's disposal. While the Romans were able to find and annihilate in battle every British army that gathered against them, William's forces needed castle walls to shelter them from the English weight of numbers. The sources are full of accounts of Normans hunkering down and simply waiting for rebellions to subside, before sallying out to hunt down the ringleaders and punish the population. The most balanced account

BY THE TWELFTH CENTURY, ONE CHRONICLER REFERRED TO CASTLES AS 'THE BONES OF THE KINGDOM'

of the Conquest is the *Ecclesiastical History* written by the monk Oderic Vitalis, who had a Norman father and an English mother. His assessment of how the Normans annexed what had been the most powerful state in Western Europe was simple: 'The king rode to all remote parts of his kingdom and fortified strategic sites against enemy attacks. For the fortifications called castles by the Normans were scarcely known in the English provinces, and so the English – in spite of their courage and love of fighting – could put up only a weak resistance to their enemies.'

Rarely in history has an annexation proved so enduring. The Norman grip on England held strong and Norman influence and power slowly spread, with varying success, through Wales, Scotland and Ireland. By the twelfth century, one chronicler referred to castles as 'the bones of the kingdom'. But the warlords with their mighty castles that underpinned this dominance brought their own problems. Castles had begun as a response to the breakdown of central control, and a lord in his castle was a king in his own domain. To live in a castle bred, and still breeds, an independence of spirit, a suspicion of distant rulers or central government. Conquest and occupation was led by an active warrior king, but it was often enforced by a patchwork of local, autonomous warlords. To a king of William's stature this was not a problem, but to his successors, castles, and the men who guarded them, would often prove less like bones that gave kingdoms their integrity, and more like rocks on which the ship of state could founder.

William's descendants would learn that castles were loyal only to the men who held the key to their gate. His son, William II, was immediately faced with a rebellion by his father's greatest nobles, who preferred the prospect of his brother's rule. He was forced to conduct a gruelling siege of Pevensey Castle, once the symbol of his family's claim to the English throne, as well as sieges of other castles, before a mixture of generous promises and the non-appearance of his brother's army allowed him to secure the throne. Castles were the weapons of occupation, but not the tools of orderly royal rule.

ABOVE *Pevensey was one of the first sites to be fortified when William the Conqueror came to England. Under the Normans it was updated to include a stone keep*

Across Europe similar trends were seen. As the principalities of Western Christendom chipped away at the ring of pagans and Muslims that surrounded them, they built castles on their expanding frontier zones. Against the English, William the Conqueror had believed himself to be on a Crusade, carrying the Pope's banner into battle. The Pope encouraged this, knowing that the English Church was frustratingly insubordinate. In Iberia, the Baltic and Eastern Europe, relatively small Crusader forces would annex land and then lock it down with a network of castles exactly as William had done in Britain. The Christian toehold in the north of the Iberian peninsula, initially part of the Frankish kingdom, first broke away from French control and then became a base for the conquest or 'reconquest' of the rest of modern Spain and Portugal. In Catalonia, in the far north-east, the massive castle of Cardona and the magical Quermançó Castle, built in the late eleventh century on a dizzying rocky outcrop, are testament to a refusal to be dominated by their neighbours – Christian or Muslim. Further south, the sprawling central area that would become the Kingdom of Castile was so defined by castle building that its very name was derived from them. Desperate to cling onto their gains, Crusaders built castles relentlessly – and their Muslim opponents did too. At Málaga, on the peninsula's southern coast, the great castle of Gibralfaro – clinging to a hill above the town – would prove one of the last bastions of resistance against the resurgent Christian armies (see Chapter 6).

Other Christian Crusaders pushed north and east. The warlike Normans travelled widely, building castles as they went. As William was crossing the Channel, his countrymen travelled also to southern Italy, first, it seems, as religious tourists, then as land-hungry warriors. Men like William de Hauteville, who won the nickname 'Iron Arm', arrived as adventurers and died as sovereigns. His half-brother Robert invaded Sicily and built San Marco d'Alunzio, the first Norman castle there, before capturing Rome itself.

ABOVE *Margat Castle's black walls contrast starkly with the white limestone of Krak. Built of hard basalt, it was one of the Knights Hospitallers' most important strongholds*

In November 1095 Pope Urban II proposed a military expedition to 'recover' Jerusalem, the holiest site in the Christian faith – a call which unleashed wars of terrible ferocity across Eastern Europe and the Middle East. Kingdoms and principalities were carved out, besieged, captured and recaptured. In what was already a heavily-fortified landscape, the Christians built the most perfect castles in the world: Kerak, Krak des Chevaliers, Marqab and Saone to name a few (see Chapter 3). To visit them today is a truly awesome experience. At Saone, now known as Salah Ed-Din's (Saladin's) Castle after the Egyptian military genius who eventually captured it, there is a 30-metre-deep ditch cut into the rock either by the Crusaders or their predecessors, guarded by a monumental Crusader bastion with walls 5 metres thick. As I approached these castles, panting in the heat, the walls seemed to grow ever more formidable. I was overwhelmed by the lengths to which the Crusaders went to protect their conquered territory. But I also could not help thinking that these vast edifices bear witness to the fury and vigour with which the Muslims tried to drive them back into the sea.

With a supply chain stretching over thousands of miles, a hostile unfamiliar climate and a dizzying array of enemies close by, these castles were needed as 'force multipliers' more than anywhere else. Despite the utterly different terrain, they were doing the same job as castles everywhere else I had visited. A group of armed outsiders, invaders, surrounded by hostile territory, sought refuge and strength behind stone walls, gatehouses and towers. The process was universal. I saw the same thing in Syria that I had in Wales, France and Spain.

In the West, war and anarchy continued to promote the building of castles. When King Henry I of England dared to die without a male heir, despite having fathered over twenty acknowledged illegitimate children, England was again plunged into chaos. Camps formed around his daughter Matilda and her cousin Stephen. War followed. Local lords looked to their own defence. Fortifications were raised. 'Christ and all his saints were asleep,' a chronicler observed, and 'the land was filled with castles'.

Castles appear to have made civil war all the more intractable. Neither side had the resources to besiege their enemy's castles one after the other and so two competing weak regimes were eclipsed in the provinces by local powerbases. For the first time in British history, sieges really came to the fore. During a siege of Newbury Castle, Stephen demanded the surrender of the garrison and said if they held out he would hang the son of their defiant leader in broad view. The warlord defied this threat: 'I still have the hammer and the anvil,' he declared, 'with which to forge still more and better sons!' Fortunately for the child, and fortunately for England, Stephen did not carry out his threat. The boy, William, would grow up to become the supreme English knight of medieval history, the Marshal of England and saviour of the kingdom at its lowest ebb. Matilda herself was no less lucky if folklore is to be believed. Twice she escaped from being besieged, once across the frozen Thames in winter in a white cloak, and once as a corpse being taken out for burial.

The so-called 'Anarchy' came to an end when Matilda's son Henry Plantagenet invaded England from France in 1153, and forced the ageing Stephen to negotiate. The death of Stephen's heir opened the door to a deal and Stephen named Henry as his successor. Through his marriage to Eleanor of Aquitaine, Henry II would control a vast empire from the borders of Scotland to the Pyrenees. To secure it he tore down troublesome castles and built mighty royal ones, like that at Dover which rose above the white cliffs and which would endure the attacks of Prince Louis, another claimant to the throne of England (see Chapter 1).

DOVER WAS A GLITTERING ADORNMENT TO THE CHANNEL COAST, VISIBLE TO SHIPS PASSING THROUGH THE NARROWS, A SYMBOL OF HENRY'S MASSIVE EMPIRE

Henry spent vast amounts of money on his royal castles. It was not unusual for half the annual royal budget to be spent either on building new castles or repairing old ones. An eyewitness observed of the building work at the Tower of London that 'with so many smiths, carpenters and other workmen, working so vehemently with bustle and noise […] a man could hardly hear the one next to him speak'. Under Henry we know that an unskilled labourer moving earth and stones on a site like this would have been paid a penny a day. For the King these castles were about prestige as much as security. Dover was a glittering adornment to the channel coast, visible to ships passing through the narrows, a symbol of Henry's massive empire. It was also one of many seats of government. Medieval kingship was peripatetic: kings and courts moved constantly. Since rule was personal it was wise for a king to show himself to his subjects, dispense justice and redress grievance as widely as possible. But logistics also played a part. The King and his court soon consumed all the supplies in one castle and it was easier to move to the food than to bring the food to them. Henry would have recognized the description of medieval kingship offered by his namesake, Henry IV, King of France: 'I rule with my weapon in my hand and my arse in the saddle.' His royal castles really were residences for him and his court on these huge progresses and they were appointed with all the finery demanded by the royal court.

The castles also served their most obvious purpose. When Scottish King William the Lion invaded England in 1173, he marched on Newcastle but did not even attempt to besiege the castle because he lacked the necessary, cumbersome siege engines. When he tried to besiege Alnwick, he was captured by English knights and eventually forced to sign a humiliating submission to the English Crown. Henry's castles defended his northern frontier while he focussed his attention on unrest in other parts of his empire.

That empire grew wider: Ireland was sucked into the orbit of the Plantagenet Crown when Henry himself invaded and captured Dublin, and received the submission of its bishops and kings. Castles like Kilkenny, Killeen and Dunsany were planted by Henry's subordinates, and his son, John, started work on Dublin Castle, a building that was to remain the seat of English and then British rule in Ireland until 1922. Ireland remained largely beyond the writ of English government, however, as other targets distracted English kings. It was never fully annexed, the chronicler Gerald Cambrensis lamented, because of the failure to build castles 'from sea to sea'.

Henry's sons utterly failed to guard their vast inheritance. Richard was a warrior, but no ruler, and John may have been a ruler, but he was no warrior. Richard died while pressing home the siege of a castle in France. His younger brother John's reign saw Philip of France pushing to expand his kingdom at the expense of Plantagenet lands – laying siege, most notably, to Château Gaillard, the extraordinary castle Richard had built above the small town of Andely, on a bend of the River Seine (see Chapter 2). Failure and losses in France led to unrest in England itself, where rebels tried vainly to hold out in Rochester Castle ('Living memory,' a chronicler wrote, 'does not recall a siege so fiercely pressed, and so staunchly resisted'). The French intervened in this English civil war and the loyal knight Hubert de Burgh led King John's garrison at Dover in defiance of Prince Louis' invading army (see Chapter 1).

The years following the death of Henry II witnessed a protracted struggle about the nature and limits of kingship, and castles were the physical manifestation of an aristocracy that felt themselves more than simple subjects. John, his son Henry III and even Henry's warrior son, Edward, were no strangers to being besieged and even captured by rebels. Eventually the monarchy, in the person of Edward I, emerged victorious, but only after he had promised to abide by the restrictions placed on his grandfather and father by the Great Charter or Magna Carta.

Edward's peace within England lasted long enough to turn his attention to unfinished business in the rest of the British Isles. Edward fought several campaigns in Wales, initially punitive but eventually of outright conquest. As always, castles were to be the method of subjugation. Edward spent a staggering £80,000 in twenty-five years, considerably more than his father had spent on the magnificent Westminster Abbey. Edward's engineers built castles that are regarded around the world as some of the finest ever built, including Harlech, Caernarfon, Beaumaris and Conwy – a ring of steel around the recently-independent mountain region of Gwynedd in north-west Wales. To this day, a castle like Conwy dominates its surroundings. Caernarfon was built on a site with powerful Roman associations, and in its architecture and brickwork it deliberately echoed this earlier empire. This was Edward staking his claim to be the modern incarnation of the Caesars, just as his ancestor William had done centuries before. The Welsh understood the message, and when they rose in rebellion, it was these castles – symbols of hated English rule – that were a prime target (see Chapter 4). King Edward attempted to bring Scotland and Wales under the English Crown and yet again castles were used to enforce occupation. Scotland already had a wide network of castles built by Anglo-Norman settlers who had integrated themselves at the Scottish court through marriage and service to the Scottish Crown. These castles Edward sought to control as his forces dealt with widespread rebellions across the countryside led by William Wallace and Robert the Bruce. The Bruce knew just how important these castles were and rarely lost a chance to 'slight' or render them defenceless by collapsing an important section of wall. Scotland was never truly pacified by Edward, who died on his way north to deal with the latest of the Bruce's victories.

As the chapters in this book explain, the design for these castles had evolved greatly since the arrival of the Normans in England. The key defence was no longer, as at Dover, a central keep, but the outer layers. Towering walls, lofty round towers and a massive gatehouse were in vogue, allowing the interior to be laid out with palatial magnificence. The gateway had always been a weak point, but by the thirteenth century changes had made it almost the strongest point of the castle. Round towers on either side in castles like Framlingham in Suffolk or Caerphilly in South Wales were pushed forward with embrasures, allowing the defenders to rake the entrance with crossbow bolts and arrows. Above the gate murder holes and 'machicolations' could be used to pour boiling water or incendiaries on the attackers below. Some castles were given a barbican or additional defensive layer in front of the gates, which might be offset to prevent an attacking force using a battering ram.

Scotland eventually secured independence thanks to a crushing victory at Bannockburn in 1314 in the shadow of Stirling Castle, held by the English, besieged by the Scots, and the key to central Scotland. Castles played a huge role in the nature of Scottish kingship thereafter. A geographically-disjointed state with a poor central treasury, Scotland had little choice but to delegate political authority. Lords ruled isolated areas with the powers of kings. Castles were the choice of these aristocrats, partly because Scotland was occasionally torn by civil strife (although it does not seem to have been endemic as was once thought), but partly also because of fashion. The Bruces, the Comyns, the Balliols all had Anglo-Norman blood, owned land in England, and employed the same architects and engineers as their peers had south of the border. Their castles reflected their status as demi-kings: in their own lands dispensers of justice, collectors of revenue and protectors.

Further north the kings of the Scots pursued their own imperial project, with the same vigour with which they defended their independence from the English. James IV fought long and hard to bring north-west Scotland under the control of Edinburgh. One of the most iconic castles in Britain, Urquhart, teetering on the edge of Loch Ness, was strategically vital and constantly changed hands between the Scottish Crown and the Lords of the Isles who dominated the north and west highlands of modern Scotland.

Eastern Europe, meanwhile, became a giant frontier between Christendom and the pagan, often nomadic, tribes of the steppes. The 'Teutonic Knights' who began operating in the Crusader States of the Holy Land pursued God's enemies instead in the north-east of the continent, helping to convert (and conquer) Prussia on the Baltic coast. Behind them they left towering castles in red brick – strongholds like Malbork, which allowed them to dominate the region and to grow rich off its trade (see Chapter 5). The German brickmakers and engineers that they used were some of the most proficient in Europe, and further west, in Germany itself, it was said that there was a castle to every square mile, helping to frustrate the ambitions of anyone who sought to unify the hundreds of autonomous statelets, bishoprics,

> THEIR CASTLES REFLECTED THEIR STATUS AS DEMI-KINGS IN THEIR OWN LANDS: DISPENSERS OF JUSTICE, COLLECTORS OF REVENUE AND PROTECTORS

margravates, duchies, and the like which covered central Europe in a bewildering patchwork.

By the time Malbork came under siege in 1410, a new technology had emerged which radically changed the way castles were built, and attacked. Gunpowder, invented in China around the ninth century, gradually spread west. By the late fourteenth century it was used widely in Europe. In 1453 the Hundred Years' War was brought to a successful conclusion by the French at the battle of Castillon, the first pitch battle in European history in which cannon played a decisive role. Weapons now existed which could pound even the mightiest walls into dust: a development which in turn triggered a series of changes in government, society and fashion, and which led eventually to the eclipse of castles.

As improvements were made to gunpowder itself, and to the weapons it powered, artillery became ever more dominant. It was also, however, vastly expensive. Effectively, only those with access

BELOW *The middle and inner wards of Caerphilly Castle in south Wales which was not a royal project, despite its size. The leaning tower (centre-left) was a product of damage during the English Civil War*

introduction

to the public purse could afford to use cannon, which became the weapon of kings. This significantly undermined the autonomy of the provincial aristocracy. No longer were they free to act as petty kings behind impenetrable walls. During the civil war in England in the fifteenth century, known as the 'War of the Roses', even the greatest castles in the land were eventually battered into submission. Bamburgh, which had been thought to be impregnable, fell when two cannon named 'Newcastle' and 'London' smashed a breech in its walls in 1464. Dunstaburgh, Alnwick and even Harlech all fell, though Harlech had held for seven years.

Bolstered by the power of gunpowder, the nature of central government changed in Western European kingdoms like England, Scotland, France and Spain. The Crown has less need for a military elite, with private armies ready at an instant to march against enemies domestic or external. Instead, the ability to tax their subjects to pay for musketeers, artillerymen or ships carrying heavy guns became paramount. Strong regimes emerged which showed a determination to gain a monopoly on the use of military power. Courtiers, administrators and lawyers were required, not warlords. The court travelled less as government grew more complex and immobile. The elite came to the court, not the other way round. Courtiers built comfortable houses and palaces using sophisticated new building techniques and materials like glass which were more enjoyable to inhabit and also embodied their status within a modern political system.

Castles survived. Many people continued to regard crenellations and fortifications (however fake) as the hallmarks of aristocracy. A few people even continued to build them, but these modern castles were subtly different from their stark Norman predecessors. A castle like Bodiam in Sussex was built as a stately home in the architectural style of a castle, but with its shallow, easily drainable moat and its windows in the curtain wall it would not have withstood a siege. Edward III spent a vast amount of money on Windsor Castle in the mid-fourteenth century, none of it on improving its defences. Instead he built palatial accommodation for himself and his queen and a set of buildings in the lower bailey for his new Order of the Garter. His son John of Gaunt entirely rebuilt Kenilworth Castle with comfort uppermost in his mind and Carew Castle saw its powerful defences hobbled by the renovations of its owner at the end of the fifteenth century.

In Scotland, the Stuart dynasty slowly eroded the power of the local elites. King James II was a great fan of artillery. He reduced several castles and increased the power of the Crown before being killed by an artillery piece exploding next to him at the siege of Roxburgh in 1460. Buildings were still built that look like castles – such as Borthwick, south-east of Edinburgh – but in reality they were indefensible. (Borthwick has beautiful machicolations but no crenellations, so anyone actually trying to use them to defend the castle would be exposed to the enemy below.)

In Spain, Ferdinand and Isabella, who completed the *Reconquista* or removal of Islamic rule from Iberia in 1492, ordered all the castles in the realm to be handed over to royal control. Although this was only partially enforced, they did order the destruction of many of them. There could be no more tangible a symbol of the assertion of royal, central control over the periphery.

The process was not irreversible, of course, nor was it universal. Far-away Japan saw a surge in castle building during the anarchic Sengoku period which lasted for around 150 years from the mid-fifteenth century onwards. From this maelstrom of violence a very similar military caste to that in the West came to dominate Japan. Showing a remarkable synchronicity, they chose castles as the totems of their power. It was centuries before central government was able to assert itself fully. The capture and destruction of Osaka Castle in 1868 was a hugely symbolic end to the period of rule by the military elite and a resurgent central government confiscated thousands of castles, destroying around 2,000 of them.

The British Isles would also see one more rush to fortify as its three component kingdoms descended into a bitter, unanticipated

ABOVE *Osaka Castle was raised in the sixteenth century. The siege in 1614–15 is considered by many to be one of the most important events in Japan's history*

civil war in the seventeenth century. Old castles were suddenly reoccupied and modern earthworks were added. Taking the lead from Italy, fortifications were built with a low profile and arrow-shaped bastions projecting from the walls denying enemy cannon a clear shot at a towering wall. Huge earth ramparts were erected to deflect cannon balls, and complex geometric shapes were adopted to maximize fields of fire of the defenders. King Charles I's followers fought supporters of Parliament in a drawn-out conflict as these new strongholds sprang up across Britain. With modern improvements to their defences, many medieval castles proved a match for the ad hoc artillery trains of the Parliamentarian forces. Castles like Basing House, Raglan and Pontefract proved a serious obstacle to final Parliamentarian victory. As a result the new Commonwealth regime that succeeded the deposed and executed King Charles ordered the destruction or 'slighting' (weakening) of some of the finest castles of the medieval world. Pontefract was wiped off the face of the earth, Nottingham and Montgomery were destroyed. Corfe, Caerphilly and Kenilworth were slighted. Thankfully castles deemed important for coastal defence were left standing. Dover, Arundel and Rochester are evidence of the new regime's fear of foreign intervention.

As I have toured the world looking at some of the most powerful castles ever built, I have been struck by the fact that, eventually even the most perfect castle will fall to its enemy. As the axe fell on the neck of King Charles in Whitehall in January 1649, the defenders of Pontefract Castle were still holding out for the royalist cause. When the news of his death reached them, the defenders negotiated a surrender. Castles can delay or grind an attacker's force down and they can bolster a cause, but when that cause totally disappears, even the garrison of the greatest castle must submit to the inevitable. Castles may appear to sit, eternal and unshakeable above the fray, but in fact their survival and that of their garrisons depends ultimately on the wider strategic situation.

Following the war, a new, highly centralized unitary regime sought to bind Britain together as one nation and it was highly significant that they focussed on castles as representing the greatest physical obstacle to this process. Castles were seen, correctly, as the symptom of a political system dominated by an autonomous warrior elite. From now on, even after the restoration of the monarchy and Stuart family, defence would now be left to the State. The Crown built coastal forts and barracks for a national army while the vast majority of aristocrats lived in comfortable modern buildings rather than expensive, dingy, old castles.

In Western Europe gunpowder, government and fashion brought the era of classic castles with towering battlements to an end. But in many ways their story continues to this day. Man still fortifies. The massive forts in France and Belgium that stalled the Germans in World War One, the Atlantic Wall built by the Germans to protect the coast of Europe from the allies in World War Two, the contemporary walls around Israeli settlements, and the compound at Sangin in Helmand with its Hesco ramparts today, are all born of the same basic urges that drove early man to build the walls of Jericho. These defences, like castles, are force multipliers, they do the job of countless men; they provide a secure base from which to conduct combat operations and prevent an area falling into enemy hands. Perhaps we will never truly see the end of the castle.

What follows are chapters which feature the six mighty castles that I encountered during the production of the TV series *Battle Castle*. The contributors to the chapters in the book are leading authorities on each of the castles. Every chapter tells the story not only of the castle in question, its construction and character, but of the historical context behind its creation. Perhaps most importantly of all, each castle was tested in a terrible siege, the result of which would have a very real impact on subsequent history. These are some of the pivotal moments of history seen through the lens of a castle, and the battle for its control.

BELOW *Hesco fortifications are pop-up containers into which materials such as sand or stone can be poured. The ones shown here protect a Dutch military base in Afghanistan*

THE CONTROL OF ENGLAND:

DOVER CASTLE

On 22 May 1216, King John stood disconsolately on the Kent shore at Sandwich. A few days earlier a terrible storm had scattered the powerful fleet which he had gathered to defend his realm and to keep an invading army at bay. From his vantage point he could now see, anchored off the coast a little to the north, the invasion fleet of Prince Louis, the son of the French King and claimant to his own throne. The prince had landed safely on the Isle of Thanet the day before. Exactly 150 years after the first Norman invasion, an army from France was yet again trying to unseat the King of England. With a sizeable fifth column to assist him, the prince came at the invitation of an English rebel army, determined to make John pay for what it deemed his arbitrary and tyrannical rule.

After sounding his trumpets on the beach, King John fled south back to Dover, leaving his bewildered followers behind. His formidable castle – begun by his father, Henry II, continued by his brother, Richard I, and latterly King John himself – would become a crucial stronghold in the coming struggle. The castle was besieged not once, but twice, by Louis' substantial armies. At times it seemed that this great bastion was all that stood in the way of Louis' formal recognition as King of England. It was in relation to the events of 1216 that the chronicler Matthew Paris later described Dover Castle as '*clavis Angliae*' or 'the key of England'.

THE MURDER OF BECKET AND THE BUILDING OF DOVER CASTLE

The origins of Dover's construction and pre-eminent status are to be found in the reign of Henry II, and a political crisis even more famous than that which afflicted his son. At dusk on 29 December 1170, the Archbishop Thomas Becket was brutally hacked to death by a party of knights in his cathedral church at Canterbury. According to an eyewitness, his brains were scattered across the floor while the monks sang Vespers in the choir above.

Whether or not he had deliberately incited the murder, Henry II was universally held responsible and was later to make an astonishing public penance. This formidable man, described by a contemporary as having 'a large, round head, grey eyes that glowed fiercely and grew bloodshot in anger, a fiery countenance and a harsh, cracked voice', submitted to three lashes from each member of the cathedral's eighty-strong monastic community.

Within days of the archbishop's sensational murder, word spread that Becket was working miracles from beyond the grave, encouraging a cult that attracted international attention. In 1179 the King of France landed at Dover to make a pilgrimage to Canterbury and was conducted to and from the shrine by Henry II himself. The following year the saint's tomb was made the centrepiece of a new cathedral being built at Canterbury.

It can hardly have been a coincidence that Henry II started to pour money into the castle at Dover soon after Louis' visit. This strategically-placed castle straddled the approach to Canterbury from the Continent. Here at Dover, the hub of one of Europe's most important communication routes, Henry needed to respond architecturally to the burgeoning cult of his great rival and critic. The sheer scale of the project in financial terms speaks clearly of its perceived importance. Over the following eight years, the royal financial accounts record a total expenditure of nearly £6,000 on Dover Castle, from an estimated royal income of about £10,000 per year. These accounts, known as the Pipe Rolls, got their unusual name from the tradition of attaching each year's record to the last and the document being rolled into a pipe shape. Dover could plausibly claim to be the single most expensive secular architectural commission of Henry II's long reign.

The castle's location and site had been chosen carefully by Henry. It offered the shortest sea-crossing between England and the European mainland. Set on a hill above the mouth of the

BELOW *Henry II, King of England (1154–89) is frequently hailed as one of England's greatest monarchs. Under his rule the Crown's dominions on the continent grew rapidly and the English legal system evolved considerably*

MAGNA CARTA AND THE ROAD TO CIVIL WAR

When King John inherited the vast Plantagenet Empire, the power of the French Capetian monarchy was on the rise. He soon lost important continental territories, and critics compared him unfavourably to his brother and predecessor, Richard I. They ridiculed him as 'softsword' (see Chapter 2).

John desperately needed money for campaigns to win the lands back. Like his father and brother before him, he resorted to both new and archaic taxes, highhanded behaviour such as the seizing of land without legal process, as well as arbitrary imprisonment. All the Plantagenet kings considered themselves largely above the law. But unlike his predecessors, John failed to redeem himself with military success. Negative personality traits – ingrained suspicion, cruelty and a vindictive temper – saw important baronial allies in France and England desert his cause.

Plans for campaigns were repeatedly foiled by baronial unrest. Northern barons in particular had little to gain from warfare in France and resented the burden of debt placed on them by the king. Finally, when John's campaign in 1214 failed – culminating in the decisive defeat at Bouvines – a group of barons broke into open revolt. They massed an army which moved south to hold London. In June 1215 John met the rebel leaders in a meadow by the Thames at Runnymede, west of London. An agreement was reached whose terms were written into a document called the 'Magna Carta', or the Great Charter, to distinguish it from a small charter containing additional terms.

This was no universal declaration of rights. The charter's terms were intended to protect the baronial classes against specific abuses by an overbearing monarch, closing loopholes in feudal law which successive kings had exploited to raise money. Importantly though, its talk of the rights of free men (earlier drafts had specified barons), the right to trial by peers, and other terms intended to uphold the rights of the barons, made it open to a later, broader interpretation – of inviolable rights held by all men as opposed to merely the privileged few.

John never intended to abide by a charter which so constrained his authority, consenting to it only through short-term necessity. From the outset he worked to recruit mercenaries and to have the Pope condemn the agreement. This lobbying was successful, resulting in a papal letter which duly proclaimed the charter 'not only shameful and base but also illegal and unjust'. Meanwhile, the more extremist barons were set upon a military resolution. The rebel army refused to disband or give up London. When the rebels seized Rochester Castle, a full-scale civil war broke out that would dominate the remainder of John's reign.

PIPE ROLLS

The Pipe Rolls, or Great Rolls, are financial records kept by the Exchequer, as the Treasury was previously known. Sheepskin parchments were stitched together, both sides used for writing, then rolled for storage – their resemblance to pipes giving them their name. Running from the twelfth to the nineteenth centuries, they are the longest, almost-unbroken run of records preserved by the English government. The first surviving roll dates from the year 1129–30, and exhibits the confidence of an established practice, leading historians to think that such records were created before, perhaps even in the time of William the Conqueror and the Domesday survey. In 1834, the Pipe Office, then responsible for the creation of the annual rolls, was abolished and the sequence came to an end.

Each roll contains the audits for a financial year, based on the submissions of sheriffs and other officers and preserved on a county-by-county basis. Each annual record was known as 'the great roll' or the 'roll of the year'. The rolls were the responsibility of the Treasurer's clerk, known as the Clerk of the Pipe, and were stored in the Treasury for easy consultation by the Exchequer clerks.

For the earlier centuries in particular they comprise an invaluable record of administration in England – testimony, like the Domesday records, to the centralising drive of the Norman and Plantagenet kings. In this regard England was more advanced than comparable monarchies like that of France, which kept no similar records until the 1190s. Since items of expenditure and debts owing can be traced, much can be learnt about the construction of royal castles like Dover or Conwy, about the order in which the work was done, for instance, or the identity of important individuals, like Maurice the Engineer, who carried out the work.

RIGHT *The Roman 'pharos', or lighthouse, within the grounds of Dover Castle. It was one of two beacons for guiding sea traffic, and may have stood at almost twice the height it does today*

River Dour it was a natural place to fortify, and previous castles are known to have existed on the site. There may have been an Iron Age hill fort. By about the year 1000 there was certainly a fortified settlement, if not a castle, within the U-shaped ditches, dropping to the sea, which still define the modern site. Not long after the Norman Conquest a chaplain of William the Conqueror, William of Poitiers, wrote of a castle at Dover which 'stands near to the sea on a rock which is naturally steep on all sides', and which had been

ENGLAND

LINCOLN

NORWICH

CAMBRIDGE HEDINGHAM

ORFORD

COLCHESTER

BERKHAMSTEAD HERTFORD PLESHEY

WINDSOR

MARLBOROUGH GUILDFORD REIGATE

ROCHESTER

FARNHAM

WINCHESTER

DOVER CASTLE

PORTCHESTER

'patiently chipped away with iron tools, so that it is like a wall of towering height equal to the flight of an arrow on the side washed by the sea'.

What Henry II created here was a massive keep, or great tower, within its own enclosure or bailey. At over 27 metres high and 30 metres square it was one of the largest ever constructed in Britain. It was the pinnacle of a building tradition in which castles were built with a powerful central keep (the walls at Dover were in places nearly seven metres thick) which both provided accommodation for high-status residents and served as the core defence in times of crisis (see The Keep box, p.50). Dover was the final link in a chain of such fortifications which ran along the route between London and this most important port for shipping to the continent: from the Tower of London through Rochester and Canterbury to Dover. Its form, moreover, echoed and was echoed by royal castles across the Plantagenet Empire.

PLANTAGENET EMPIRE

From the mid-twelfth century, after the accession of Henry II in 1154, the Plantagenet kings of England ruled over a large strip of European territory stretching from the northern borders of England and parts of Ireland to the Pyrenees. At its height this empire included all the western side of modern France. The dynastic name 'Plantagenet' derived from a nickname of Henry's father, Geoffrey. He liked to wear a sprig of yellow broom flowers in his hat – a plant the French called *genet*; the kings, and their empire, are also known as 'Angevin' because Geoffrey and his family had come from Anjou.

Not an empire in the modern sense, this was a disparate group of territories acquired largely by inheritance rather than conquest. They were separately administered by Henry in his capacity as king, duke, or count. He succeeded to the throne of England because his mother, Matilda, was the daughter of Henry I. Henry II was thus a great grandson of William the Conqueror. Henry also inherited from his mother other territories, like Normandy; and from his father Anjou and Maine. Territories such as Aquitaine and Poitou, he governed in right of his formidable wife, Eleanor of Aquitaine.

While England was a sovereign kingdom, Henry's duchies and counties in modern France were – according to feudal tradition – held in varying degrees of vassalage (bonds of duty and allegiance) to the King of France. In practice, however, this overlordship was largely nominal: Henry refused to undertake the act of homage expected by the French king for his Duchy of Normandy and other holdings. In fact he even tried to capture more French territory by force, including the great cities of Toulouse and Bourges.

1066 had changed everything: by their conquest of England the Dukes of Normandy had made themselves crowned and anointed kings and henceforward met their French counterparts as equals. Even when they did acknowledge kings of France as overlords for the Duchy of Normandy, they began to run the duchy, as one contemporary chronicler put it, as 'almost a kingdom'. It was a situation which the increasingly powerful Capetian kings of France were determined to address. They knew, as Henry did, that the Plantagenet lands had been brought together through acts of marriage, and could fall apart easily.

The fact that the buildings at Dover were laid out to the north of the old castle enclosure removed the need to demolish the most important of the existing buildings. There was a small Anglo-Saxon church, known as St Mary-in-Castro. Immediately next to it, there was also an ancient lighthouse, or 'pharos', wrongly believed to have been built by Julius Caesar as his treasury in Britain, which lent prestige and symbolism to the site (though it was probably built between AD 117 and 140).

THE KEEP

The keep was a central area in many castles in the Middle Ages, built to be the last line of defence for a garrison under siege. It also often contained comfortable accommodation for royal or lordly owners.

Those which survive today are made of stone, but timber was also a primary building material. Both were used in the medieval period depending on local resources as well as the needs and wealth of lords. In an area short of stone, the Teutonic Knights were still building timber castles in the 13th century (see Chapter 5). Technological advancements in siege weaponry played their part, as timber gave way entirely to stone or brick.

In the time of the Norman dynasty in England, two main styles of keep emerged in north-western Europe: the *shell-keep* and the *great tower*. The former consisted of a walled fortification built around the top of a motte, or artificial mound, sometimes containing buildings arranged around the interior. Although much altered from its original form, the most famous shell-keep in the world is perhaps that of Windsor Castle.

Great towers, meanwhile, were square-based structures with soaring walls often crowned with corner-turrets. Between London and England's south-east coast a magnificent chain of four great towers still stands. The earliest and most iconic is the White Tower at the Tower of London, begun by William the Conqueror in the late-eleventh century. Rochester Castle's great tower is the tallest in England, while those at Canterbury and Dover complete this network.

As time passed, keeps in north-west Europe, particularly in France, were built round rather than square. It is difficult to say how far military concerns fuelled this change (see Towers box, p. 117) but it must have been informed to some extent by the design of earlier shell-keeps. Philip II of France is known for building round keeps, known as *Tours Phillipienes*, while his rival Richard I of England built Château Gaillard with a broadly round keep.

By the end of the thirteenth century the keep's heyday was over. Favoured styles of castle-building abandoned it in favour of walls whose towers contained apartments, as seen in the majestic castles such as Conwy, built by Edward I in North Wales.

PREVIOUS PAGE *Dover Castle's Great Tower. The walls of Henry II's keep are over six metres thick in places – wider, on average, than the top of the Great Wall of China*

Unusually for the period, the walls of Henry II's great tower and inner bailey were punctuated by a multitude of rectangular towers. Pale Caen stone from Normandy, in precisely-cut blocks, was used to finish the central section of the entrance façade and to create stripes across the other three sides. A late-twelfth-century traveller arriving across the Channel, being confronted by this fantastical, turreted structure rising up from the white cliffs, must have found this hugely striking and impressive. The fact that these bailey towers incorporated arrow loops within their lower storeys created a second level of defence beneath the wall walks – a novel idea in mid-twelfth-century English castle design. The configuration today reflects the fact that in the eighteenth century the loops were reordered to cater for muskets.

To either end of Henry's new bailey were two gates, each protected by a walled outwork. Such gateway fortifications, or 'barbicans', were a relative novelty in castles of this period. The term derives from the Arabic words *bab* (gate) and *khan* (courtyard or enclosure) – perhaps the most convincing connection made between the European Crusades in the Middle East and English castle architecture.

The southern barbican formed a combined defensive structure with the older defences in the area of the Roman pharos. There

ABOVE *A reconstruction of how Dover Castle's defences may have looked in the early thirteenth century*

TOP *On the north side, Henry's keep was laid out with stripes of light Caen Stone and dark Kentish Ragstone, used for strength but also for decorative purposes*

ABOVE, LEFT *Arrowloops in the lower section of an inner wall tower. With the advent of gunpowder weaponry, crenellations were removed from the top of the tower*

ABOVE, RIGHT *The Palace gate on the south side of the inner wall*

RIGHT *A stone bridge now stands where a timber bridge once led to the inner wall's northern barbican*

is evidence of changes to the ancient buildings at this period: architectural fragments from St. Mary in Castro are similar to those found in the great tower. Beyond the northern bailey gate and barbican, meanwhile, was a timber bridge, one support of which remains encased in a later masonry ramp. This bridge probably led to an outer gate on the landward tip of the castle enclosure, the site of the castle's future great north gate.

Besides the new fortifications, Henry was evidently concerned to create domestic apartments that could accommodate royal visits and important guests. The rooms of the great tower itself were luxuriously appointed, with their own piped water supply. The private rooms, furthermore, reveal an intriguing insight into the castle's early history. Among the rooms of the great tower were two chapels, with rich architectural sculpture identical to that found

in the works at Canterbury Cathedral (which were being carried out at the same time). Revealingly, we know from a slightly later document that one of the chapels became dedicated to the man who had enraged Henry in life, but whose death had forced him to repent and to confront a growing international pilgrimage network centred on Canterbury: St Thomas Becket.

The Pipe Rolls record that the senior mason responsible for the work at Dover from 1181 was Maurice 'the engineer'; he was, most likely, also the principal architect. This was almost certainly the same Maurice 'the mason' who worked on Henry's great tower at Newcastle-upon-Tyne from 1168. In fact, however, though there are points of similarity between the planning of Maurice's towers at Dover and Newcastle, in terms of architectural detail they are quite different. The contrast suggests that in both cases locally engaged masons influenced the architecture of the respective buildings. At Dover, the style of the architectural sculpture suggests, as we have seen, that the masons working on the castle were drawn from the ongoing operations at Canterbury Cathedral.

It is not easy to tell where the works carried out by Henry end, and those carried out by his rebellious sons Richard and then John, begin. In a recurrent pattern within the Anglo-Norman dynasty, with no clear tradition of primogeniture, Henry's sons had fought their father, and each other, to secure a significant slice of the huge Plantagenet Empire. It is generally presumed that Henry completed the great tower and the inner bailey before his death in 1189. His expenditure on the castle peaked in 1185–86 and tailed off slightly thereafter. Nevertheless, the amount spent on Dover in the last recorded financial year of his life, £185 in 1187–88, still represents a very large sum of money. Both Henry II's surviving sons continued their father's lavish investment on works at Dover. While some aspects of John's work are separately documented, to all intents and purposes Richard I's building at Dover is indistinguishable from that undertaken by his father.

ABOVE *With painstaking attention to historical accuracy, the domestic apartments in the keep have been laid out as they may have appeared in the late twelfth century*

PREVIOUS PAGE *The northern barbican as seen from the inner wall. Attackers were confronted by a long diagonal route to the King's Gate while under attack from the wall's defenders in this 'killing zone'*

Whatever the case, around 1190 either Henry or Richard completed the great tower and also began a new stone wall punctuated with towers along the line of the main castle ditch. In the Pipe Roll for 1195–96, specific mention is made of payments for the wall of the castle, which is presumably a reference to this operation. Work may have begun on the large, faceted tower – known today as the Avranches Tower – which filled the gap in the eastern ditch left by the original castle entrance. A polygonal structure, this was among the castle's most powerful fortifications, its walls laced with firing galleries for crossbowmen. Unusually, not enough space was left for the drawing and firing of longbows, making it perhaps the first purpose-built crossbow tower.

Following his accession to the throne in 1199, John appears to have pressed on with the stone fortification of the ditch round the northern tip of the castle. In line with the latest architectural

fashion, the new towers along the wall were D-shaped in plan, rather than rectangular, as those previously built had been. The curved surface meant that missiles were more likely to strike only a glancing blow (see Towers box, p.117). The creation of such a long line of fortification in this way can be compared to John's similar work at several other castles, including Corfe in Dorset and Scarborough in Yorkshire.

John's building operations at Dover are poorly documented and any chronology is tentative. But we know that in 1205 a master miner and twelve associates were employed at the castle – perhaps constructing the network of defensive tunnels at its northern tip. This work must in turn have been carried out in tandem with work to the centrepiece of John's building operation: a new north gate to the castle. The miners created a system of galleries and tunnels cut out of the chalk beneath the north gate. Though later changes have made it difficult to understand their original extent and form, there

ABOVE *On the outer wall's northern stretch, the Avranches Tower guards a vulnerable patch of high ground (centre left), which is believed to be evidence for the Iron Age fort at Dover*

LEFT *The Avranches Tower in the outer wall. It was provisioned with a vast number of arrowslits to cover multiple fields of fire to the east*

certainly existed a tunnel beneath the gate passage which dropped into the castle ditch to create a sally port.

John's north gate was a large stone building fronted by two D-shaped towers pierced with arrow loops that overlooked the castle ditch. It probably stood three or four storeys high in the manner of similar twin-tower gatehouses of the period, such as Warkworth, Northumberland (c.1200) and Pevensey, Sussex (c.1190). Descending from the threshold of the gate across the outer castle ditch, there must have existed a massive timber bridge dropping to an outer fortification or barbican. This barbican was circular in plan; its earthworks survived into the 18th century, before being cannibalised to create the present bastion outside the castle walls. It is described in 1216 as being enclosed by a ditch and an oak palisade.

John certainly extended the outer wall southwards along the western side of the castle as far as Peverell's Gate. This internal gate separated the lower area of the castle, towards the cliffs, from its upper, northern parts. The construction of Peverell's Gate was probably connected to the refortification of the pharos and St Mary

ABOVE *To reach the keep, besiegers had to overcome the outer ditch, the twin towers of the north gate (now the Norfolk Towers – the row of towers in the outer wall), the wooden bridge to their right (now stone), the barbican and the King's Gate (right, in the inner wall)*

in Castro: by cutting away the sides of the hill on which they stood, John created an imposing new semi-circular rampart around them.

By the time John faced the massive threat to his authority from the rebellious barons and invading French army in 1215–16, Dover had become a formidable stronghold, with two circuits of stone walls around an imposing great tower and a subsidiary inner bailey around the Roman pharos. To either side of the castle, the ditches and the natural fall of the land made the fortifications unassailable. Only to the north, at the tip of the defences, was the castle approachable – and here it was protected by a massive new gate with its two towers, as well as a deep ditch and a heavily-fortified barbican.

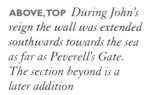

ABOVE, TOP *During John's reign the wall was extended southwards towards the sea as far as Peverell's Gate. The section beyond is a later addition*

ABOVE, BOTTOM *At the time of the siege in 1216, the mound on which the Roman and Anglo-Saxon buildings perch is thought to have been protected by wooden fortifications*

R bell ogreffio menfe iulio vi. kl. auguft r.

Rex fracoz philippus.

REBELLION AND INVASION

John cannot have anticipated that his great castle at Dover would face a large-scale foreign invasion so soon. However, although the conflict with his barons was a civil war and led to the signing of Magna Carta at Runnymede in June 1215, this was also a war that had taken place in a European context. The ruthless manner in which John raised money by taxing his leading subjects might not have caused the upheaval it did, had not John seemed to spurn this wealth in disastrous wars which caused the loss of much of his continental empire (see Plantagenet Empire box, p.47). As the power of the Capetian dynasty in France revived under Philip Augustus in the late-twelfth and early-thirteenth centuries (see Philip box, p.102), a combination of misfortune and misjudgement brought about the humiliating loss of huge swathes of territory, including Normandy,

PREVIOUS PAGE *Dover has been adapted and augmented to meet new threats. The keep and inner wall are twelfth-century, the Constable's Gate (far right) is thirteenth-century, and the triangular spur (foreground) dates from the eighteenth century*

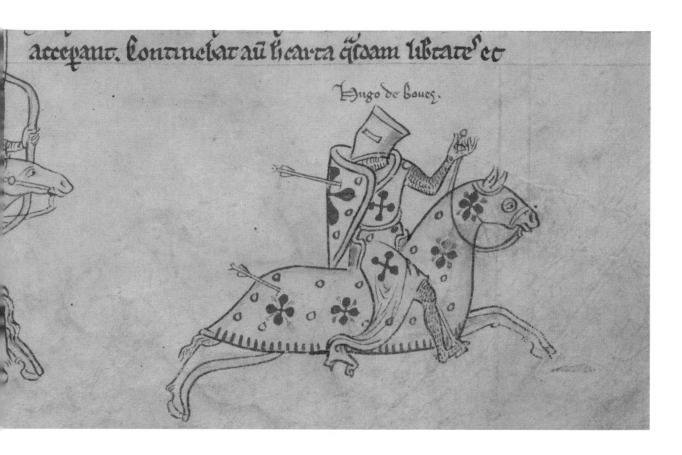

accepant. Continebat aū ħ carta quōdam libtatḗ et

Hugo de boues.

to the French king (see Chapter 2). And in 1214 the decisive French victory at Bouvines dealt a final shattering blow to John's hopes of reconquest. Key territories of the Plantagenet Empire – Anjou, Brittany, Maine, Touraine, Normandy – were lost to France.

Magna Carta was in some ways a direct product of John's blasted reputation on the international stage. Its failure, for John never intended to abide by its constraints, had ramifications beyond the borders of the kingdom. As England descended into civil war, John's first act of the conflict was to summon to his aid an army of mercenaries from Flanders. Leaving his queen and eldest son in the safety of Corfe Castle in Dorset, he travelled to his stronghold at Dover to await their arrival. From the outset, however, John's luck was poor. The mercenary force departed for England on 24 September 1215, but sailed directly into a great storm that battered the fleet. Many of the ships foundered and the English shore was reported to be awash with the corpses of drowned soldiers. Those that did survive struggled to safety at any port they could reach and travelled onwards to join up with John's army. Though deprived of most of the mercenary reinforcements he had relied upon, John was driven to commit his small army to the field.

The 'Northerners', as John's opponents were sometimes known, had occupied London and made it the centre of their operations – the city making little effort to oppose their entrance. With John at Dover, they hoped to bottle him up in Kent, and to this end a rebel army marched southeast, taking the town and castle of Rochester, on the main London road beside the Medway crossing of the Thames estuary, before pressing onward to confront the king.

Reluctant to be forced into a corner, John left the security of Dover and marched towards Rochester. On reaching Canterbury, he paused and began to erect barriers across the road. As news of the rebel advance from Rochester reached him, his nerve failed and he turned back for Dover. Meanwhile, having heard of John's departure from Dover, the rebels had then also retreated. John was the first to recover from this mutual panic and, encouraged by his enemies' loss of nerve, he marched directly for Rochester. There he seized the town and destroyed the bridge, isolating the castle from London.

A garrison of about ninety rebel knights was caught in the castle which, like Dover and others of the period, was centred on a great tower or keep. (Rochester Castle's tower, still standing today, was the tallest built anywhere in England – see The Keep box, p.50.) The intensive siege would last over seven weeks, and ultimately starvation – as at other sieges of the time – would prove the key to success.

> **THE INTENSIVE SIEGE WOULD LAST OVER SEVEN WEEKS, AND ULTIMATELY STARVATION WOULD PROVE THE KEY TO SUCCESS**

After the outer defences had been demolished, the great tower alone resisted the stone barrage from John's catapults. Miners succeeded in bringing down one side of the tower, but a thick internal wall allowed the defenders to shelter on the other side. 'Never in our age', wrote the chronicler Walter of Coventry, had 'a siege been driven so hard, or resisted so bravely'. In spite of this, ravaged by hunger and forced to eat horseflesh, the garrison finally succumbed. First the weakest were thrown out, and some of these unlucky men had their feet cut off at John's command. Soon afterwards, the remainder were captured and put in chains, unless they could claim Benefit of Clergy. Such was John's fury that many were afraid he would put the entire army to death. In fact, Walter reported, 'he only ordered the hanging of one man', a crossbowman said to have been fostered by John since childhood. According to Walter, the fall of Rochester made a great impression, with many concluding that castles no longer offered the protection they once had:

> *All the other rebels were desperate at this news; some fled in fear back to London, others took refuge in monasteries, and now there were few who cared to put their trust in castles.*

After the fall of Rochester, John planned an expedition to ravage the territories of his opponents. After celebrating Christmas at Nottingham Castle he marched north by way of Pontefract, York, Durham, Alnwick and Berwick, before raiding into Scotland to punish King Alexander for an attack on Newcastle. At the end of January he returned south through Suffolk and Essex. In the course of an extraordinarily rapid campaign, John's army seized all the rebel castles on its route, massacred the population of several towns and pillaged the countryside with a ferocity that made a deep impression on contemporaries (and contributed to John's poor reputation).

Holding out in London, the Northerners were demoralised by word of John's brutal campaign. Seeking to regain momentum, they made overtures to Prince Louis, the son of John's arch-enemy

Philip Augustus, King of France. They promised Louis the English throne if he would support their cause. For the French, it was a difficult situation. John had previously placed England under the protection of the Papacy, and so a French invasion would risk placing them at loggerheads with the Pope. The solution was to cook up for Louis a largely fanciful claim to the English throne through his wife Blanche of Castile (a grand-daughter of Henry II). This gave him the excuse to come to England on his own initiative, contrary to his father's public prohibition, though in reality he acted with Philip Augustus' approval and military backing.

As Louis mustered forces in Calais, John returned once more to the adjacent port at Dover. With a powerful fleet at his command he intended to fight the French at sea. Again, however, the elements conspired against him. On the night of 18 May 1216 a storm scattered his fleet and left the sea clear for the French to cross. More happily for John, the calm weather brought to England a crucial ally, Cardinal Gualo, an emissary from the Pope. Furious at Louis' temerity in invading a kingdom under Papal protection, Gualo excommunicated all those who supported Louis, and placed all rebel-held locations under interdict – prohibiting the practice of most religious ceremonies. The whole of England had been under interdict between 1208 and 1213, while John refused to accept Stephen Langton as

HUBERT DE BURGH

The career of Hubert de Burgh was an illustration of how far it was possible to rise from relatively humble origins in medieval England (even if older baronial families scorned him at times as a 'new man'). Born around 1170 to a family of minor Norfolk landholders, he would become one of the great knights of the age and, as Chief Justiciar of England, the second most important man in the realm.

His elder brother had served Prince John in Ireland and may have provided Hubert with an entry to royal service. By the time John became king in 1199, Hubert was the chamberlain of his household. From 1202 Hubert became closely involved in French affairs on John's behalf, as Philip Augustus, the King of France, made huge inroads into John's continental possessions (see Chapter 2). Early in 1203 he was sent to take command of one of the crucial Anglo-Norman frontier castles at Chinon. There he conducted a long and heroic defence of the castle which culminated in the summer of 1205 with the garrison riding out from the ruined fortifications and fighting until they were killed or captured. Hubert himself was injured and held for ransom as a prisoner.

John contributed towards his ransom and when Hubert finally returned to England, later in 1207, his career quickly revived. By 1215 he was dignified with the office of Justiciar of England, which made him the second figure in the kingdom after John, and effective ruler during the king's absences abroad. In the preamble to Magna Carta, Hubert is listed among those lay barons who advised the king to grant it. As relations between the king and his rebel barons worsened, Hubert was made castellan of the key castle of Dover – a loyal ally to John, with a clear vested interest in upholding his cause. An experienced soldier, he was a formidable opponent to Louis when the French prince laid siege to Dover in July 1216.

After John's death Hubert remained loyal to his young son, becoming the effective Regent of England after the death of William Marshal in 1219 and remaining one of the realm's most influential men. In 1228 Henry III made him Justiciar for life and granted him the English castles of Dover, Canterbury and Rochester as well as a number of castles in Wales. In the 1230s, his enemies managed to have him deprived of his lands and briefly imprisoned, but he was restored, and died as an old man in 1243.

Archbishop of Canterbury. The rift had since been mended, and Stephen in turn angered the Pope by supporting the rebel barons.

Having observed Louis' fleet, John fled Dover leaving this, his most important stronghold, in the hands of a trusted ally. He filled it with a large garrison and plentiful supplies, before travelling to Winchester, the second city of the kingdom. Louis marched from the Kent coast towards London, taking the sympathetic Canterbury without a fight, and Rochester – scene of the rebel defeat a few months previously – after a short siege. On 2 June 1216 he entered the capital itself, and stayed at Lambeth Palace, the seat of the Archbishop of Canterbury.

John rejoined his queen at Corfe in Dorset – a castle he had refortified, borrowing ideas from his brother Richard's Château Gaillard. Meanwhile, Louis seized Winchester, along with two castles in Hampshire: Portchester and Odiham (the latter one of the few John built from scratch). As his campaign gathered momentum, Louis began to attract important defectors from John's following. He also won the support of two powerful figures from beyond the borders: King Alexander of Scotland, and Prince Llywelyn of North Wales.

Increasingly secure in his position, Louis sent one of his captains to besiege Windsor, while he turned his attention to Dover – the castle which controlled his communications with France. To take Dover would place Louis in a very powerful, perhaps unassailable position. As he neared what he knew to be a formidable stronghold, Louis must have hoped that the garrison, disheartened by the weakness of John's position, might surrender the castle – or that the castle's commander might be persuaded to shift his allegiance. But he knew enough about Hubert de Burgh, the man John made his constable at Dover and Justiciar (second-in-command of the kingdom), to know that neither of these scenarios was probable. Hubert de Burgh had been tested under siege before and had proved himself to be determined and loyal.

THE KNIGHT

Knights formed the fighting core of all major armies in medieval Europe. They were the social and military elite: mounted warriors who enjoyed the prestige long associated with horsemanship, and who provided kings with a certain period of military service annually in return for grants of land. It was from their training as horse riders or 'chevaliers' that their particular code of conduct termed chivalry derived, with its emphasis on honour, courtesy and courage.

From manuscript illustrations and tomb effigies a considerable amount is known about the equipment of knights at the time of the Dover siege. Each would have possessed a coat of chain-mail – a vastly expensive object in its own right. This would have been worn over heavy, padded clothing to prevent the metal from chafing the skin, and was complemented by chain-mail covering for the legs and feet. The head was protected by a hood of mail, a padded steel cap and a great helmet worn over the whole with slits for seeing and breathing.

By the early thirteenth century it was common for knights to wear a light overmantle called a surcoat, which could be emblazoned with a distinguishing device or coat of arms. It was at this time that heraldry was coming into general use. A device might also be painted on the shield carried by a knight, which in this period would have been shaped like an inverted teardrop. During sieges knights would have dismounted and served as formidable foot soldiers. Their weapons on foot would have included swords, daggers, maces and axes. The sword was the knight's principal weapon. From the early fourteenth century it became enhanced with an extended grip and a double-edged blade to improve the cutting blow and the sharper thrust necessary to overcome the increasing weight and strength of armour.

Such was the greater value placed upon knights as the social elite among fighting forces, that they were frequently captured alive in order to be ransomed, often for substantial sums. The more lowly men-at-arms, worthless as prisoners, were usually killed.

One contemporary account in particular – the *Histoire des Ducs de Normandie et des Rois d'Angleterre* – offers an exceptionally detailed and accurate account of Louis' siege of Dover. It seems likely that its anonymous author was either there or knew somebody who was. According to this version of events, de Burgh had carefully prepared for the siege by provisioning the castle with plentiful supplies. His garrison comprised more than 140 knights – the elite fighters of a medieval army – along with 'a great number of men at arms'. Other

members of the garrison, such as the crossbowmen or the specialist workmen, like the carpenters and miners, are not mentioned. All in all, a formidable force had been installed at Dover, greater than that which English castles usually contained.

Louis appears to have begun his siege of Dover in a relaxed manner. On arrival he lodged himself in the priory within the town. This was conveniently placed beside the harbour, and was separated from the castle by the Dour estuary. In times of peace the monastery was a popular place to stay for eminent individuals passing through Dover on business, on their way to or from the Continent. As the most comfortable available residence, it was the obvious choice for the prince and his retinue. Much of Louis' army was billeted in the town, with the remainder camped in tents nearby. A number of senior French knights left Louis' army while it was based at Dover. These men were offering their services to Louis by choice and he chose to accommodate their coming and going. In this regard, as

PERRIER

Machines designed to hurl stones and other missiles date from ancient times. Throwing-machines appeared in the Greek and Roman world in the fourth century BC. These were often 'torsion-powered' – utilising the energy contained in a twisted cord to fire arrows as well as stones. Such machines were given the common name 'catapult'. Developed to target enemy soldiers, by 332 BC at the siege of Tyre they were being used to destroy fortifications. Construction and trajectories were calculated with mathematical precision. Ancient balls have been found on which their weight is carefully marked.

From about the seventh century AD a new man-powered stone-thrower appeared in Europe, having spread gradually west from China. Arabs used the name *manjaniq* for all stone-throwing machines which used a large beam, while adapted forms such as *manganon* and *manganikon* appeared in Europe. The French later used the word *perrière*. Anglicised, these terms became 'mangonel' or 'perrier'.

Ropes were attached to the short end of the firing arm. A trained crew of pulling men – often dozens, sometimes even hundreds – would pull on the ropes simultaneously, causing the throwing arm to rotate rapidly upwards. At the end of the arm was a sling in which the ball was placed. This whipped round, producing additional acceleration before releasing the projectile.

This man-powered 'perrier' was simple to construct and quick-firing (at three or four shots per minute). At between 100 and 150 metres, however, its range was not large enough to exceed that of enemy archers. As a result the pulling team was invariably targeted and casualties were high. Some larger perriers were built in a pyramid shape, with covered sides beneath which the pullers could shelter. Mongol armies got round the problem simply by using prisoners and local peasants as expendable slave labour. It was also difficult for teams to pull on the ropes repeatedly with equal force, particularly on slippery or uneven ground. As a result accuracy was comparatively low.

in others, the prince acted his part as an overlord to perfection – in stark contrast to England's King John.

If this relaxed behaviour was intended to express the calm confidence of Prince Louis, the Dover garrison responded in kind. They frequently paraded in full armour outside the castle barbican beneath the north gate, in full view of the besieging army. The intention, presumably, was to show their exceptional strength and express their appetite for the fight. The *Histoire* tells us that during these parades, the crossbowmen of Louis' army approached within range to fire arrows at the garrison. On one occasion a crack crossbowman named Ernaut crawled so close to the garrison's parade line that several of Hubert's soldiers ran upon him. Having advanced too far to be supported by his comrades he was captured. One may assume that he met with an unenviable fate – not being entitled to the consideration, or worth the ransom, that an eminent knight might command.

In mid July the siege began in earnest. Louis divided his forces: one part remained in the town, while the bulk of the army moved up the hill to the castle, to a large encampment which must have stood outside the barbican and north gate. Louis also sent his fleet to sea in order, as the chronicler explains, to shut in the castle on all sides – to ensure that no supplies or reinforcements could be landed by water. Massive siege engines were then set up to bombard the walls and gate (see Perrier box, p.76), while a wattle tower – described as 'a very high castle made of hurdles' – was erected (see The Carpenter box, p.82). This would have been sufficiently tall that Louis' crossbowmen, from its upper levels, had a clear sight over the castle walls, and so could harass the garrison more effectively. Since both the tower and the siege engines must have been within bow-shot of the walls, they

THE DOVER GARRISON FREQUENTLY PARADED IN FULL ARMOUR OUTSIDE THE CASTLE BARBICAN

*During the siege,
French miners undermined
one of the north gate's
towers. The Norfolk
Towers (background)
and St John's Tower
(foreground) were later
constructed to strengthen
this vulnerable side*

must themselves have been provided with a protective screen,
and perhaps have incorporated earth and timber fortifications
of their own.

In addition Louis built a covered gallery (known as a 'cat')
which was moved towards the wall of the barbican. Placed
across the ditch, it provided cover for miners busy working,
probably at ground level, to undermine the oak palisade of the
barbican. The chalk on which Dover was built was certainly
easier to dig than other rocks and the miners succeeded in
creating a breach in the palisade, which was stormed by Louis'
knights causing the barbican to fall (see Undermining box,
p.135). We are told that Huart de Paon, a mounted soldier
who bore the banner of the Lord of Bethune, was the first to
scale the breach. We know also that the captain of the gate and
barbican, Pierre de Creon, received a terrible wound during the
fighting and died soon afterwards.

Louis now pressed his attack, sending miners to dig beneath
the castle gate. 'They mined', the chronicler relates, 'so that
one of the towers fell, of which there were two'. The surviving
remains of this gate are preserved within the Norfolk Towers

which today occupy this part of the outer wall. These show that it was the eastern tower that was undermined. Internally, the walls of the surviving tower are tinged red, an indication that the stones were exposed to intense heat during the siege. Presumably a second cat was constructed up the inside face of the castle ditch, the levels precluding the excavation of a full tunnel.

Once the supporting timbers had been ignited and had given way, the huge tower collapsed to the ground in a thunderous crash of falling masonry, accompanied by the screams of soldiers within. Large numbers of Louis' men surged through this breach into the castle. As steel clashed with steel his knights stormed inwards as the knights of the garrison tried desperately to limit the incursion, and for a short while Dover's defence hung in the balance. Fortunately for Hubert, the design of the castle, with its inner bailey, meant that there were as yet unpenetrated layers of defence for his men to fall back upon, and from which they could harry the attackers as they pushed through the narrow gap in the outer walls. It seems that eventually, after a period of savage fighting, the garrison managed to kill or repel Louis' advance party. Timbers (some described as crossbeams) were ripped from the castle's internal buildings,

LEFT *Once the French had penetrated the outer wall, they encountered fierce resistance from the garrison here in the outer bailey*

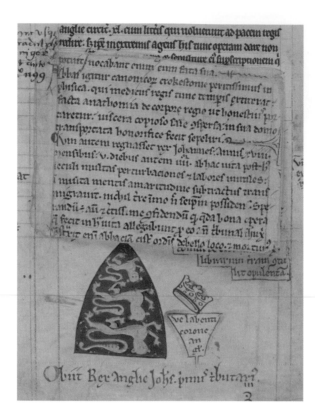

wherever they could be found, to block the breach. With the failure of this attack came a stalemate, followed on 14 October by a truce.

While Louis was engaged at Dover, John, having heard various pieces of welcome news, was tempted to launch a campaign in East Anglia. Several of his leading opponents had been killed: one shot in the head by a crossbow bolt while inspecting the fortifications of a castle loyal to John; another killed accidentally in London while taking part in a tournament. At Lynn in Norfolk, however, disaster struck. Either through overexertion, or overindulgence at a feast hosted by the town, John contracted dysentery. Then on 11 October, while his baggage train struggled across the Welland Estuary of the Wash into Lincolnshire, it was overwhelmed by the tide. Famously, all his treasure was lost to the sea and the quicksand. Word of this disaster, combined with the news that Dover had struck a truce with Louis – at which John was reported to be furious – made his condition worse. Early in the morning of 18 October 1216, as he lay at Newark Castle with a howling gale outside, King John died. There were many who did not mourn him. One of his critics remarked bitterly 'foul as it is, hell itself is made fouler by the presence of John'.

LOUIS AND THE AFTERMATH OF INVASION

The death of John transformed the political situation. On 28 October his nine-year-old son and heir was crowned Henry III in Gloucester Abbey – Westminster was still controlled by rebel forces – under the supervision of Gualo, the Papal Legate. At the same time, the elder statesman of English politics, William Marshal the Elder, Earl of Pembroke, was appointed regent of the kingdom. There was concern that the Justiciar, Hubert de Burgh, might take offence at being passed over for the post of regent, but the difficulty was patched over.

Ultimately John's death was to prove a blessing for the cause of his allies. For many of his opponents, John was a personal enemy – loathed for the abuse of his position, rather than because he was not rightfully king. His son had offended no one, and William Marshal was highly regarded for his long experience and prowess as a knight. For the rebel barons, too, support for Louis was proving increasingly irksome. Louis' French followers expected to be rewarded for their service with substantial landholdings, but nearly all the grants that he made to them were openly contested by his English supporters. This vicious competition for prizes would prove an important incentive for counter-defections from Louis' service to that of the young Henry III.

Some accounts of the Dover siege state that when news of John's death reached Dover, Louis briefly thought that he had won the crown. The chronicle of Roger of Wendover describes a conference called by Louis at which he offered Hubert de Burgh lands and substantial power in return for his loyalty. Hubert, it is said, deliberated with his fellows but decided to reject the overture, 'lest [the garrison] might be branded with treachery for a cowardly

THE CARPENTER

Carpenters played a key role in all aspects of medieval life, with the building and maintenance of castles being no exception. Timber had long been a primary building material: relatively light and strong. Into the thirteenth century even a royal castle like Northampton was still constructed largely from timber and earth. Once the principal walls of a castle were being built in stone, basic structural elements like roofing and flooring as well as furniture were the responsibility of specialist carpenters, who made up part of the huge army of craftsmen and less-skilled labourers required to build a castle. Among those important enough to be mentioned by name in the royal accounts relating to the construction of Edward I's castle at Conwy was an English carpenter, Henry of Oxford. The materials with which they worked were gathered by less-skilled woodcutters. Among those mobilised to build Edward's castles in Wales during 1282–83 were some 1600 woodcutters, from English counties near the border like Shropshire, Herefordshire and Gloucestershire.

James of St. George, the man with overarching responsibility for the construction of Edward's great castles in Wales (see Chapter 4), wrote to justify the cost of his work at Beaumaris:

In case you should wonder where so much money could go in a week, we would have you know that we have needed – and shall continue to need – 400 masons, both cutters and layers, together with 2,000 less-skilled workmen, 100 carts, 60 wagons and 30 boats bringing stone and sea coal; 200 quarrymen; 30 smiths; and carpenters for putting in the joists and floor boards and other necessary jobs. All this takes no account of the garrison … nor of purchases of material. Of which there will have to be a great quantity.

For besieging armies, carpenters were no less important. They were the men who were set to work constructing temporary towers, siege engines, and the great weapons that were used to bombard castle fortifications. Kings on campaign sometimes resided in elaborate timber buildings. Outside Dover, Prince Louis would have set his carpenters to work building the huge wattle tower – the 'high castle made of hurdles' – from which his crossbowmen could shoot over the walls, as well as the covered gallery under which his miners could work under shelter from arrows and other missiles.

Carpenters were highly skilled and respected craftsmen, having served long apprenticeships in a guild acquiring the knowledge of basic mathematics, woodwork and the use of tools, which was essential for their trade.

submission'. Whether this exchange took place, or was a patriotic fiction cooked up later, Louis left for London after nearly three months spent outside the gates of Dover. Ultimately, all he had achieved was a truce, but this did at least give him the peace of mind to launch another campaign through East Anglia. He took castle after castle: Hertford, Berkhamsted, Colchester, Orford, Hedingham, Pleshy and Cambridge. The ease with which his army captured these smaller castles is testament to Dover and its large and well-trained garrison. Norwich also surrendered to Louis, but he was checked at Lincoln, where the redoubtable Lady Nicola de

BELOW *Key castles taken by Prince Louis of France (blue) prior to the siege of Dover Castle in 1216*

ENGLAND

DOVER CASTLE

positions of some kind. His intention may have been to blockade the castle and starve the garrison into surrender. Very soon after the siege had resumed, however, a naval force loyal to Henry arrived which in turn blockaded Dover harbour, cutting off Louis' supplies. Then, just as he was feeling the pressure at Dover, word reached Louis of a disastrous battle at Lincoln on 20 May.

Louis' forces had placed Lincoln as well as Dover under siege. At Lincoln they had occupied the city and continued to assault the castle. William Marshal took a gamble, gathering all the forces he could muster to relieve the siege. Louis' men opted to remain within the security of Lincoln's walls when they saw the size of William's army. The bishop of Winchester, however, took it upon himself to assess a blocked gate in the city walls and discovered that it could be opened. Under cover of an assault to the north of the city, the blocked gate was forced open and a second force drove into the heart of Lincoln. So complete was the surprise, that one French engineer managing a catapult mistook William's men for allies and was decapitated 'mid shout' as he fired his engine at the castle. In the confused battle that followed, Louis' supporters were driven through the precipitous streets of the city, his chief followers either killed or captured.

LEFT *The medieval tunnels were enlarged in the aftermath of Louis's invasion. Hubert de Burgh supervised the repairs and improvements himself*

ABOVE *The circular St John's Tower (centre right), constructed after the siege, was connected to the medieval tunnels which led to the outer bailey*

This battle transformed the political situation, as Louis was quick to realise. When word reached him at Dover he promptly disassembled his trebuchet and held a council. At the same time he lifted his long-term siege of Windsor. With his hopes of further reinforcements from Calais dashed, Louis moved to London, which remained loyal to his cause, where he took up residence in the safety of the Tower. There he managed a deteriorating political situation and limited his military activities to raiding forays.

The final disaster for Louis was yet to come. On 24 August, a French fleet sailed for England packed with reinforcements raised by Louis' wife, Blanche. In response, a force loyal to Henry set sail from Sandwich, including – and perhaps led by – Hubert de Burgh. The principle French ship, armed with its own trebuchet, was surrounded by English vessels and its crew blinded by clouds of pulverised quick-lime as it was hurled onto the decks in pots. The English climbed aboard to hunt down the French captain, a notorious pirate and renegade monk called Eustace, in the hold of his own ship. He offered huge sums of money for his life but was offered the grim choice of execution at the ship's rail or on its trebuchet – catapulted at bone-breaking velocity into the open sea. It seems he took the former of the unenviable options, which offered a quicker end. A seaman called Stephen Crave, who for some reason bore him a personal grudge, stood up to wield the blade. Eustace's head was brought back to shore as a symbol of triumph. In the aftermath of the Battle of Sandwich Louis finally admitted defeat. He gave up his attempt to take the English throne and peace terms were agreed in early September 1217. At Sandwich, as at Dover, it was Hubert de Burgh who proved Louis' nemesis.

THE CASTLE REBUILDING PROGRAMME

Immediately after the siege at Dover, a massive programme of repair was initiated on behalf of Henry III. The work was probably overseen directly by that great supporter of John and his son, Hubert de Burgh, and it can be compared in technical terms with similar programmes at Windsor and Lincoln. The influence of French architectural ideas is apparent in all these projects. At Dover and Lincoln, for example, drum towers were created that come to a point or beak. This form is otherwise unknown in England, but is found from the late twelfth century in a number of French castles, such as Loches, thirty miles southeast of Tours, and Coudray Salbart, near the coast a hundred miles or so southeast of Nantes.

To make good the damage inflicted by Louis' miners, the north gate at Dover was rebuilt and its entrance blocked to create the present curious trinity of towers at the northern tip of the castle – the so-called Norfolk Towers. Meanwhile the tunnel network beneath the gate was greatly enlarged and connected to the former barbican through a tower built in the bottom of the moat.

With the northern tip of the fortifications re-ordered in this way it was necessary to create new entrances to the castle. Two new gatehouses, both conceived on an unprecedented scale, were built along the line of the walls to the east and west. That to the east, known as the Fitzwilliam Gate, had a triple-towered façade. From this a covered passageway extended, interrupted by a gate and a drawbridge that crossed the double ditches of the castle and issued out beyond them. To the west, an existing tower in the wall was enclosed by new structures to create Constable's Gate. This became, and remains, the main entrance to the castle, as well as the residence of the Deputy Constable of the castle. It is a vast building, its main entrance set in the middle of a façade nearly 120 feet high. It was approached across a bridge from a stone barbican set on the bank between the castle double ditches.

In the same period the domestic apartments of the castle were altered and the fortification in stone of the full line of the outer castle ditch was completed. The strengthened castle evidently became an object of particular pride for Henry III, and in November 1247 he instructed the constable to show it to a visiting

ABOVE *After the siege, the north gate was closed off. The Norfolk Towers now guard the castle's northern approach*

MEDIEVAL COMMENTATORS PRAISED DOVER CASTLE FOR ITS ROLE IN THE CRISIS OF 1216–17, HAILING IT AS AN IMPREGNABLE FORTRESS

dignitary 'in eloquent style so that the nobility of the castle shall be fully apparent to him, and that he shall see no defects in it'.

Medieval commentators praised Dover Castle for its role in the crisis of 1216–17, hailing it as an impregnable fortress. Modern writers have often echoed this judgement. Four decades later during another civil war, the so-called Barons' War of 1258–66, the castle was again besieged: this time by the forces of Henry III and his eldest son, the future Edward I. The attacking force had allies within. A group of fourteen captured royalist knights were held in chains within the great tower. Thanks to the complicity of three guards, one of whom secretly collected food from the town, they broke free. A siege within a siege took place as the knights barricaded themselves inside the tower, while the castle garrison attempted to force access. Immediately sensing an opportunity, Prince Edward rushed from London to Dover, gathering a force and attacking the castle from the front. The rebels now faced assault simultaneously from within and without, those inside the tower, according to the chronicle of Thomas Wykes, 'hurling down from above spears and crossbow bolts with great forcefulness, of which they had an abundant supply in the tower'. Crippled by this 'divided assault' they were compelled to submit. The castle fell, in other words, only in a highly untypical situation, in which the garrison was set upon by well-armed prisoners let loose within the central keep.

The architectural bones of the medieval castle created by Henry II, Richard I, John and Henry III at Dover between the 1180s and 1240s still survive. Later changes to the buildings, however, have transformed their character. Through the later Middle Ages, the castle was occasionally occupied by the king.

RIGHT *The Constable's Gate (right) was built far from the northern high ground in the 1220s as the castle's principal entrance*

Edward IV reordered Henry II's great tower in the 1470s as a luxurious residence; in 1520 this building provided the setting for Henry VIII's meeting with the Emperor Charles V. It was last used by an English monarch when Charles I lodged there with his new French bride, Henrietta Maria, in 1625.

The castle was captured in the Civil War of the 1640s by a Parliamentarian force that managed to scale the cliffs – an approach thought impossible by the royalist garrison. Henceforth, Dover was developed exclusively as a military base, its fortifications being adapted for the needs of cannon. As part of this process, the medieval castle became one element in an ever growing complex of military installations in and around the town. These were subject to bewildering and repeated changes as the technology of war developed through the eighteenth and nineteenth centuries. Their sheer scale is astonishing, and most now lie derelict. During both world wars the castle operated as a military headquarters and was further fortified. It was from within the tunnels beneath the castle that the Dunkirk evacuation was planned, and the D-Day invasion partly overseen. When the army eventually left in 1963, the castle was handed over to the State as a historic monument. Tunnels beneath the castle were retained and converted into a secret Cold War bunker, which would have acted as a seat of regional government in the event of a nuclear war. To a modern visitor it offers an unexpected insight into almost every period of English history.

What the history of Dover shows is that no castle, however impressive its fortifications, can be considered in isolation from the political and military context of a conflict in which it became embroiled. In the war that beset England during 1216 and 1217, Dover was, like numerous other castles, a fixture in a grand political game where allegiance and political fortune played a bigger role than fortifications. No castle, moreover, could function in isolation from its garrison; none, however mighty, was impregnable if its garrison lacked the will for the fight, or harboured traitors in its midst. But when a supreme structure like Dover was in the hands of a leader as

LEFT *During World War II, the Dunkirk evacuation was coordinated from Dover Castle. Prime Minister Winston Churchill is photographed here leaving its tunnels*

competent, loyal and strong-willed as Hubert de Burgh – a leader who had at his disposal a large, well-trained and well-provisioned garrison – it proved itself able to withstand the sternest tests that the warfare of the age could throw at it.

If its garrison spent longer observing truces with Prince Louis than it did actively opposing him, this was because Louis recognised the extraordinary effort that would be required to take the castle. He opted to campaign elsewhere, hoping to shift the political game in a manner that would force Hubert to agree to terms. Had he taken Dover at the moment when his position was strongest – when he controlled much of England, including its capital, and would thereby secure the shipping route to the continent – it seems reasonable to think that the outcome, and English history, might have been different. Dover's pre-eminent position as protector of England, and its throne, is well deserved.

THE BATTLE FOR NORMANDY:

CHÂTEAU GAILLARD

AN ENGLISH CASTLE

IN FRANCE

2

hâteau Gaillard was a source of immense pride to its builder. During the 1190s the King of England, Richard the Lionheart, had lavished money and attention on a castle he had constructed with astonishing speed to fortify the eastern border of his Duchy of Normandy. 'How beautiful', he is said to have remarked, 'is my one-year-old daughter'. He also called it his 'Castle on the Rock', and claimed he would hold it against besiegers 'though its walls were made of butter'.

1203 – The Lionheart had been dead for four years. A huge number of civilians as well as soldiers were sheltering within the castle's walls. Wracked by hunger, they might have wished the walls were made of butter. The vast caverns dug out of the chalk (beneath the main bailey) to house provisions were increasingly bare. Beyond the walls the encircling French army ravaged the surrounding countryside and cut off supplies.

As war loomed in the months before the siege, King John, Richard's brother and heir, had provisioned the castle well. He had sent good French wines and English cheeses in such quantity that the soldiers occupying it could have held out for a year. However, while the stores were sufficient to feed a garrison, they could not supply the townspeople of Petit Andely. At least 1,500 of them had scrambled in panic up the steep slope to take refuge within the castle as the forces of King Philip of France crossed the Seine. An attempt to re-supply Château Gaillard using armed ships to sail upriver had failed when the current proved too strong. Meanwhile, a small force led by the great Angevin knight William Marshal had tried without success to relieve the castle. After attacking Philip's main army encamped on the south bank, it was beaten off and withdrew to the west.

The living conditions for those forced to live week after week, crammed into a space that was never intended for such a large number of inhabitants, deteriorated. Members of the garrison who accessed the basement store-rooms were painfully conscious of the diminishing food supplies. As elsewhere, civilian settlement and castle had lived together in a symbiotic relationship – the one

deriving security, the other a source of food and services. Personal relationships had developed, and many of the garrison must have had family members among the town population which had joined them within the castle walls. Nevertheless, resentment mounted among the soldiers as resources were rapidly depleted by the 'useless mouths' of civilians who could play no worthwhile defensive role.

Increasingly the castellan, Roger de Lacy, rued his decision to admit them. The stakes, as de Lacy knew, were huge: with Gaillard would fall the whole of eastern Normandy and probably the rest of this key English possession on the continental mainland. A fortification could be impregnable – Gaillard itself was often considered as such – but this would be of little use if the garrison lacked the means to feed itself. Hunger was the most effective of all siege weapons. In November, de Lacy made a painful but perhaps inevitable decision. In a dramatic bid to hold out he rounded up five

hundred of the terrified civilians and sent them out of the castle into the no man's land between the outer walls and the besieging army.

THE RISE OF MEDIEVAL FRANCE

For some decades now the power of the French kings had been on the rise. Increasingly they chafed at the rule in the west of modern France by upstart Angevin kings who refused to pay the French king homage (see Plantagenet Empire box, p.47). Henry II had been a powerful and resilient king who fought to hold off alliances between his own rebellious sons and Philip II. One of these sons, Richard I, was a formidable military campaigner. But under John, Richard's brother and heir, the land of the English kings in France had shrunk dramatically after sustained assaults by Philip. This one-time friend and ally became a bitter opponent of Richard and John in turn.

Castles in Normandy's defensive chain, of which Château Gaillard formed the key – Conches, Le Vaudreuil, Gournay – had surrendered to Philip's forces without much of a fight. Important barons who held territory in the borderland switched their allegiance. While King John was away, having travelled west then sailed for England, the French imposed their control on the Seine valley and advanced on the great castle Gaillard itself. John's absence was a serious abdication of personal responsibility for a key fortress in a key territory and one that his elder brother would have found unimaginable, and unforgivable.

When Richard came to the throne back in 1189, he paid his last respects to his dead father. The nostrils of Henry's corpse were said to have gushed blood at this visit by his disloyal son and heir. Richard wasted no time having himself invested as Duke of Normandy and Aquitaine and crowned as King of England. As yet there would not be the fracturing of the Angevin empire for which Philip had hoped. Richard had earned renown as a brilliant warrior, and as a knight and troubadour poet with all the courtly virtues. However much Richard and Philip had once made common cause against Henry II, as king Richard was as determined to defend his realms against French encroachment as his father had been.

In 1190, Philip and Richard went together on Crusade. It was not a successful collaboration. Philip found himself overshadowed by this ideal Crusader king. Richard knew how to show largesse, paying his knights (according to one chronicler) at a higher rate, leaving Philip looking mean in comparison. Philip could not compete on the field of battle;. behind his back, men mocked his squeamishness and cast doubt on his nerve.

THE NOSTRILS OF HENRY'S CORPSE WERE SAID TO HAVE GUSHED BLOOD AT THIS VISIT BY HIS DISLOYAL SON AND HEIR

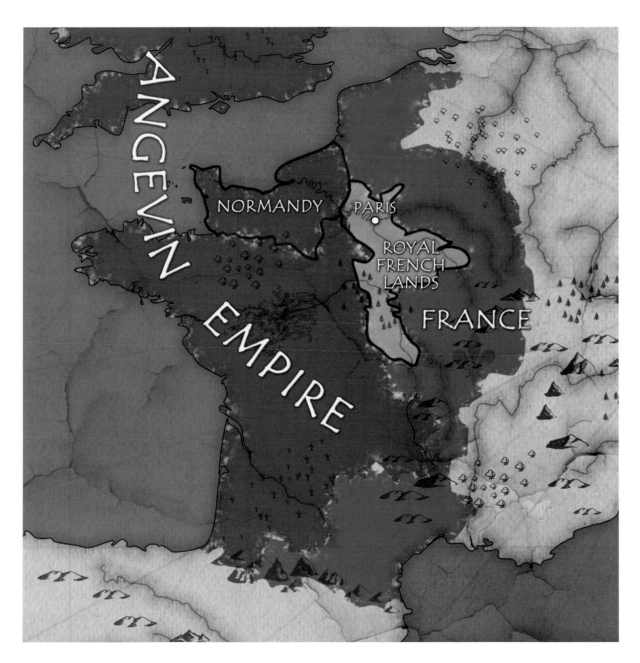

ANGEVIN EMPIRE

NORMANDY

PARIS

ROYAL FRENCH LANDS

FRANCE

ABOVE *France and the Angevin Empire in the late twelfth century. At its height the empire stretched from the Scottish border to that of modern-day Spain*

CHÂTEAU GAILLARD

PHILIP OF FRANCE

Philip II – Philippe Auguste, or 'Augustus' as he was admiringly nicknamed – was one of the greatest French kings. His administrative reforms put the French state's finances on a surer footing. He curbed the power of the nobility and promoted urban growth by supporting merchants, fortifying and improving Paris, and establishing new towns. His reign saw major territorial gains from the Plantagenet kings, as well as from other rivals.

Aged only thirteen, Philip became lost in the forest while hunting. Cold and afraid, he was forced to spend the night out before being found. When he contracted a dangerous fever, his father made a pilgrimage to the recently-created shrine to Thomas Becket at Canterbury, which was reported to be working miracles (see Chapter 1). Philip recovered, but his father suffered a stroke on his return journey and Philip found himself crowned king. In spite of his young age, he frustrated leading nobles by his unwillingness to be guided as his father had been.

Soon after his accession Philip began military campaigns against Henry II of England, often in collaboration with Henry's rebellious sons who fought their father to extract guarantees of a generous inheritance. Close to Geoffrey, Richard and John in turn, Philip was reportedly devastated by Geoffrey's early death. He fought alongside Richard against Henry, inflicting a rare defeat on the latter before he died. His legitimate sons, the dying Henry was reported as saying, were 'the real bastards'. He joined Richard again on Crusade, but fell out with him – as with his brother John – once they had assumed the English throne.

Philip struggled to compete with Richard's revered status as a model of the chivalric king – bold and decisive on the battlefield, high-minded off it – but in the long run it was he who won the upper hand. His careful husbanding of resources and insistence on value in his castle-building proved decisive.

Having left the Holy Land early to go back to France, Philip could scarcely believe his good fortune when his bitter rival was captured on his return by the Duke of Austria. It was 1194 before Richard was released, on payment of the quintessential king's ransom. In the meantime Philip had found Richard's younger brother John equally happy to take advantage of his imprisonment. Philip made deep inroads into Normandy, pushing back the frontier. When Richard returned, he soon reasserted himself, but had no choice but to accept some of Philip's conquests. Under treaties of 1195 and 1196, he acceded to a revised border between Normandy and France which ate into his duchy.

More important than the territory alone was the fact that he lost the fortifications which had secured the old border. This had bristled with Angevin castles – Nonancourt, Château sur Epte and Gisors among them – all rebuilt or improved by Henry II to secure Normandy against the French king. His works at Gisors were particularly impressive. The chronicler Gerald of Wales recounts a meeting between Henry and Louis VII at which the French king and his entourage were overcome by admiration for the soaring towers of Henry's new works. All, that is, except the young Philip, who muttered that he wished it were built of gold and precious stones so it would be more valuable to him when he took it. Now Philip had indeed captured this line of castles protecting Normandy, and Richard was forced to set about fortifying the new border.

Close to the new Norman line, on a great bow of the River Seine, lay the manor of Andely, a property of the Archbishop

BELOW *Key castles guarding the Norman border from French incursion in 1193. Later that year, King Philip of France seized almost all of them during the Lionheart's imprisonment*

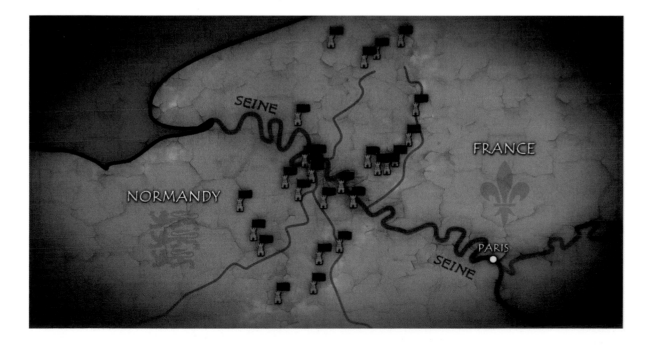

of Rouen. In a small valley a stream, the Gambon, ran into the Seine opposite an island in the middle of the great river. Above, overlooking the confluence and the island, towered a precipitous chalk cliff. Until now this great cliff above Andely had been well behind the Norman border. It may have been fortified in the distant past, but neither the dukes of Normandy nor the archbishops of Rouen had ever tried to do so, despite its commanding position above the Seine. Suddenly, however, it was in the midst of disputed territory and its potential for fortification was obvious to both Philip and Richard. The treaties of 1195–96 declared that Andely should remain neutral, unfortified by either side.

In practice, the temptation was too great. Richard had the advantage, for the Archbishop of Rouen was head of the Norman church. In 1195, the archbishop was Walter of Coutances, a loyal Angevin administrator who had acted briefly as justiciar of England when Richard was imprisoned in Austria, and been one of the hostages for the payment of Richard's ransom. Richard offered the archbishop some attractive lands in exchange, and moved to possess Andely, assuming Walter would have no objection. The archbishop, however, was furious. When Richard insisted, Walter fled Normandy and took his case to Rome.

The pope took the line that Richard should be able to defend his dominions, and in 1196 Walter returned and accepted the generous exchange of lands Richard had offered him. In any case he was presented with a fait accompli. For Richard had already begun to build a great castle on the cliff above Andely.

BUILDING CHÂTEAU GAILLARD

The castle on the rock was the centrepiece of an immense building project. On the island in the middle of the river, Richard built himself a fortified palace. On the meadows below the cliff, where the valley of Andely met the Seine, Richard founded and built a new town, Petit Andely. Fortified bridges linked the palace on the island to the new town, and to the south side of the river. The new town

was walled, and the river Gambon was diverted to provide it with a protective moat. The walls of the town stretched up the steep cliff to encompass the great castle on the rock in a single defensive entity. Where this outer curtain wall met the Seine upstream of the island palace, the town and the castle, Richard had the river itself fortified with lines of sharp stakes driven into the riverbed.

The entire complex was built with astonishing speed. Works were clearly well underway when Archbishop Walter got back from Rome in 1196. The project was largely complete by 1198, for the building costs were accounted for in the Norman exchequer rolls for that year. Corners were cut to get the great project finished on time: some walls were built too quickly for the mortar to have time to set properly. The exchequer rolls not only reveal how quickly the vast project was built, they also reveal how costly it

ABOVE Richard's town of Petit Andely, opposite the island in the River Seine. Built over eight hundred years ago, the church of Saint Sauveur (right) still stands today

RIGHT *Steep chalk cliffs made an assault on this western side futile. Once a wall ran down to the water where three rows of wooden stakes barred the river to French ships*

FAR RIGHT *Chalk and flint infill between the stone facings of Château Gaillard's keep. This practice would have saved substantial time and resources during the castle's construction*

PREVIOUS PAGE *Today the castle lies in ruins. The large tower of the outer bailey and the corrugated walls of the inner bailey still dominate the valley*

was. A huge workforce, including many specialist masons and carpenters, was required. Flint and chalk infill for walls could be sourced at the site itself – a by-product of the digging of substantial ditches – but the fine squared stone to finish walls, along with iron and enormous quantities of timber, had to be transported, often some distance. During the castle's construction Richard spent around 45,000 Angevin pounds – the currency of Angevin Normandy. In 1195 the total annual income of the duchy was 80,000 Angevin pounds. Richard was spending between a third and a half of the revenues of Normandy on this single great project.

THE MASON

Among the skilled craftsmen involved in the construction of medieval castles, masons were perhaps the most essential and the most respected. Experienced masons were in great demand and were relatively few in number in comparison with the vast armies of less-skilled labour recruited, or press-ganged, to help build a castle. Nevertheless, the fact that castles were constructed under more extreme time pressure than was the case with cathedrals, did mean that much larger teams were involved. In July 1286 no fewer than 227 masons were recorded as working on Harlech Castle in north Wales, with the help of 115 quarriers to provide the stone (as well as 546 general workmen).

When a suitable local stone was not available, good stone was often brought long distances – particularly if transport by water was possible. The Norman kings made significant use of the stone from Caen in Normandy, for instance, at the Tower of London and Canterbury Cathedral. In general, though, local quarries were chosen where possible. Château Gaillard was built, in part at least, from the rock on which it sat.

The mason's work began in the quarry, since stone was often supplied to the site pre-cut. The knowledge of geometry and measurement that was required for the daily work of the mason may have been the 'secret' information passed between masons which would later give rise to the traditions of Freemasonry. The master-mason is often portrayed with his set-square and compasses. The 'lodge' was originally a covered area on a building site where the masons could work, measuring and making alterations to blocks of stone.

Unusually among medieval tradesmen, masons were not closely controlled by a guild before the fourteenth century. Since large-scale projects did not occur regularly in a given area, they had to travel widely to learn their trade and to find work. They were, literally, journeymen; a journey, in its original sense, could be a day's work as well as a day's travel. They had, of course, widely varying pedigrees: freemasons were skilled craftsmen; rough-masons, as the name suggests, less so.

Long before the modern notion of an 'architect' developed, it was the 'master-mason' who took overall charge. He was responsible for the design, the engineering and for contracting the workforce. He answered directly to the patron who had commissioned the project. Unlike a modern architect he had worked up from being an apprentice mason, learning his trade through direct, hands-on building experience. Leading master-masons were eminent and sought-after individuals. James of St George, the man Edward I employed to oversee his great series of castles in Wales, was summoned from Savoy. In 1290 Edward appointed him Constable of Harlech Castle, and he lived for three years in the gatehouse accommodation he himself had designed.

The Château Gaillard complex was never meant to stand alone. Richard linked it in to a chain of fortresses protecting the new Norman border, just as his father had previously done. In time of war, garrisons and provisions could be moved rapidly between castles. If one castle was besieged, garrisons from other castles could ride out to attack the besiegers. To further strengthen Château Gaillard's position, Richard built two new castles as outposts. The small castle of Cléry could provide advance warning of an attack across the rolling uplands of the Vexin – the fertile plateau on the right bank of the Seine that straddles the Norman border. On the Seine itself, Richard constructed the advance tower of Boutavant (meaning 'pushing forward').

The great castle on the rock was the centrepiece of a formidable defence network. It occupies an irregular triangular spur of chalk cliff rising above the Seine and looking out across the Vexin. Deep ditches, natural in part but made steeper by Richard's engineers, surround it on the landward sides. Towering over these is the outer curtain wall, strengthened at various points by round towers, with a particularly large tower at the apex of the triangle, like the prow of a ship. This wall is faced in two different types of stone, a pale chalky clunch, and a darker-toned tufa, laid in alternate courses, to give a striped effect which recalled the Roman buildings which still abounded in twelfth-century France. The Angevin king-dukes would have been familiar with the striped Roman walls of their city of Le Mans; Henry II had used striped masonry to evoke the power and grandeur of Rome in his great square keep at Dover; and Edward I would later do the same at Caernarfon. Parts of the wall have holes for the wooden hoardings or machicolations, which would have lined the top of the walls, allowing defenders to drop missiles and to unleash

THE GREAT CASTLE ON THE ROCK WAS THE CENTREPIECE OF A FORMIDABLE DEFENCE NETWORK

their crossbows against potential attackers (see Machicolations and Crossbow boxes, pp. 214 and 274).

The apex of the triangle was used to create a sort of barbican or advance work (outer bailey), separated from the rest of the castle by a deep moat crossed by a drawbridge. Within the moat was a middle bailey which contained some of the practical buildings a garrison required, such as stables and storage areas. It had a deep well, and a substantial and skilfully-designed latrine tower. Beneath it, huge and elaborate cellars were hollowed out of the chalk cliff to hold the grain, wines and other provisions a castle would need to withstand a siege, or simply to supply a lengthy royal visit. Within the middle bailey a second steep-sided ditch isolated the centre of the castle. The inner bailey, with its keep and grand apartments for the king when in residence, was enclosed on the landward side by an inner curtain wall.

The inner curtain wall, towering above the inner ditch, undulated as if with a succession of very shallow towers, at the same time merging with the sloping bedrock to form a massive base. Large windows in the apartments and the keep provided magnificent views over the precipitous cliff to the Seine, out across lands disputed with the king of France. Like the inner curtain wall, the walls of the keep – already immensely thick – widened into a huge glacis at the base. Rounded on the side facing the Seine, the keep came to a sharp point on the landward side from which stone buttresses emerged to carry the wooden machicolations.

With its machicolations in place, its keep and all its mural towers crowned with steeply-pointed slate roofs, Château Gaillard must have looked impregnable. It incorporated all the latest ideas in defensive design. Some of the walls have archery slits built into them, so that archers could fire from within the walls themselves, as

CHÂTEAU GAILLARD INCORPORATED ALL THE LATEST IDEAS IN DEFENSIVE DESIGN

CLOCKWISE FROM TOP LEFT *The limestone walls shine a brilliant white in sunlight. It took roughly a year to quarry, transport and mortar the stone into place, where construction of other castles has taken decades*

Very little of the middle bailey wall survives today (left), but when the castle was built, domestic buildings and workshops stood against its inner facing

Vast cellars beneath the middle bailey where provisions were stored. Although blockade and starvation could minimise loss of life among the besiegers, it could also prove a very lengthy tactic

The semi-circular bulges of the inner wall are an unusual design, but they allowed the garrison more comprehensive fields of fire than a flat-faced wall

well as from the wooden machicolations above. Though wooden machicolations were commonplace, those supported on stone buttresses, as at Gaillard, were very unusual. Count Philip of Flanders had experimented with them at his castle in Ghent in the 1180s, and Edward I would later incorporate them in his great castle at Conwy.

The projecting spur of the keep was also unusual. Two other keeps with this design exist today: at the French castles of La Roche Guyon, on the Seine towards Paris, and Issoudun in the Berry. Neither is firmly dated. Issoudun also occupied an important border area between the Capetians and the Angevins. It came into Capetian hands as part of a treaty in 1200, and it is usually assumed that the castle was built subsequently by Philip Augustus. It is just possible, however, that Issoudun is another of Richard's castles. At all events, castle-builders in France were experimenting with the projecting

spur design at the time, perhaps because they thought that it could deflect missiles. Most of the lower parts of the walls of Château Gaillard – particularly the keep and the inner curtain wall – have a sloping glacis, so the base of the wall is very thick indeed. This too has often led to theories about missile deflection. In fact, in an age when mining had become an important element of siege-craft, it is more likely to do with stability. The thicker the wall, the further besiegers had to tunnel to bring it down. Richard and his engineers would have been acutely aware of this at Château Gaillard, for the chalk cliff on which the castle stands is soft and crumbly. If it was easy to dig ditches and foundations for the castle, it was also easy to undermine.

Access to the castle had been carefully considered. Anyone wanting to gain entry would have to ride or walk up the steep slope from the town under the eyes of the guards on the outer curtain wall. Eventually, a drawbridge would take them across the outer ditch through a tower-flanked entrance into the advanced work, or outer bailey, within the apex of the triangle. From there, they would cross another drawbridge to reach the service court of the middle bailey. A third drawbridge would then give them access through

ABOVE *A reconstruction of what the castle may have looked like from the east. The main entrance to the outer bailey can be seen below Château Gaillard's towers, crowned with wooden hoardings and turrets*

TOWERS

Towers which project outwards from castle walls are known as *mural towers* or *flanking towers*. The projection allowed defenders to target enemies with a greater field of fire than the arc of less than 180 degrees which a straight wall permitted. Multiple towers allowed interlocking fields of fire. Men in adjacent towers could shoot at the same target between the towers, and along the walls without having to lean out over the side. Provided the garrison comprised sufficient men, the greater the number of towers, the better covered the ground outside the wall would be – an important consideration in preventing the enemy from scaling the walls with siege ladders or undermining the foundations.

At the beginning of the thirteenth century, it became fashionable for castles to be built with round or D-shaped towers instead of square ones. At Dover Castle it is broadly possible to determine the sections of wall built by Henry II's son John because they are punctuated with round towers.

Round towers gave their defenders an improved field of fire. They were more difficult to bombard because projectiles were more likely to glance off at an angle, whilst the force of the impact was distributed throughout the structure more effectively. They were also harder to undermine because they lacked the vulnerable corners projecting outwards from the building. However, they were by no means invulnerable, as the sappers of Philip II proved at Château Gaillard in 1204, as did those of his son Prince Louis at Dover in 1216.

Arrow loops, crenellated battlements and turrets completed a tower's defences. One of the most famous defensive towers in Western Europe is the Avranches Tower at Dover Castle. Its multiple arrow loops and polygonal walls gave large numbers of crossbowmen deadly coverage over the relatively vulnerable ground to the east of the castle.

Towers could serve many more purposes than the obvious military ones, particularly in castles without keeps. The towers at Edward I's Conwy Castle in North Wales, for example, are named today after the roles they fulfilled: the Kitchen Tower, for instance, or the Prison Tower and Chapel Tower.

Sadly, large numbers of the towers we see today are nothing like as impressive as they would have been when built, thanks to the emergence of gunpowder artillery in the late Middle Ages. Unlike earlier siege weapons, in order to be effective, cannon had to be mounted on lower platforms than many early towers provided and as a result towers were cut down to lower heights.

the undulating inner curtain wall to the heart of the castle: the inner bailey, the apartments and the keep. Gaillard had, however, one glaring weakness. The castle occupied a spur of cliff above the Seine; but it only occupied the end of the spur. Behind the castle, beyond the triangular outer bailey, the chalk hill continued to rise, so that it was possible to set up an attacking position looking down on the castle. An experienced soldier, Richard must certainly have been aware of this weakness.

He perhaps thought it unimportant. He may in fact have felt that he was unlikely to have to defend his magnificent new castle. Money had been lavished on it more as a statement of power than the confession of weakness that castles often were. The large number of impressive castles built by the crusading orders in the Holy Land, or by Edward I in Wales, were an overt sign of the vulnerability both felt in foreign lands. But here, Richard felt himself to be merely fortifying his own territory.

Since his return from captivity, Richard had put Philip onto the defensive and he now had real expectation of pushing the Norman border back to the earlier line, making Château Gaillard not a border castle, but a great town, castle and palace complex in the midst of the Norman Vexin. Richard had his new port town of Petit Andely laid out with spacious streets, substantial stone houses and an elegant parish church. The latter was built by the same masons

who had worked on the magnificent Cistercian Abbey of Bonport, founded by Richard beside the Seine before he went on Crusade.

Richard seems to have expected his new town to become a thriving and prosperous port rather than a stressed front-line settlement. He used his castle not as a garrison but as a place to hold court. Its large windows offered glorious views over the lands he meant to re-conquer, and he issued many charters from his castle on the rock. With its striped Roman wall, its curving inner curtain wall, its buttressed tear-drop keep, its deep ditches and drawbridges, and its steeply-roofed towers, Gaillard must have looked the embodiment of a romantic castle straight from the contemporary pages of Chrétien de Troyes, the poet and composer known for his themes of chivalry and courtly love.

No doubt King Philip watched the building of the great castle with rising, but impotent, fury. He had no illusions about its significance. He fully appreciated the strategic importance of its position; it was for this reason that he had tried to ensure Andely remained unfortified. He was aware, too, of Gaillard's importance as a political statement: it clearly declared that Richard was now on the offensive, and that he expected to prevail. It proclaimed Richard as the King Arthur or Alexander of his age. Philip and his circle understood the importance of the glamour of kingship. His courtiers and court poets – above all William the Breton, who was writing a heroic account of the king's deeds – continually compared Philip to the great Frankish Emperor Charlemagne. But here, once again, Richard was setting the pace. Philip sourly declared of Château Gaillard that he would take it

> ITS LARGE WINDOWS OFFERED GLORIOUS VIEWS OVER THE LANDS RICHARD MEANT TO RE-CONQUER, AND HE ISSUED MANY CHARTERS FROM HIS CASTLE ON THE ROCK

though its walls were made of iron, eliciting Richard's famous boast that he could hold it were its walls made of butter.

Philip himself was already an experienced castle-builder, building, rebuilding or making major additions to a large number of castles; on occasion he personally directed their layout. He carried this out not just in old Capetian lands – at Paris, Orléans or Bourges – but also, as might be expected, in lands he brought under royal control for the first time: in the north-east of France and above all in Normandy. Where Richard's castle-building was hugely expensive – intended to display not only the king's brilliance as a military strategist but also his vast wealth and largesse – Philip kept building costs under tight control. Although he personally ordered the building of a wall round Paris, he persuaded the citizens themselves to pay for it. Philip's accounts survive for the period 1205–1212, a time of extensive castle-building as Philip imposed his rule upon newly conquered Angevin territories. Some fourteen castles were rebuilt or profoundly altered for approximately two-thirds of the cost of the Château Gaillard complex.

Philip controlled costs by sticking to relatively simple designs. While Château Gaillard was a one off, Philip's castles were built to a pattern, often with similar dimensions, by a small group of specialist masons. By medieval standards they were almost mass-produced. Castles were laid out as regular polygons: usually rectangles, but occasionally triangles if the lie of the land demanded it. Corners were defined and guarded by round towers, as were the gates. Long sections of curtain wall were provided with regularly-spaced round towers. The centrepiece of the castle was always a great cylindrical tower, usually set in the middle of the inner bailey, as at the Louvre, but occasionally on the inner bailey wall. So distinctive an aspect of Philip's building were these towers that their raising alone signalled his appropriation of castles. He did this to powerful effect in Normandy at the proud ducal castles of Gisors and Falaise. These plain cylindrical towers are powerful symbols in landscape and cityscape alike, and are so distinctive that historians have coined the term 'tour philippien' – the philippic tower.

Making bold and effective statements on a reasonable budget, Philip's castles employed simple masonry: rectangular blocks for the straight walls, simply-curved blocks for the round towers. Since all the round towers (mural towers, gate towers, the keep itself) were built to almost standardised measurements, stone could be ordered from the quarries in large quantities, and stored, if necessary, for the next castle. Philip's castles had none of the complex stone-cutting required to provide the undulating inner curtain wall of Château Gaillard, or the built-in stone machicolation buttresses of the keep. Nor did Philip demand the use of two different types of stone to produce the striped Roman effects of Richard's outer curtain wall at Château Gaillard (though the regularity of his castles was itself reminiscent of Roman city walls). His great towers advertised his wealth not by costing a fortune to build but simply by resembling the famous round tower his grandfather Louis VI had built in Paris as a treasure store.

CASTLES AS MILITARY STRATEGY

Philip's castles were practical from an economic and also from a military perspective. The bailey around the great cylindrical tower was usually quite spacious, providing ample room for stabling, storage for weapons and provisions, kitchens and accommodation for the garrison. A raiding party could ride out of them quickly, and if necessary return to the security of the castle with equal speed. However, in the mid-1190s, while Richard built Château Gaillard, much of Philip's castle-building lay in the future and he aspired to prove his pre-eminence not only by building but also by taking the finest castle of his leading rival.

Death, though, would deprive Philip of the chance to inflict decisive defeat on the Lionheart. In April 1199, Richard raced south to the Limousin to control a potential revolt. During the siege of the castle of Châlus, a stronghold of one of the rebels,

Richard was wounded by an arrow fired from a crossbow. The wound turned septic, and it was clear to Richard and his entourage that he would not survive. On his deathbed he left his great complex of lands – the throne of England, the duchy of Normandy, the counties of Maine and Anjou, and the overlordship of Brittany and Aquitaine – to his younger brother, John. Richard's body was taken to Fontevraud, to be buried at the feet of his father. His mother, Eleanor of Aquitaine, living in semi-retirement at Fontevraud, commissioned two fine effigies for the tombs of her husband and her son. John wasted no time in having himself invested as Duke of Normandy and then crowned King of England.

John's succession was not straightforward because John's older brother Geoffrey had fathered a son, Arthur of Brittany, who had a claim to succeed Richard. It was not clear whether the rights of an older brother's son should take precedence over those of the younger brother. Initially, Philip supported Arthur. When he agreed, by the Treaty of Le Goulet, to accept John's right, it was in return for the huge sum of 20,000 marks, at least half John's entire annual income for that year. With this payment John had acknowledged, in a way his predecessors as kings of England had refused to do, that the French king was his overlord for lands held in mainland Europe.

Philip knew John well and knew not to under-rate him. John was clever, meticulous and capable occasionally of brilliant generalship but he was also suspicious and given to intrigue. In a chivalric culture in which loyalty mattered, John's reputation had suffered by his attempts (encouraged by Philip) to weaken his brother's rule while Richard was a captive in Austria. Far from cultivating the loyalty of the great lords and barons of the Angevin lands, John actively undermined it. The Angevins were famous for their fierce tempers, but John seemed also to possess a streak of deliberate cruelty. When his young nephew Arthur disappeared while in John's custody, rumours spread that his uncle had had him blinded, murdered and dumped in the Seine – an outrage to the morality of his day as to that of ours.

When John eloped with and married Isabelle of Angoulême, betrothed to an important baron of Poitou, Philip had an excuse to take the offensive. Summoned by Philip to account for this mistreatment of his vassal (one beneath him in the feudal chain of allegiance), John refused, as Philip had probably expected him to do. Philip then declared John forfeit of his French lands and undertook to seize them, announcing his intentions by attacking and destroying Boutavant, the advance castle built to protect Château Gaillard.

For the remainder of 1202 and 1203, both kings prepared for war. John ensured that his Norman castles and their garrisons were prepared and provisioned, supplementing his Norman revenues with money raised in England. Philip had increased his riches as king, reforming the administration of his expanding lands and fostering the vitality of his capital city, Paris. Wealth meant a great deal in war. A rich king could employ large numbers of mercenaries, including the specialist military engineers who played a vital role in siege warfare – the sappers who undermined walls, and the men who constructed and fired the great catapults and siege engines. The well-judged distribution of gifts, moreover, could decide the allegiance of a baron, and great barons brought substantial retinues of their own.

Both kings built alliances. John tried to rebuild the alliances which had served Richard well: with his nephew, the Emperor Otto of Brunswick; his brother-in-law, the king of Castile; and the count of Flanders. Above all, he seems to have depended on Pope Innocent III. It was the Pope who

THE ANGEVINS WERE FAMOUS FOR THEIR FIERCE TEMPERS, BUT JOHN SEEMED ALSO TO POSSESS A STREAK OF DELIBERATE CRUELTY

had approved Richard's decision to build Château Gaillard in order to protect his lands from attack; now John hoped he would order Philip to cease harassing his great vassal. But when the Pope wrote to urge both kings to make peace, Philip replied tartly that this was a matter of feudal law, and lay outside the competence of the Papacy. Philip's alliances were less grandly international than John's, but their local nature made them devastatingly effective. He played to Breton sensibilities, continually demanding that John hand over the vanished Arthur, and courted any who might be disaffected within the Angevin Empire – barons, churchmen and townsmen.

The great lords of Normandy were faced with a difficult decision, especially those whose lands and castles lay in the extensive Norman border zones. Many of them had married into the great families of Capetian France, and thus had landed interests in both France and Normandy. If they backed Philip, and he won, they would be able to enjoy all their French and Norman lands in peace. John had alienated too many of them, and they felt none of the personal loyalty to John that they did to the chivalric Richard, or even to old King Henry. As soon as Philip began to make serious gains in Normandy, important members of the Norman baronage deserted John.

Norman towns and cities whose wealth depended on trade with England, especially Rouen, Caen and Dieppe, remained in close alliance with John. But many in the areas which had suffered the ravages of twenty years of fighting were weary of the continuous war. The Angevin defence of Normandy had placed huge financial strains on the duchy. Every ducal custom and privilege, along with ingenious new ones, had been exploited in order to raise revenues from the lords, towns, church and people. It was clear where most of that income went: into the building of castles, and especially Château Gaillard. Philip played cleverly on the war-weariness and economic concerns in the region. Wherever he made gains, he confirmed the trading rights of towns and the privileges of the church.

Philip laid his plans for the attack carefully. In the summer of 1202, while John spent time in the Seine Valley, fortifying his

defences, including Château Gaillard, Philip captured a set of
castles in the north-east of the duchy. In July he took Gournay, not
by an extended siege, but by adjusting the elaborate waterworks
which filled the moat, and flooding the castle itself. Briefly John
regained the initiative when he seized the ill-fated Arthur of
Brittany, deflecting Philip from his attack on north-east Normandy.
But he soon lost the advantage.

His treatment of Arthur alienated the Angevin lords.
Repeatedly, and to good effect, Philip called on John to produce
his nephew. By March 1203, Philip had persuaded all the lords of
Maine, Anjou and Touraine away from their allegiance to John,
and was building an active alliance with the Bretons. Philip's
control of the Loire isolated Normandy from the rest of the

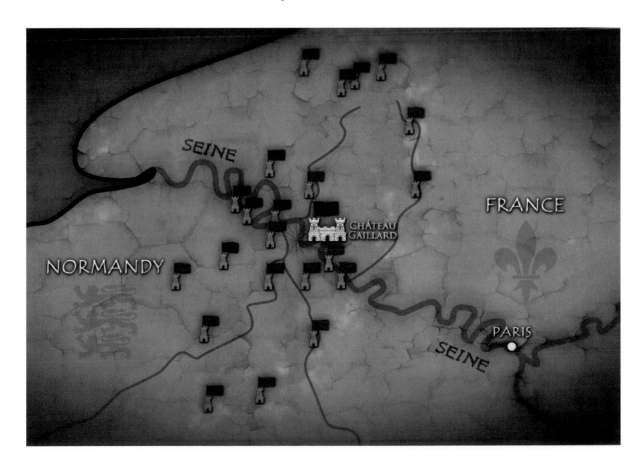

Angevin lands. In Normandy itself, early 1203 saw the defection of key barons like Robert of Alençon who controlled important border territories. In May he took the castle of Conches; in June the important, well-provisioned and well-fortified ducal castle of Le Vaudreuil.

These castles were vital elements in the fortification network of which Château Gaillard was the key, and their loss left the latter much more vulnerable. John did little to respond. Contemporary chroniclers attributed this inaction to an energy-sapping passion for his young wife. In fact John probably hoped the Pope would come to his rescue, but when the Papal legate finally arrived with Innocent's demand for peace, Philip responded by holding a great council on 22 August. This secured him the support of the barons and church in France for an invasion of Normandy which had the express aim of depriving John of his French lands. By September 1203, Philip controlled the land in the bow of the Seine opposite Château Gaillard, and had surrounded and begun to besiege the great castle itself.

While Philip imposed his control on the Seine Valley, John was absent, leading his troops away to the far west, though he did little more than sack a couple of settlements on the Breton frontier when he got there. John must have realised that eastern Normandy was all but lost, and made plans to cede this valuable land, with his capital city of Rouen, to Philip. A new border would be fortified, and Caen would become the new ducal capital. John announced he would go back to England, ostensibly to raise more money and men. His hold on the loyalty of the duchy was so precarious that he was forced to travel west in secret and at night. When he sailed from Barfleur on 5 December 1203, most believed that he had deserted his duchy, leaving Philip to attack Château Gaillard at his leisure.

The siege which began in September 1203 is described in vivid detail by William the Breton, who was Philip's chaplain, and who was with Philip throughout his invasion of Normandy.

THE HEROIC POEM

Very often what we know of medieval sieges has
to be pieced together from chronicles and prose
histories. We are fortunate, though, that for the
siege of Château Gaillard in 1203–04, one
eyewitness wrote not only a prose account but
also a much more substantial poem. It survives
today in three different manuscripts and covers
the events of the siege in considerable detail.

The poet, William the Breton, was a highly
educated man. He served as a chaplain to Philip II
of France and was tasked with writing the
'official' account of the deeds of his king. His
prose account of the siege is contained in
his *Gesta Philippi Augusti*, 'The Deeds of Philip
Augustus' (written 1216–1220). Then, between
1222 and 1223, he turned this into a Latin poem,
called the *Philippidos*, completing his final version
after Philip's death in the latter year.

The poem itself is a medieval epic, written
in complex Latin and modelled on a story of
Alexander the Great, the *Alexandreis*, by Walter of
Châtillon, as well as classical authors such as Virgil
and Homer. In similar fashion to Virgil's great epic,
the *Aeneid*, William divided his poem into twelve
parts and wrote it in hexameter with high-register
vocabulary and an elevated tone, all of which
served to glorify his patron.

In most cases William's account is
corroborated by the site of Château Gaillard
itself, by the lie of its land, and by the remains of
the castle. However, the narrative is not entirely
without problems for the historian. Philip is
presented throughout as the perfect chivalrous
knight, the new Charlemagne; King John is an
almost pantomime villain. William put lots of
new and interesting detail into the *Philippidos*,

but he was writing almost two decades after the
event and it can be difficult to tell when he is
describing real events and when he is fabricating
experiences worthy of classical heroes at classical
sieges. Nevertheless, his account is compelling. He
describes the fortifications, the siege engines and
the fighting with relish, and he makes the siege the
centrepiece of Philip's capture of Normandy.

CHÂTEAU GAILLARD UNDER SIEGE

Philip approached the castle from the south bank of the Seine. His first move was to attack the palace on the island and Richard's new port-town of Petit Andely. These he took relatively easily. To take the palace on the island, and then to attack the town on the other side, Philip employed a team of trained swimmers to remove the stakes which Richard had used to block and control the river. The French swimmers set fire to the palace and in terror the townspeople fled up the great cliff to take refuge in the castle itself, the gates opening to receive them.

Gaillard was now isolated from its fortress network (Radepont was another link in the chain which fell to Philip's forces). Attempts to relieve Gaillard by boat and by a relief force led by William Marshal both failed. By the end of September 1203, Philip had

RIGHT *This image of Château Gaillard was drawn over a hundred years after the siege. It bears little resemblance to the castle, but the story of the siege was clearly still being told*

surrounded and laid siege to the castle itself, digging extra ditches all around and lining them with his own wooden fortifications – an extended structure lined with watchtowers. With provisions unable to reach the castle by land or river, Philip settled down to starve the garrison into submission.

John had assigned the defence of the castle to Roger de Lacy, the constable of Chester. De Lacy had forty knights, supported by sergeants, crossbowmen and engineers – a full garrison estimated at about three hundred people, though that had now been swollen by the terrified townspeople who had taken refuge in the castle. Three wells provided water for the castle, but they must have been sunk deep into the chalk cliff to reach the water table, and raising water in large quantity from such a depth was laborious and slow.

Alarmed at the rapid depletion of his resources, as winter set in during November 1203, de Lacy took the fateful decision to start expelling non-combatants, starting with five hundred of the sheltering townspeople. He assumed they would be allowed though the siege lines, as indeed they were, the French army seeing no threat from the line of bedraggled and unarmed civilians. A few days later, another five hundred were similarly evicted, and again were allowed to pass. Philip was not present; he was away campaigning elsewhere in Normandy. When he was informed about what had happened he gave clear instructions that nobody else was to be allowed to pass. Non-combatants they might be, but Philip realised that living within the castle they were actively assisting his cause by helping to reduce the garrison's supplies.

When a last large group of the townspeople was forced out of the castle gates – at least four hundred, perhaps as many as twelve hundred – they made their way down the slope as their predecessors had done. Expecting to be allowed through the French lines as previous groups had been, the horrified crowd was met with an impenetrable line of soldiers who shot arrows as they approached, forcing them back up the hill. De Lacy, desperate to

ABOVE *One of Château Gaillard's three wells. No castle, however robust, can withstand a siege without an adequate supply of water*

RIGHT Les Bouches Inutiles (*'The Useless Mouths'*) *by Francis Tattegrain. King Philip's siege engines bombard the castle as refugees outside the walls starve through the winter*

preserve his supplies, would not admit them back into the castle and here too they were beaten back by the sentries.

The miserable group were forced to spend the winter on the inhospitable hillside, attempting to eke out a subsistence on grass, dead dogs and the occasional chicken (eaten, feathers, bones and all when it flew out of the castle). In desperate hunger, and cruelly tormented by the rain, snow and biting winds of winter, they even resorted to cannibalism, a new-born baby among the victims. Many died there on the rocky hillside of starvation and exposure. Finally, Philip took pity on those who survived, though most of them were by now in such a desperate condition that they went into shock and died as soon as they ate any food.

With their numbers dramatically reduced, Roger de Lacy and his garrison continued to hold out defiantly until Philip finally lost his patience. In January 1204, after four months besieging Château Gaillard, he ordered the construction of great siege engines, catapults and stone-throwers. He had already dug ditches and constructed an encircling wooden wall. Now on the shoulder of land which looked down onto the Château he built his own counter-fortress. This had always been the obvious weakness of Richard's great castle. Richard had done what he could to counter it. His small castle at Cléry had acted as an advance post to prevent attack from that side, but this, along with others, was no longer in Angevin hands. His triangular advance fort, or barbican, reared up towards the higher shoulder of land; the elaborate buttress machicolation and the spur of the keep faced towards it. From this shoulder of land, the full ingenious complexity of the defensive system of the great castle was manifest. Richard must have calculated that it would be more than enough to deter anyone who had somehow managed to get so close from besieging his fortress. But Richard would never have let Philip get to this position in the first place, and John was not there to stop him.

Between them, Philip's specialist military engineers who worked the great siege engines, and the sappers who mined beneath

RIGHT *The French besiege Château Gaillard from the high ground in Viollet-le-Duc's nineteenth-century drawing. The aerial view gives a sense of the many defensive layers which made up Richard's fortified system at Andely*

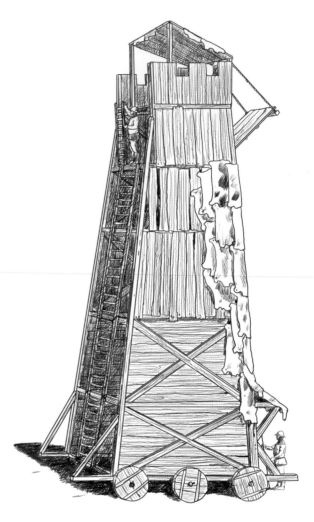

the walls, brought down the tower at the prow of the castle's outer bailey. Philip's men swarmed into the triangular enclosure, while the Angevin troops retreated into the middle bailey, setting fire to any wooden structures they were abandoning. However, Roger de Lacy still firmly believed the great castle to be invincible and had no intention of handing it over to the king of France. Philip continued to pummel the castle walls with missiles from his siege engines; and his miners continued their work in the soft chalk. However, the massive walls of the central part of Richard's castle stood firm.

UNDERMINING

From ancient times mining, or digging tunnels, was an important strategy of static siege warfare where time was available (as opposed to quick-moving conflict on the battlefield). Though it would later become synonymous with the use of explosives, before the advent of gunpowder its purpose was generally either to allow besieging troops direct access through the tunnel to a walled town or castle, or to cause the collapse of part of a fortification by removing its underpinning.

In the medieval period, when stone castles (invulnerable to fire) constituted vital symbols of power, mining was one of the principal weapons in a besieging army's arsenal. Specialist teams of miners would dig tunnels beneath points of a castle's defences that seemed weakest, such as the corner of a square tower. Mining for iron ore increased substantially during the thirteenth century as demand for the metal grew, and the same miners – highly skilled at tunnelling and excavating – were often employed in a military context. As they dug, the roof of the tunnel would be propped up using thick blocks of wood.

When the tunnel was complete it would be filled with combustible material like brushwood. The props themselves were often coated in the fat from slaughtered pigs. King John issued an order for pigs when undermining a corner of the keep at Rochester Castle in November 1215: 'Send to us with all speed by day and night, forty of the fattest pigs of the sort least good for eating so that we may bring fire beneath the castle'. It would be the dangerous job of a 'torch man' to enter the tunnel after others had left to start the fire which would burn through the roof supports. As the fire ate away the props, the tunnel would cave in, causing the collapse, if successful, of the fortification immediately above.

Those manning a castle had to find ways to respond to this threat. When possible castles would be sited on a base of hard rock which was more difficult to mine. The soft chalk underlying Dover and Château Gaillard made them much more vulnerable; Krak des Chevaliers was built on hard basalt, but even then was not invulnerable to skilled and determined miners.

The concentric castle design meant that any attacking army forcing a way through the outer wall would find itself trapped in an outer bailey overlooked by garrison troops from the high walls of the inner enclosure.

One common means of defence was to dig deep ditches – sometimes filled with water as moats – around key fortifications. Another was to dig defensive tunnels which any mine dug by attackers was likely to meet before it achieved its aim. When mining was suspected by a castle garrison, a counter tunnel was often dug – carefully moving towards the sound of digging – in an effort to meet it and to enable soldiers to confront the miners before they had got too far. For attacking forces, concealing the large quantity of earth and rock extracted from a tunnel was sometimes a problem in keeping the work secret.

Where a castle was built on hard rock in particular, attacking sappers would sometimes dig directly into the base of a castle wall, rather than creating a tunnel, with the same intention of damaging the foundations. It was to confront this threat that machicolations developed – allowing the garrison to drop rocks and shoot arrows on any men beneath the wall (see Machicolations box, p. 214). Sappers would sometimes work underneath protective structures designed to shield them from missiles, as Louis' miners did at Dover.

ABOVE *A south-west section of the middle bailey, where Boggis and his men are reputed to have snuck in through a window*

Philip rethought his strategy, turning from power to guile. One of Philip's foot-soldiers, a man named Boggis – 'snub-nosed' in the French slang of the day – noticed a potential weakness in the apparently impregnable fortress. The south-west section of the middle bailey, which overlooked a steep ditch that ran down to the Seine on that side of the castle, was less heavily fortified than the rest of the curtain wall; not only that, but it contained quite large openings. At this corner was a latrine tower with large vents at the base to clean out the waste. Further to the east, buildings had been set against the curtain wall, lit by generous windows which opened within the curtain wall itself. The designers of the castle seem to have been more concerned with amenities than defence in this area of the castle, perhaps because they thought the steep slope here would provide natural protection against attack. The impregnability of the castle was designed to be admired by those approaching from the town below, or higher up, where Philip had stationed his siege engines. From those perspectives, this section of curtain wall would not have been visible. But Boggis had clearly scouted more widely around the castle.

Under cover of darkness, Boggis and a small group of intrepid companions scrambled up the steep cliff to the south until they reached the base of the curtain wall. The windows were set high, but not so high that Boggis, standing on the shoulders of his companions, could not reach them. He climbed in, finding himself in a dark undercroft, and one by one his colleagues followed him – into the middle bailey. A small group, not capable of taking on the garrison, they then deliberated about what to do next, before deciding to make as much noise as they could in order to sound a more formidable force than they were.

Surprisingly, the ruse worked. The castle garrison was focused on the threat from Philip's forces in the advance work. Attack from the south-west was clearly totally unexpected. Panicking, the defenders opted to set fire to their own buildings, fleeing in the ensuing smoke and confusion across the drawbridge over the inner ditch. As they took refuge within the inner citadel, Boggis and his men opened the gate to the middle bailey, allowing Philip's men to pour in, seizing whatever remained of the Angevin provisions.

Weary and now starved of their remaining provisions, de Lacy and his men could not hold out for long. The drawbridge from the middle bailey to the inner was fixed, and supported in the middle by a huge chalk pillar. Both the drawbridge and the pillar gave Philip's sappers protection as they worked away at the chalk beneath the massive, undulating curtain wall. When the towers flanking the entrance to the inner citadel began to crumble de Lacy accepted at last that resistance was useless. On 6 March 1204, after an epic siege lasting almost six months, de Lacy and his men finally surrendered. De Lacy's ransom of £1000 was paid with John's assistance.

ABOVE *The bridge leading to the undulating inner wall was solid stone in the early thirteenth century – a major weakness in the castle's defensive system*

Abandoned by its king, and cut off from all hope of relief, Château Gaillard had been shown not to be invincible after all.

Philip did not push straight for Rouen. He took his time in decommissioning his camp and his siege engines. When, in May 1204, he set the final Norman invasion in train, he swept in an arc through western Normandy, taking the great ducal castle of Falaise. At the same time, the Bretons invaded from the south west. Philip and the Breton army met at Caen, the duchy's second capital. This was where the Norman exchequer had sat, and where William the Conqueror lay buried. The city soon surrendered. Now, at last, with most of Normandy already under his control, Philip turned to Rouen. The capital held out for the best part of a month. Urgent messages were sent to John in the hope that he would send a fleet up the Seine to relieve them. But relief was not forthcoming, and in June 1204 Rouen surrendered.

The king of France now ruled Normandy and the Loire. Only Poitou and Aquitaine remained under the sway of the Angevin king of England. King John refused to accept Philip's victory. He spent the next decade planning invasions, and rebuilding an anti-French alliance with the count of Flanders and his nephew, the Emperor Otto. In 1214, Otto and the count of Flanders, with a substantial contingent of English troops, invaded north-eastern France but they were decisively defeated by Philip at the battle of Bouvines. For Philip, this was the greatest triumph of his reign, greater even than the taking of Château Gaillard. In commemoration the normally parsimonious king founded and built an abbey just north of Paris, named La Victoire.

For John, meanwhile, Bouvines was an unmitigated disaster. Once again, he had levied every tax he could devise to fund the anti-French alliance. Now that it was finally defeated, his barons and the church forced him to abjure such tyrannical exploitation in the Great Charter, signed at Runnymede in 1215 (see Magna Carta box, p.43). After John's death his son, Henry III, remained hopeful of regaining his father's French territories. He planned several invasions of Normandy, and encouraged disaffection among Norman nobles and merchants – although there was not much of it. Finally in 1259, at the Treaty of Paris, Henry III gave up all claims to Normandy, the Loire fiefs and Poitou, leaving only Gascony in English hands.

Given the enormous expense of the six-month siege, and the fact that Philip's final invasion of central Normandy by-passed the Seine valley and Château Gaillard altogether, it is difficult to avoid the impression that Philip's determination to take the castle was personal. Richard, Philip's great rival, had set up his castle to be impregnable. Philip was determined to show that it was not and knew that doing so would profoundly unsettle those still prepared to defend Normandy for the Angevins.

Did Château Gaillard deserve, then, its formidable reputation? It had defensive weaknesses, and Philip, with help from Boggis, found them. Isolated and cut off from supplies or relief, all the garrison could do was to retreat into their central bunker, where starvation or submission were ultimately their only options. When Philip finally invaded Normandy, he swept far to the west of Château Gaillard. Roger de Lacy and his forty knights could have been left, isolated within the castle, unable to do much damage. However Philip, normally so parsimonious and calculating, was determined to take it at any cost – and the cost of building a wooden fortress around it, and maintaining a besieging army for six months, must have been immense. Richard the Lionheart's castle was a great architectural statement of defiance; Philip knew the power of that statement and was determined to answer it with a statement of his own. Normandy would not truly be his until he had taken it.

RICHARD'S CASTLE WAS A GREAT ARCHITECTURAL STATEMENT OF DEFIANCE; PHILIP KNEW THE POWER OF THAT STATEMENT AND WAS DETERMINED TO ANSWER IT

CRUSADER CASTLES:

KRAK DES CHEVALIERS

Towards the end of February 1271 a colossal army began to arrive outside the walls of the greatest castle in the Middle East. From the walls and towers of Krak des Chevaliers, the Christian knights who gave the castle its name looked out with a mixture of defiance and apprehension at the dust-clouds being stirred up by thousands of approaching soldiers. The garrison at Krak had faced down besieging armies before, secure within the seemingly impenetrable walls of this massive fortress. Krak was perched on a spur of dark basalt hills and presided over a narrow pass linking the Mediterranean coast with the Syrian plain to the east. One Muslim writer had referred to it as 'this bone in the throat' of Muslim armies who had tried to take it.

During the last two decades, the tide had been turning against the Christian crusading orders in the Holy Land, including the 'Knights Hospitaller' who had made Krak their base.

The Hospitaller order's numbers had steadily declined. At their height they had maintained some 10,000 knights active in the 'Crusader states' which clung to the eastern shore of the Mediterranean. In the early thirteenth century great castles like Krak, or the stronghold of the Knights Templar at Atlit, were effectively large military towns. The latter was defended in 1220 by some 4,000 men, while at Krak the Hospitallers maintained a garrison 2,000 strong which dominated the surrounding area and extracted tribute payments by force from neighbouring Muslim powers. But by 1268, according to the Master of the Hospitallers, Hugh Revel, the order as a whole could support only 300 knights.

By this time Muslim raiders were roaming practically unhindered through the territory surrounding the great castle. In 1252 a vast horde of Turkmen had torn through the fertile plain, plundering and laying waste to the land and terrorising the population, many of whom fled, never to return. Lands on which many thousands had lived and worked, Revel lamented, now lay deserted – a depopulation which grievously affected the knights' revenue. In 1270 Sultan Baybars, the ruler of Egypt who had united

LEFT *Krak des Chevaliers, the 'castle of the knights', was the headquarters of the Knights Hospitaller in the Holy Land*

Muslim forces in the region, led a force into the vicinity of Krak, allowing his horses and men to feed with impunity on the crops and fertile grasslands of the plain which were relied upon by the garrison. On that occasion he retreated, when word reached him of the arrival of St Louis (King Louis IX of France) on Crusade. Early the following year, after Louis had died, Baybars was back.

Sultan Baybars had made it his mission to extinguish the European 'Crusader states'. His troops had been joined, in what was effectively a Muslim holy war or *jihad*, by others loyal to the Lord of Hama, al-Malik al-Mansur; the Lord of Sahyn, Sayf al-Din; and the Lord of the Isma'ili territories, Najm al-Din. Their army comprised between five and ten thousand men: horsemen, foot soldiers and crossbowmen, as well as technical experts and all those who supported a massive army on campaign. Late in February, Baybars' force began a siege of the nearby castle of Safita – the 'White Castle' of the Knights Templar – visible on the skyline fifteen kilometres to the north-west. His strategy was to strike fast and hard, and after leaving a small contingent to pursue (successfully) the siege of Safita, he moved on with his main army to Krak, reaching the vicinity towards evening on the same day.

THE CRUSADES

From the seventh century, Muslim armies spread rapidly out of Arabia, uprooting Christian rulers in the Levant – the fertile region between the Mediterranean's eastern coast and the Syrian desert which included Christianity's 'holy land'. As the Christian Byzantine Empire was pressed back into Anatolia and further towards the borders of Europe by the Muslim Seljuq Turks in the eleventh century (when large-scale settlement of Turks in the lands of modern-day Turkey first took place), the Emperor made a plea to the Pope in Rome for help in beating back the Muslim advance.

Western Europe responded, and the first of many Crusades was launched by Pope Urban II in 1095. The recapture of the Christian holy lands and of the city of Jerusalem in particular became a central goal. Early success was not followed by the restoration of the Levant to Byzantine rule. Catholic knights, principally Normans from modern France and Italy, owed no allegiance to the Orthodox Emperor. Instead, over the following decade, four new states were founded based on ancient cities and ruled by dynasties of European knights. These were: inland, to the north-east, the County of Edessa; adjacent to it, on the coast to the south-west, the Principality of Antioch; south of this the narrow County of Tripoli; and most prestigiously of all, the Kingdom of Jerusalem.

The early success and expansion of these states, however, soon gave way to an effort to survive. The number of castles built in the region by Christian rulers was a testament to their weakness rather than their strength, as it invariably was elsewhere during the Middle Ages, from English-ruled Wales and Normandy, to the Baltic Teutonic State. The conquest of isolated Edessa by Seljuq armies in 1144 prompted a disastrous Second Crusade (1145–49) which was routed by Muslim forces. Under Saladin, who united the previously divided forces of Egypt and Syria, Muslim armies reconquered most of the cities in Crusader hands, including in 1187 the most important by far: Jerusalem.

The Third Crusade (1189–92) was a direct response and it enjoyed some success. Richard the Lionheart won back coastal territory – but he failed to regain Jerusalem. The truncated Kingdom of Jerusalem was now based on the Mediterranean port of Acre. The Fourth Crusade soon afterwards was a notorious failure, leading to the siege and sacking of the Christian city of Constantinople in 1204 and the entrenching of the divide between Western and Eastern Christianity.

From Europe and from the Christian state of Cyprus which had been established as a base by the Crusader knights, repeated efforts were made to shore up the remaining Christian presence in the Levant. (The Crusader States were always dependent on support by sea and the domination of the Mediterranean by European naval power in the thirteenth century was critical to their survival). But successive major expeditions produced no lasting shift in the general trend. One Templar knight who fought in the Seventh Crusade (1248–54) bemoaned God's apparent neglect of the Christian cause:

> Rage and sorrow are seated in my heart ... so firmly that I scarce dare to stay alive. It seems that God wishes to support the Turks to our loss ... ah, lord God ... alas, the realm of the East has lost so much that it will never be able to rise up again. They will make a Mosque of Holy Mary's convent, and since the theft pleases her Son, who should weep at this, we are forced to comply as well ... Anyone who wishes to fight the Turks is mad, for Jesus Christ does not fight them any more. They have conquered, they will conquer. For every day they drive us down, knowing that God, who was awake, sleeps now, and Muhammad waxes powerful.

With the Ninth Crusade in 1271–72 – attended by the young Prince Edward, later Edward I of England – they came to an end. The final loss of the port city of Acre after a siege in 1291 effectively marked the end of the Crusader States in the Levant.

Initially, Baybars was impeded by the weather. Heavy winter rains lashed the exposed Muslim army for several days. This prevented them setting up the massive siege engines with which they planned to batter Krak's formidable walls. Time, however, was on Baybars' side: no relieving force was on hand that could seriously threaten him. Once the rains subsided men got to work assembling the array of huge counterweight trebuchets – lining them up on the south side of the castle, where the lie of the land offered no natural protection. We do not know precisely how many of these huge weapons Baybars had at his disposal in 1271, but when the Muslims laid siege to the Hospitaller castle of Margat fourteen years later they used ten trebuchets of differing kinds. Crossbowmen on the castle walls could harry any who came within range, but those working on the trebuchets sheltered behind protective stockades. Others in the Hospitaller garrison could do little except wait for the inevitable onslaught.

CRUSADING COUNTRY: EARLY HISTORY

The strategic importance of this location had long been recognised. Its elevated site dominated one of the few passes providing easy access from the inland cities through the mountains of modern Syria and Lebanon to the Mediterranean. The first surviving historical record relating to the location reveals that during the year 1031 the Emir of the ancient city of Homs established a military settlement composed of Kurdish soldiers on a site known as Hisn al-Safh or the Castle of the Slope. The aim was to control traffic through this narrow valley between Homs and Tripoli, the Mediterranean port which then controlled the flow of trade from Damascus. The fortification became known as Hisn al-Akrad, the Castle of the Kurds, and lasted until the close of the eleventh century.

CRUSADER ARMIES ARRIVED FROM EUROPE BENT ON WRESTING JERUSALEM AND THE HOLY LAND FROM ISLAMIC CONTROL

Not much is known about this structure, although a recent archaeological mission found traces of a mid-eleventh century defensive wall and buildings in an upper and lower bailey.

At the end of the century the region's history shifted decisively. Crusader armies arrived from Europe bent on wresting Jerusalem and the Holy Land from Islamic control. In January 1099 an army under Raymond of St Gilles, the Count of Toulouse, appeared in the narrow plain beneath Hisn al-Akrad. This area was known as the Buqaia, and contained the castle which was still in the hands of Kurdish soldiers. In fear of the marauding Christians, local inhabitants drove their herds within the defensive walls. Desperate for supplies, the Crusader army laid siege to the castle, and on 28 January made an assault on its defences. Their cohesion was disrupted, however, when the garrison released some of their cattle through a gate. Unwilling to let these prizes escape, the hungry soldiers broke off their attack to pursue the animals. So fragmented did the attacking army become that the castle garrison spotted an opportunity to launch a sortie which almost succeeded in capturing

BELOW *A map showing the location of Krak des Chevaliers in Syria*

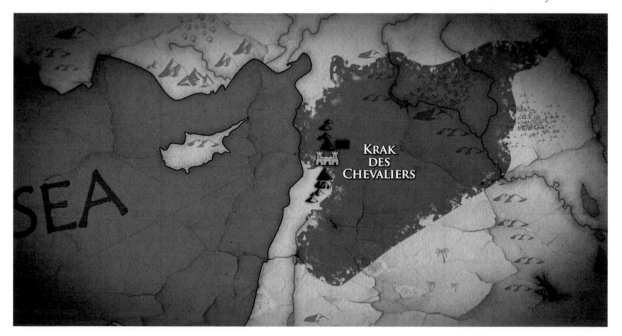

Knights Hospitaller

During the eleventh century, before the coming of the First Crusade, a hospital was founded by Italian merchants in Jerusalem to provide care to Christian pilgrims visiting the holy sites. Strictly speaking, it was re-founded, for an earlier Christian hospital had been destroyed by the city's Muslim rulers. Initially this hospital dedicated to John the Baptist was run by Benedictine monks whose role was peaceable.

Two events transformed the ethos of the movement. In 1099 the First Crusade succeeded in wresting Jerusalem and other areas in the Holy Land from Muslim control. Then, in 1119, a group of knights established themselves in the 'Temple of Solomon' in Jerusalem. They took monastic vows of chastity, poverty and obedience. But rather than adopt a life of peaceful contemplation, they devoted themselves to protecting pilgrims, using force if need be. These 'Knights Templar' were formally recognised by the Pope and other influential figures in Europe, receiving substantial patronage and financial support.

Under the French knight Raymond of Le Puy, the Hospitallers moved to follow the Templar example, establishing a martial wing which provided armed escorts to pilgrims and which became largely distinct from those who tended the poor and sick. Granted privileges by the Pope, such as an exemption from tithes, and generous endowments from the aristocracy of Europe, the Hospitallers (or Knights of St John, as they were also known) became, like the Templars, immensely wealthy and influential. In 1185 they were granted a charter of privileges by the Holy Roman Emperor, Frederick Barbarossa.

The Hospitallers rapidly acquired and built castles in the Holy Land: among them Belvoir, Kerak and Belmont in the Kingdom of Jerusalem (before the region was ravaged by Saladin in 1187), and the great fortresses of Margat and Krak des Chevaliers in the County of Tripoli to the north. Answering only to the Pope – and even he found them on occasion difficult to control – they were granted effective independence in vulnerable borderland, from where they extracted further revenues from surrounding Muslim rulers.

With the final defeat of the Crusader States on the eastern Mediterranean mainland, the Knights moved to take up residence first in Cyprus, then Rhodes and ultimately – in the sixteenth century – Malta, where they resisted the efforts of larger Ottoman forces to unseat them.

RIGHT *A rich illustration depicting Crusader knights and Saracens battling in the Holy Land*

Count Raymond. When the Crusaders attacked again the following day, they found the castle deserted. Under the cover of darkness the garrison and the sheltering local inhabitants had slipped quietly away – but in the rush they left most of their possessions behind. On 2 February the Christians celebrated the Feast of the Purification within the walls of the castle.

The Crusader army's real target was Jerusalem, however, and after barely a month they moved off, allowing the Seljuk Turks to reoccupy the castle for a whole decade. It was only in 1110 that it was brought under the control of Tancred, the Norman knight who had become Crusader prince of Antioch and who created the fief of 'Crat' around the former 'Castle of the Kurds', integrating it into his properties. The castle was held by the rulers of Antioch until 1144 – with new buildings and possibly a new defensive wall being built – when it was granted to the Knights Hospitaller to use as their principal base on Tripoli's eastern frontier.

The castle's structure at this time remains relatively unknown. Neither Arabic nor Latin texts make mention of it. The archaeological evidence suggests that initially little in the way of defensive improvement was undertaken, beyond some

LEFT *The hard black basalt at the wall's base is difficult to work into high-quality blocks. The white masonry is a softer limestone – ideal for castle-building*

BELOW *A vaulted chamber within the upper castle*

development in the upper bailey. This was perhaps a consequence of the limited financial means of the Hospitallers, who were only then acquiring their first properties and income from land taxes in the region. They had also suffered from the destructive impact of the first of several massive earthquakes which struck the Levant in the twelfth and early thirteenth centuries.

The first shock struck in 1157. Worse was to come thirteen years later, on 29 June 1170, when a violent quake struck in the early morning, wreaking havoc. One chronicler lamented that 'there was no place undamaged even as far as the ends of the earth'. Both Christian and Muslim writers were likely to view the disaster as divine justice exacted on their religious enemy and therefore to exaggerate the devastation suffered by rival communities. This was a tendency also recognisable within the divided Christian ranks, where it was the cause of some gloating among Catholic Franks that a dome of the Cathedral Church of St Peter in Antioch had collapsed upon the Greek Orthodox patriarch and his clergy.

Most fortified sites were completely destroyed as a result of the earthquake, and the Hospitaller castle at Krak was no exception.

ABOVE *The castle chapel*
on the north side of the
upper castle, which became
a mosque under the
Mamluks

Its walls, according to the Arabic chronicles, were entirely ruined.
The complete destruction of the fortifications of the upper bailey
was recently confirmed by archaeologists. They discovered that
the earthquake caused the collapse of the buildings at the top of
the upper bailey and cracked their foundations. An Arab source
mentions that the chapel was destroyed and this was probably
construed as a sign of God's allegiance. What the earthquake did
provide, at least, was a relatively blank canvas. Once the rubble and
ruins strewn around the upper and lower baileys was removed, a
new and ambitious construction campaign could be launched by the
Hospitallers on a site now largely free of building constraints.

MILITARY ARCHITECTURE: REBUILDING

A new defensive complex was built in the inner bailey, consisting of an outer wall, built in dressed (ashlar) limestone blocks. This surrounded the whole area of the inner bailey, and another, concentric wall 10 metres inside. The gap between these walls was vaulted and roofed to create a continuous hall which looked onto a central courtyard. Similar continuous halls were developed by the Hospitallers and the Templars at some of their other castles, such as Belvoir, Torsosa and Margat. Within this circuit two principal structures were built. To the east there was a rectangular gate-tower protected by a frontal arrow-loop, a slot machicolation, a portcullis and a wooden double door reinforced with iron nails. To the north-east there was a chapel – a key element in any Hospitaller castle, the order being religious as well as military (see Knights Hospitaller box, p.148). This was built in a Romanesque style with a single nave, a pointed barrel vault and upper-level narrow windows providing light. Other functional rooms, like the hospital, the latrines area and the kitchen were created within the hall using partition walls.

At the same time lower baileys were created to act as buffer zones between the central castle and any potential attacker. The slope on the south side of the castle immediately outside the wall was not steep at that time – only a gentle slope linked the upper bailey with the cliff to the south of the castle. The knights therefore decided to enclose the area with an outer defensive wall, the remains of which have recently been excavated. Its southern section followed the line of the current southern curtain wall. There was one gate at the southern end of the eastern wall, and perhaps another which opened from the southern front to allow direct access to the lower bailey from the outside. To the east of the upper bailey a wall was built to enclose the important area in front of the gate-tower and so to control access to the high castle.

By 1188, the rebuilt castle at Krak must have been considered formidable. In that year Saladin, the great sultan of Egypt and Syria

ABOVE, TOP *The ornately vaulted cloisters in the central part of the upper castle*

ABOVE, BOTTOM *A Latin inscription by the cloisters from the time of the Knights Hospitaller which means, 'May abundance, prudence and beauty be given to you; pride befouls all foundations, if it follows (you)'*

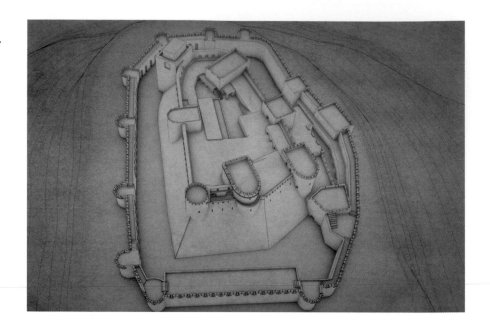

who led the Muslim fight-back against the Crusader states in the Levant, came to Krak with a large army. The previous year he had won a major victory over the Christians at the Battle of Hattin. It was the second time his forces had ravaged the County of Tripoli. When they did so in 1180, the Knights Hospitaller sought refuge in their castle at Krak, and did so again in 1188 – trusting that Saladin would pass through without pausing to lay a siege.

Saladin had gathered an army of between five and ten thousand soldiers near Homs and on 30 May he led his troops up to Krak des Chevaliers and established an encampment on a hill facing the castle. In June he launched several raids against Hospitaller possessions in the area between Krak and Tripoli but refrained from attacking Krak itself. He did spend a day blockading the castle in order to test the strength of its fortifications and the resolve of its garrison. He soon realised that the castle was well-defended and that a siege would tie his army down for several months.

Saladin had hoped that the Hospitaller garrison might launch an expedition from the castle to defend the region against his army. Had they done so it might have given him an opportunity

ABOVE *A moat between the 'talus' and the outer wall provided the castle with an additional layer of defence against any would-be attackers*

to conquer Krak itself. For a whole month, however, the knights remained within the castle while the Muslims pillaged at will. Saladin had another objective in mind: the conquest of Antioch and its territory. By early July, he decided to break camp, and to lead his army north along the Syrian coast, leaving the castle at Krak unscathed. He made the same decision at the Hospitallers' sister castle of Margat; recognising that it was impregnable, one Arab chronicler recorded, 'and that he had no hope of capturing it, he passed on to Jabala'.

Although Saladin inflicted no serious damage on Krak des Chevaliers, nature soon did. In 1202 another massive earthquake struck the region, causing significant destruction in the County of Tripoli. Geoffrey of Donjon, the Master of the Knights Hospitaller, wrote home of the 'lamentable destructions' the area had suffered when the earthquake struck just before dawn on 20 May. In the cities of Tyre, Acre and Tripoli countless citizens were killed and buildings destroyed. The great Hospitaller castles of Krak and Margat were badly damaged (though they would, Geoffrey hoped, still withstand an enemy attack). This 'horrible bellowing from the earth' – as Philip du Plessis, the Master of the fellow Crusading order of Knights Templar described it – was accompanied by a poor harvest and a devastating plague which ravaged the survivors. Such, wrote Geoffrey, were 'the sorrows and miseries of the Promised Land'.

HIGH POINT OF THE HOSPITALLER KNIGHTS AT KRAK

At Krak des Chevaliers this earthquake triggered another construction campaign during the first quarter of the thirteenth century. Efforts were made to strengthen the foundations of the castle against the seismic threat as well as to improve its defences against Muslim raids. These raids were on the increase in the region since the earthquake had left settlements weakened and

BELOW, LEFT *The aqueduct that directly fed the castle's moat on the south-west side*

BELOW, TOP RIGHT *The southern section of the 'talus', close to a principal tower through which the entrance ramp passes (right)*

BELOW, BOTTOM RIGHT *The deadly 'Great Ramp' entrance to Krak des Chevaliers. This 180-degree turn in the middle would force potential enemies to slow the momentum of their attack*

EARLY CRANES OR SQUIRREL CAGES

The cranes employed to build large medieval structures like cathedrals or castles used the power of a man (or men) walking in a wheel to lift heavy objects like blocks of stone. They were known as treadwheel cranes, or squirrel cages. A rope was wound or unwound around a spindle by the turning of the wheel, lifting or lowering its load – similar to the function of a windlass, a less powerful medieval lifting device driven by the turn of a crank.

The technology dated back at least to Roman times, when it vastly increased the efficiency of construction. A single man could now lift much greater weights than had previously been possible, dramatically reducing the manpower demands of a construction project. A single man might now lift some 3 metric tons; during the building of the Egyptian pyramids some fifty men had moved a single 2.5-ton stone.

Treadwheel technology fell into disuse after Rome's fall, and the size of building blocks reduced as a result. It then reappeared during the medieval period, the first evidence for it dating from the first half of the thirteenth century, when the great age of Gothic cathedral construction created a strong incentive for improved techniques.

more vulnerable. The slopes of the basalt hill on which the inner castle stood were cut away vertically on all sides to prevent it being climbed by attacking forces. These steeper slopes were then covered on all sides with a 'glacis' or 'talus'. This artificial slope was faced with smooth masonry with a low-grade incline towards the top of the wall, which served both a defensive and a structural function, shoring up the walls against earthquakes and making them very difficult for soldiers to scale. This feature had been previously used in Crusader castles at Arqa, Belvoir and Balatanus, but was principally developed by Muslim builders at castles like Aleppo, Shayzar and Harim. Finally, a deep ditch 5–10 metres wide was cut through the bedrock at the foot of the northern, western and southern sides of the glacis, which was then filled with water brought by aqueduct from a nearby spring. This served both as a water supply for the garrison – important in an area where reliable sources of drinking water were a critical concern – and made it much more difficult for any attacking force to undermine these solid walls.

On the south-eastern corner of the inner castle a high pentagonal gate-tower was constructed, known as the 'Lion Tower' because reliefs of lions adorned its western façade. Its entrance was on its western wall, through a monumental gate protected – like the older eastern gate – by a portcullis, a slot machicolation, and a wooden double door reinforced with iron nails. The quality of the well-cut, bossed limestone masonry, the size of the gateway, as well as the unique presence of stone reliefs confirm that the main access to the castle was now through the southern bailey rather than the eastern one. To the east a long sloping path or ramp climbed towards the gate, heading first south towards the Lion Tower where it turned back on itself 180°, passing through two doorways, before heading north up towards a gate into the inner castle. The roof which fully encloses it was probably added later, but anyone using the ramp was nevertheless overlooked by high walls, from

ABOVE *Stone lions such as these can be found on the aptly named Lion Tower on the south-east side of the upper castle. The lion was the heraldic symbol of Sultan Baybars*

LEFT *This illustration from a manuscript shows a squirrel cage aiding construction of a tower*

LEFT *The quality of the masonry at Krak des Chevaliers is impressive throughout, even in these arches which cover a set of latrines*

BELOW *The outer-facing wall of the tower containing the latrines. A postern gate to the left gave access from the outer bailey to the upper castle*

CHAPTER THREE

which the garrison could shoot at anyone attempting to force their way through. (Such complex entrances were a favoured design of the Crusader castles of the period: at Margat, right-angle bends and alternative routes overlooked by outer walls constitute a similarly forbidding introduction to the castle.) A large oblong building to the east of the ramp was used for stabling and as a barracks and may have been built at this time.

The relative success of the Third Crusade in reversing some of Saladin's gains over the Crusader States in the Levant between 1189 and 1192 (though it failed to retake Jerusalem) meant that the Hospitaller Order flourished for a period. Muslim forces in the region – united while Saladin was alive – squabbled over his domains after his death, though Muslim raids remained a danger. The garrison at Krak swelled to 2,000 men, dominating its hinterland. They sent raids into Homs and Hama, sometimes in conjunction with brother Knights from the castle at Margat (only 60km away over the hills to the north-west), and extracted regular tribute payments from Muslim rulers. Even the fearsome Ismai'ili 'Assassins' (from whom the modern word for a contract killer derives) paid tribute to the Hospitallers for a time. It was a virtuous circle: success brought a stream of prestigious visiting Crusaders to Krak – men like King Andrew II of Hungary and Geoffroy de Joinville, who boosted the Order's fighting strength with their retinues, and left generous endowments. An attempt by the Emir of Hama in 1230 to refuse to pay tribute was initially successful, but three years later the Hospitallers led a punitive expedition, joined by parties of knights from across the Crusader States. His lands ravaged, the Emir reluctantly consented to pay up.

Rising numbers meant a need to improve the accommodation, hygiene and storage facilities of the castle. Several domestic buildings were added on the upper level of the hall, and an outer tower was built on the north-west corner, which connected to the hall only at this upper level. This provided latrines and enabled covering fire for any soldiers using the postern gate at

ABOVE, TOP *A tower rising from the 'talus'. The apparent arc-shaped break in the masonry is an illusion – the stones where the tower joins the wall are single blocks, cut into the required shapes*

ABOVE, BOTTOM *A window in an upper castle tower. No window as large as this could be built into an outer wall without dramatically increasing a besieger's chances of penetrating the castle*

this corner of the castle. This period of prosperity in Hospitaller history is reflected in the fact that the construction work of the early thirteenth century is substantial and of a very high quality. This can be clearly seen in the highly-skilled limestone masonry work – blocks which were 'stereotomic' or cut in multiple planes, which allowed the round towers of the inner castle to rise up smoothly from the sloping glacis. This improved both the strength and structural integrity of the towers, and reduced the chance of collapse during earthquakes, or when under attack.

The main project in this second construction programme, however, was the transformation of the southern front of the inner castle into a formidable central command centre and stronghold

– essentially a 'donjon' or keep. Three new towers, on three to four vaulted levels, created a protected inner sanctum for the higher-rank Hospitallers of the castle – the commander of the castle (known as the castellan) and the 'brothers-in-arms' (brother-knights and brother-sergeants) who were no more than sixty strong. The lofty chamber used by the Grand Master was elegantly finished, with ribbed vaulting, pilasters and an ornamental frieze. The shortage of wood across the region meant vaulted stone roofs were the norm, beams being unavailable. The south-western circular tower was used as a shooting position, with several loopholes, while the rooms of the two other towers were used as a refectory, a dormitory and an assembly hall.

The final significant construction campaign carried out by the Hospitallers at Krak took place around the middle of the thirteenth

century: between 1243, when Hugh Revel became castellan, until
An elite knight relied on around 1268 when his successor, Nicholas Lorgne, finished his
the important partnership
between man and horse, fourteen years in the role. They both went on to become Grand
so decent stabling was Master of the order, Revel between 1258 and 1277 and Lorgne
essential between 1277 and 1283. The climax of this construction campaign
may have been the year 1255, when Pope Alexander IV exempted the

OUTER WORKS

The term 'outer works' includes any defensive structures built outside the main area enclosed by a castle's walls. Dry ditches such as those at Château Gaillard and water-filled moats such as that at Beaumaris are common examples. They were designed to compensate for defensive weaknesses which a castle might possess.

Dry ditches increased the height siege ladders needed to be to allow a castle's walls to be scaled. This cost besiegers time and effort in constructing long ladders, and allowed defenders more time to shoot down any enemies on the ladders. The need to climb out of deep ditches also left attackers more exposed, slowing any attempt to run for cover. Soil and rock removed to create the ditch could be used to build up ramparts known as earthworks – one of the oldest forms of fortification in the world.

Water-filled moats were even more effective than dry ditches because they not only prevented attackers from scaling a castle's walls with ladders, but they also prevented sappers from reaching the base of the walls to begin undermining them. Moats reaching right up to the castle walls made undermining virtually impossible, unless the water could be drained.

Outer works also addressed specific weaknesses of an individual castle's location or design. They were raised to fortify castle entrances and strategic areas of ground which besieging armies might be able to exploit to their advantage. These could vary greatly. The outer works built in front of the North Gate at Dover Castle prior to the siege of 1216 consisted of a hastily-built palisade made from timber. Similarly, the Knights Hospitaller built timber outer works, but in the shape of a triangle, to defend a patch of vulnerable ground to the south of Krak des Chevaliers. By contrast, the outer works built by Richard I at Château Gaillard were planned at the same time as the rest of the castle, and were a much grander affair: limestone walls incorporating imposing towers on a vulnerable spur to the south-east of the castle.

Perhaps one of the deadliest outer works was the barbican, such as those built by Henry II at Dover (one of which remains) or the two built by Edward I at Conwy. A barbican was an enclosure of walls built around one of the castle entrances, often in a semi-circular shape. Some believe the word derives from Arabic *bab* (gate) and *khan* (courtyard or enclosure), and that the feature may have been noticed by Crusaders in the Holy Land and subsequently incorporated into castles in Europe. Any attackers who managed to breach the barbican found themselves in a 'killing zone'. Hemmed in by the walls yet still faced by the main gate which the barbican protected, they were vulnerable to attack from many sides at once by men on top of towers and walls.

Hospitallers from tithe payments for their properties at Krak and in the surrounding area. This was presumably because of the significant expenditure involved in construction work at the castle, which was a bulwark against Muslim incursion, meaning that its defence was holy work. Revel and Lorgne aimed to create a fortification at Krak des Chevaliers to rival the great Hospitaller castle at Margat.

THESE EMBELLISHMENTS DID NOT DISGUISE THE FACT THAT THE CASTLE'S HEYDAY AS A BASTION OF THE HOSPITALLER POWER SEEMED TO BE COMING TO AN END

The principal achievement of this phase of building was the construction of a new concentric rampart which enclosed the lower baileys and the moats, and surrounded the whole site, dramatically improving its defensive capabilities. The new curtain wall to the west, some nine metres high, was topped by a crenellated parapet and punctuated by five semi-circular towers which protruded substantially from the line of the wall. The rounded shape of the towers was itself a departure, both contemporary Templar and earlier Hospitaller building favouring the traditional square tower. A continuous wall-walk, numerous arrow-loops with triangular holes or 'oilets' at the base (to facilitate downward fire) and box machicolations enabled the garrison to man this formidable extra line of defence. The box machicolations at Krak, allowed soldiers to crouch within small stone chambers (which projected outwards from the walls) and to drop missiles on anyone attacking the foundations beneath. They had no parallel in Europe and seem to have been derived from Muslim fortifications in the Middle East.

To the south, the new outer rampart was different. It had a very thick wall (3 metres wide) which constituted the southern flank of a new building, 60 metres long, providing stabling for horses coming through the southern gate. The Hospitallers may have been the first to employ a double concentric girdle on a single castle. Their great castle at Margat had a similar double wall, as did the Templar castle at Safita, though the Templar's principal thirteenth-century castles of Tortosa and Atlit had only a single wall. To the north-east a tower was built on a rectangular plan, flanking a gate-tower which was erected over a depression in the bedrock along the eastern side.

SULTAN BAYBARS

Nicknamed Abu I-Futuh – the father of conquests – Sultan Baybars remains an iconic figure in Syria, Egypt, and elsewhere in the Middle East and Central Asia. The *Sirat Baybars*, 'The Life of Baybars', an epic poem narrating his life in sometimes fanciful form, remains popular.

Baybars was a Kipchak Turk from north of the Black Sea – tall, with fair hair and blue eyes (one of them clouded by a cataract). Around 1241 his life took a fateful turn when vast Mongol armies tore through the Eurasian steppe, conquering his homeland. The young Baybars, like countless others, was snatched to be sold as a slave.

Bought by a Mamluk officer, his outstanding military abilities were noticed and he became a bodyguard to the Sultan of Egypt. Having fled to Syria after involvement in the assassination of one sultan, Baybars later played a leading role in the murder of another, who had not rewarded him for his part in the defeat of a Mongol army. This time his ambition led him to seize the throne for himself and he became the fourth Mamluk Sultan.

Like the revered Saladin before him, Baybars united the Muslim realms of Egypt and Syria before turning his attention on the Crusader States. Between 1265 and 1271 he launched raids against the Christians almost annually, seizing towns – including Antioch in 1268 – and leaving the states fatally weakened. Captive populations were shown no mercy: the citizens of Antioch had been promised that their lives would be spared, but they were brutally slaughtered. In a letter to Antioch's absent ruler, Bohemond, Baybars taunted him with the details of his conquest:

> *Death came on them from all quarters. We took the city by the sword on the fourth hour of Saturday, the 4th of the month of Ramadan [19 May] ... If you had seen your churches with their crosses broken and rent, the pages from the false Testaments scattered, the graves of the patriarchs rifled, your Muslim enemy trampling down the sanctuary ... Had you seen these things, you would have said: 'Would that I were dust. Would that no message had come to give me news of these things'... Since no one escaped to tell you of what has happened, we have told you ourselves.*

His cruelty meant that, unlike Saladin, Baybars was reviled in the Christian world as fiercely as he was revered among his Muslim subjects.

At the same time Baybars had to confront an ongoing Mongol threat from the north and east. He personally led numerous campaigns, and worked to convert many of the Mongols to Islam. He managed to sponsor the building of canals, harbours, libraries and schools, some of which still bear his name.

He died in 1277 in Damascus after mistakenly drinking poison intended for someone else.

All these embellishments to the castle did not disguise the fact that the castle's heyday as a bastion of Hospitaller power seemed to be coming to an end. It was Hugh Revel who, as Master, lamented the decline of the Order and the depopulation caused by massive incursions after 1250. With the rise of Sultan Baybars, Muslim

THE TREBUCHET

In late twelfth-century Europe references first appear to a new siege weapon called a 'trabuchus' or 'trabuchellus'. Use of the 'trebuchet', as it soon became known, spread rapidly across the continent thereafter. A witness of the Norman siege of Thessalonike in 1185 recalled a huge trebuchet fondly known as 'The Daughter of the Earthquake'.

While its origin is uncertain, the trebuchet may have first emerged in the Middle East some time earlier, at the time of the First Crusade. The Byzantine Emperor Alexios I Komnenos (1081–1118) is said then to have pioneered new types of artillery which astonished those who witnessed them – and which were used to assist the Crusaders in bombarding the city of Nicaea. Muslims were quick to adopt the technology, but did not claim the credit. A manual written for Saladin in the 1180s contained one of the first detailed descriptions and noted that the device had been 'invented by unbelieving devils'.

In basic structure the trebuchet was similar to the 'perriers' or 'mangonels' which had existed for centuries. This consisted of a framework supporting an axle from which a large casting arm could rotate. It relied for its throwing power, however, not on a team of men but on a massive counterweight attached to the short end of the arm, often consisting of large rocks or stones in a net or box.

The longer end of the beam was pulled down to the ground, raising the great counterweight. This heavy work was achieved either by means of a pair of windlasses – geared crank devices for lifting heavy weights – or a pair of manned squirrel cages (see Early Cranes or Squirrel Cages box, p.158). Using the latter, a 10–ton counterweight could be hoisted into firing position in about five minutes. The beam was then fixed fast in position using a trigger mechanism, while a ball was placed into the sling. Generally around a dozen men were required in the team operating a large trebuchet – significantly fewer than had been needed for the earlier man-powered devices.

Initially the counterweight was often fixed to the end of the beam, but a movable, free-hanging counterweight which fell more steeply downwards proved more powerful as well as more durable and from the thirteenth century trebuchets were typically built this way. So devastating did these weapons become that they transformed static warfare, and tilted the balance in a prolonged siege between defence and attack. Trebuchets could be positioned to be used by defenders too, but a powerful leader like Sultan Baybars who could deploy large numbers of them in attack showed how irresistible they could be. Sieges which had dragged on for months were now resolved within weeks: either the garrison was relieved, or it was pounded into submission. Where Saladin had come to Krak and moved on, not wishing to become tied down in a long siege, Baybars knew he had the firepower to succeed without that happening.

in-fighting in the region came to an end and a united front was presented to the Christian Crusader enemy. Baybars was now free to put an end to the menace posed by the Hospitaller Knights at Krak once and for all. In the late winter of 1272, after taking Athlit and other smaller fortifications belonging to the Christians, he made for the great castle.

BAYBARS BESIEGES KRAK

After arriving at Krak with his army, Baybars' first priority was to conquer and contain the suburb which had grown up on the castle's eastern flank – clinging to the great fortress for protection, as towns often did in Europe. Neither archaeology nor documents reveal the exact location or extent of the suburb, but it must have been a settlement situated on the site of the present village of al-Hosn, directly adjoining Krak and defended by a rampart connected to the castle. The inhabitants and the garrison of the castle clearly put up some resistance because it took ten days for the Mamluk army to conquer the suburb and to secure the area surrounding the castle.

Around 4 March Baybars' already substantial army was reinforced by contingents from the Lords of Hama, Sahyn and the Isma'ili territories. After the persistent rains which greeted his arrival had finally eased, Baybars' men began to assemble a number of large trebuchets – the siege weapons the Sultan hoped would be able to inflict significant damage on Krak's walls and towers by aerial bombardment. They were erected behind wooden palisades to shield the craftsmen putting them together. These barriers would also protect the operators from arrows and bolts shot by members of the castle garrison who watched with foreboding as the massive weapons were erected. The palisades show that the machines were positioned within firing range of the Hospitaller archers – that is to say not more than 200 metres from the castle.

As another way of diverting the garrison from the construction of the siege weapons, foot soldiers in Baybars' army launched assaults against the main entrances to the castle. These involved the barbican (which may have been an advanced gate-tower) in front of the gate on the eastern front of the castle; and the second barbican which was situated on the rock plateau in front of the southern gate, and which was in turn defended by a palisade. These assaults were initially launched as a way of diverting the attention of the garrison from the construction of the siege machines. But they had success in their own right. On 9 March a furious attack led to the conquest of the first barbican.

This was a significant development, because the seizure of this barbican gave the Mamluk army a firm grip on the area between the eastern front of the castle and the suburb. It also dramatically increased the military pressure on this eastern front. From that point on, assaults against the main eastern gate, the southern barbican, and the third barbican on Krak's north-eastern flank multiplied. Muslim archers, meanwhile, used longbows and crossbows to target the battlement walkways, forcing defenders to retreat to lower levels. These tactics made possible the assembly

BELOW, LEFT *The high ground to the south (right) made this the castle's most vulnerable side. By 1271, it was fortified with a wooden outwork, but it did little to slow Sultan Baybars' progress*

BELOW, RIGHT *The south-west tower of the outer wall. Once the outworks had been taken, Baybars ordered his sappers to begin undermining this tower*

and adjustment of the trebuchets on the castle's eastern front. By mid-March they were finally operational and were put into action against the battlements of the eastern side of Krak des Chevaliers and the southern barbican. Their aerial bombardment was alternated with assaults by the foot soldiers. As elsewhere, the physical destruction wrought by the relentless thumping of huge rocks into the castle walls was only part of the trebuchets' impact. At least as significant was the demoralising psychological effect on the garrison, whose morale and determination to hold out were so often decisive in siege situations.

SIEGE STRATEGY

This combined approach soon brought results. On 21 March the second, southern barbican – sometimes known as the 'barbican of the blacksmith' – was conquered. Immediately the top of the basalt plateau in front of the castle to the south was occupied by Mamluk troops. Baybars looked to capitalise quickly on this success. He ordered many of his bowmen and crossbowmen to position

BELOW *The view across the castle to the north*

themselves along the northern palisade of the barbican, and from there to spray the southern front of the castle – especially the battlements – with arrows and bolts. The aim was to force the defenders posted on top to retreat behind the walls where they could return fire only at a much lower rate. So anxious was Baybars to maximise the advantage he had gained, that he grabbed a bow himself and joined his archers in this intensive shooting. Meanwhile his trebuchets kept up their relentless bombardment of Krak's eastern front.

Often, for all that siege weapons like counterweight trebuchets had become markedly more powerful and accurate, the primary threat to castle fortifications came from undermining. Even the most formidable of towers were powerless to resist having their foundations dug away. Krak was built on basalt – a hard rock that was very difficult to mine in this way. Nevertheless, Baybars had with him his specialist teams of miners and he was keen to bring them into play. While the shooting at the southern front and the bombardment of the eastern front limited the garrison's ability to observe the attackers' strategy, Baybars ordered his miners to open one or more breaches in Krak's outer wall. Two teams of mining specialists were sent along the outer fortifications, with instructions to undermine respectively the south-western circular tower of the castle and the north-eastern gate-tower. In the process, they were also to open two breaches which could be used as points of entry for the Mamluk army into Krak's lower baileys.

For a full week the two teams of miners worked without a break, operating under the cover of the pounding trebuchets and the hail of arrows sent whistling over the walls by the Muslim archers. In spite of the hard bedrock, the miners managed to dig tunnels beneath the foundations of the two towers – supporting them as they went with wooden beams. By the end of March they had completed their work and were ready to set fire to the stays holding up the roofs of the tunnels, which they did with brushwood (the pig fat often used for this purpose in Europe not being an option for a Muslim army). As the wooden props charred and gave way the tunnels collapsed in unison. In a roar of falling masonry, billowing clouds of dust and a shaking of the ground that may have made garrison members briefly suspect another earthquake, the south-western tower and the north-eastern gate-tower collapsed simultaneously. As planned, two decisive breaches were torn in Krak's defensive fabric.

Alert to the firing of the tunnel stays and awaiting their opportunity, the Mamluk foot soldiers burst en masse through the openings into the lower baileys of the castle. Their numerical advantage was decisive. The Hospitaller knights knew immediately that there was nothing to be gained in attempting to defend this outer area and so retreated into the inner castle. It was this central area which now became the final target for Baybars and his men.

During the period in which the Crusader States had successfully held off attempts at reconquest by the surrounding Muslim powers, one of the keys to their success had been the ability of Christian knights in the Levant – and the eastern Mediterranean generally – to rally a force capable of moving quickly to the aid of any castle that was under siege. This time, however, there was no prospect of relief. The Hospitallers knew it, and Baybars knew it too. Baybars' intelligence network informed him that no Crusader reinforcement would come from Tortosa or Tripoli, or even from the neighbouring Hospitaller castle of Margat. But although the defenders were alone, isolated and surrounded in their high castle, they remained determined. The inner fortifications were still formidable. Their stocks of food and water – a vital consideration for any garrison under siege – were plentiful. And they knew well that at any moment pressures or ambitions elsewhere could force Baybars to abandon the siege.

ALTHOUGH THE DEFENDERS WERE ALONE, ISOLATED AND SURROUNDED IN THEIR HIGH CASTLE, THEY REMAINED DETERMINED

They were right that the Mamluk leader was not prepared to bide his time. While he did not have to fear assault by a Christian army from the rear, Sultan Baybars did have other military objectives in mind and didn't want to waste valuable weeks besieging the high castle at Krak. There was another reason he was reluctant to maintain a long siege. A protracted campaign would involve his siege engines and mining engineers doing significant further damage to the fabric of the castle. Baybars had his eye on Krak as a future base for his own forces, from which he could continue the conquest of Crusader towns and castles along the coast.

SURRENDER

Baybars attempted to persuade the Hospitallers to surrender their castle. At first he did this by appearing menacing, hoping to demoralise the garrison into abandoning hope. He ordered the transportation of the trebuchets into the lower baileys in front of the high castle as if in preparation for a massive bombardment. Second, by contrast, he made it clear that he would treat surrendering knights mercifully. His son, al-Sa'id Barakat Khan, had determined to kill any captured Hospitallers and to keep prisoner any locals who had taken part in the defence of the castle alongside the Crusaders. But Baybars showed more indulgence by releasing a group of both local and European prisoners brought to him. Lastly he tried subterfuge. He is said to have produced a forged letter, signed in the name of the Grand Master of the Hospitaller Order in Tripoli, in which the latter ordered the defenders of Krak des Chevaliers to surrender the castle immediately.

This letter was received by the Hospitallers, still holding out within the high castle. It is quite possible that they recognised the forgery for what it was, but saw – as they were perhaps intended to see – an opportunity to surrender and to leave the castle freely without sacrificing their pride and honour. At any rate they seized the chance. On 8 April 1271 the last Hospitaller defenders at Krak

opened the gates of the high castle and were allowed to leave the site unharmed and to head back to Frankish territories on the coast. Baybars took possession of Krak des Chevaliers, the renowned 'key to the Christian lands'. It had repelled Muslim assaults for more than a century.

The loss of its headquarters was a grave blow to the Hospitaller Order, and it struggled to come to terms with this. Margat Castle

ABOVE *The western slope below the castle – possibly the knights' last view of the castle in 1271 before heading towards the coast*

remained a stronghold of the Order a while longer, but it was compelled by Baybars after 1271 to give up any claims to tribute payments from Muslim territories. As late as 1280 a large party of Knights made a raiding expedition from Margat into the plain below Krak. In the early 1280s, travellers reported that the castle remained strong and well-defended. But in 1285 a siege was begun which put an end to Margat's history as a Hospitaller castle – and an effective end to the Order's power in the Holy Land.

SUBSEQUENT HISTORY

In spite of Baybars' efforts to take Krak in one piece, the six-week siege had inevitably caused significant damage – the result both of bombardment by the siege engines and mining operations beneath certain towers. Much of this damage was along the southern and south-western fronts of the outer wall. The south-western tower had collapsed entirely after being undermined, and the upper levels of the curtain walls and towers had been pulverised by the trebuchets. On the eastern front, the upper levels of the gate-tower, the adjacent oblong tower and the curtain wall in between had all been destroyed, while the barbican to the north-east had been mined and had collapsed, along with the façades of the adjoining towers. The central 'high' castle did remain intact, however, since the garrison had surrendered after the Mamluk army stormed the breaches in the outer wall, and before the siege engines they began to set up in front of the inner towers had been fired.

Seeing the opportunity to use Krak as a new base from which to launch raids against the neighbouring towns and those castles still in the hands of the Crusaders like Margat, Tortosa and Tripoli, Baybars ensured his army did no further damage after they captured it. He entrusted Krak to a governor and appointed two Emirs as supervisors of the restoration and fortification works. These lasted for several years, and continued after Baybars' death in

RIGHT *Murder-holes line the roof of Krak's entrance ramp. Like machicolations, projectiles were dropped on the enemy through the gaps*

1277. An epigraph confirms that restoration of the curtain-wall took place under the rule of Baybars' son, al-Saʿid Barakat Khan.

The south-western semi-circular tower which had been destroyed by the mines was replaced by a larger circular tower. Continuous circuits of corbel machicolations – a defensive device developed in the Muslim architectural sphere (in contrast to the earlier box or slot machicolations) – were added to upper galleries. In several places walls were rebuilt or thickened. The ramp entrance to the east was made even more formidable, enclosed by a vaulted roof on its lower and upper sections, with 'murder-holes' inserted to allow the garrison to bombard any intruders. At the top of the higher section of the path, in front of the gate-tower of the high castle, a groin-vaulted rectangular defensive tower was built. The strength of the southern gate was improved with the construction of a semi-circular gate-tower. In some places, features that had been badly damaged or destroyed, like the northern barbican or the oblong building on the eastern front, were rebuilt according to the previous design.

After 1285 a second construction campaign took place under Sultan Qalawun and was marked by two new towers. The first was a massive square tower built in well-cut ashlar masonry, centrally-positioned on the exterior of the outer southern wall. Qalawun seems to have been keen to outdo Baybars, to judge by epigraphs glorifying him on the façade set higher than neighbouring inscriptions which mention his predecessor. The second was built within a depression on the south-east side between the Lion Tower and the outer wall, where a hammam (public bath) was also later built with the usual sequence of cold, warm and hot rooms under vaulted roofs – a sign that for future Muslim governors hospitality was often the primary concern.

Krak continued to enjoy a prominent status in the region under Mamluk rule, becoming the administrative centre of former Crusader towns and castles recently conquered in the region. It was also an important frontier post from which the campaign

ABOVE *This photograph of Krak des Chevaliers was taken by T. E. Lawrence (Lawrence of Arabia) who described it as 'perhaps the best preserved and most wholly admirable castle in the world'*

CHAPTER THREE

was continued against the remaining Crusader settlements. Its successive governors were renowned Emirs who took part in the main Mamluk military campaigns, like those which led to the conquest of Margat in 1285 and of Acre in 1291. The vast army which moved to conquer Acre – the last major Crusader stronghold in the Holy Land – had paused at Krak to pick up a siege engine aptly named 'Victorious' which joined the dozens of such weapons in the Muslim arsenal.

After the Crusades came to an end, Krak des Chevaliers lost its main military function, but remained the capital of a district in the large province of Tripoli. From then on the fourteenth-century governors who ruled the castle were little mentioned in the Arabic chronicles but were locally influential, like the Emir Batkamar Ibn 'Abd Allah al-Khazindar, who sponsored the construction of a church, a school and a hospital in the neighbouring city of al-Hisn in 1319. Nevertheless, Krak continued to play a military role until the mid-fourteenth century (as indicated by an epigraph dated 1345 carved on the façade of an eastern gate-tower, which gives details of the pay of the garrison then stationed in the castle).

After its capture by Sultan Baybars, Krak remained wholly in Muslim hands for nearly 650 years. Efforts to secure Christian rule in the Holy Land had proved a failure and for much of this intervening period the might of the Ottoman Empire dominated the Levant. Only with the collapse of this power during the First World War did European armies once again find themselves campaigning in the region. T. E. Lawrence had visited, Krak before the war, while researching a dissertation on Crusader castles, pronouncing it 'the best preserved and most wholly admirable castle in the world'.

By the time Lawrence and other pioneering students of the Crusader castles, like Paul Deschamps, visited, the villagers who had long lived in small settlements beneath the castle had moved up the hill to occupy the castle itself. Deschamps found some 500 of the local Kurdish population living as a functioning community within the walls. They had taken stone from the crenellations in building makeshift houses which obscured, and damaged, the castle fabric, while the great vaults had become packed with rubbish. As Syria was at the time a French mandate, Krak was taken into direct French care as a historic monument. The accumulated waste was cleared out – a job which took two hundred men years to complete – and the villagers themselves were likewise evicted (with some compensation). Only then did Krak become the tourist attraction it has since remained, particularly for French visitors who have most identified with the Frankish Crusaders whose fervent mission in the Holy Land left Krak des Chevaliers and other castles as a lasting memorial.

RIGHT This astonishing 28-metre needle of rock supported the drawbridge entrance to Saladin's castle, Syria (also known as Saône)

THE CONQUEST OF WALES:

CONWY CASTLE

4

THE KING AT BAY

ABOVE *A portrait in Westminster of Edward I, King of England (1272–1307). He attempted to forge the kingdoms of Britain into a single entity*

In the last week of January 1295, King Edward I of England, far from home and with only a small part of his army at hand, found himself blockaded in one of his own castles. While the magnificent fortification itself was secure, supplies were running desperately low. Marauding Welsh bands, loyal to a man who proclaimed himself a new Prince of Wales, Madog ap Llywelyn, surrounded the castle and walled town of Conwy and cut off supplies. Through the window of the royal apartment in the castle's inner ward, Edward kept a nervous eye on the heavens. For days on end the wind had shrieked through the battlements while the rain hammered down relentlessly, preventing supplies reaching the castle by sea. One English ship had been lost in a desperate attempt, and across the country conditions were terrible. One chronicler claimed that men of one hundred years old could remember no weather like it.

If the view skyward was dispiriting, the view downwards from the castle's south-eastern corner was more so. Directly beneath the king's chamber, the River Conwy – already broadening as it neared its estuary – had swelled to an impassable, fast-moving flood as rainwater cascaded off the mountains to the south. The greater part of Edward's large army, anxious to relieve the castle, was encamped on the eastern bank, unable to cross over to reinforce him.

Armed Welsh rebels besieged the castle and town, preventing vital deliveries getting through. As the days passed the situation became increasingly critical; the king and his men suffered great hunger and thirst. According to the chronicler Walter of Guisborough, Edward 'drank water mixed with honey. There was not enough bread to eat, for the Welsh captured the carts coming to him and stole away his supplies, killing all the Englishmen they could find'. Running out of wine, the garrison in Conwy vowed to save the last small barrel for their king. But Edward refused any such precedence. Now that they were in such dire need, Walter recorded him saying:

LEFT *Two of Conwy's hulking towers bear down on Castle Street. The red and yellow flag on the far left bears the heraldic device of Wales' last Welsh prince, Llywelyn II*

ABOVE *Across the waters of Cardigan Bay, the Llŷn Peninsula juts out into the Irish Sea. The reason for Edward's advance through this headland is still unknown*

PREVIOUS PAGE *The River Conwy at low tide, beneath the inner ward of Conwy Castle*

everything must be held in common, and we must all eat and drink exactly the same. For as God watches over us from on high, I am the beginning and the cause of this predicament, and I should do no better for food than you.

Edward was desperate to take the initiative. Wales was only one concern for this warrior king, who was anxious also to impose himself in Scotland and his French territories. During the previous fortnight, he had made a bold – many would say foolhardy – sortie into enemy territory. Having reached Conwy Castle just in time to celebrate Christmas there, early in the new year he had marched with the limited number of soldiers available to him west into Gwynedd. This was the old kingdom in north Wales he had abolished and broken up twelve years earlier, but which was now in open rebellion against its English overlord. Following the narrow coastal strip that skirted north of the mountains of Snowdonia, Edward's men pushed south-west into the Llŷn Peninsula. En route they passed Caernarfon, another English

BACKGROUND TO EDWARD'S CONQUEST OF WALES

While rule in Saxon England had gradually coalesced over the centuries, from multiple kingdoms into one English monarchy, in Wales the mountainous terrain and scattered population meant the country continued to be divided into distinct territories. If one Welsh ruler succeeded occasionally through military strength in establishing an overlordship, invariably he failed to secure any lasting legitimacy for his heirs, leaving the country to fragment back into smaller units.

Kings of England had long claimed overarching feudal control in Wales, which the Welsh rulers acknowledged by varying forms of oaths and tributes. After the Conquest, Norman kings endeavoured to enforce this claim more substantially. Powerful lords were granted estates in the border or 'March' land, effectively licensed to extend their territories westward. Much success was had, particularly in south Wales, and the arrival of Anglo-Norman settlers and church foundations secured English influence. Under the Conqueror's son Henry I (reign: 1100–35) 'independent' Wales was largely limited to Gwynedd in the north-west.

Over the subsequent century the strength of native rule in Wales ebbed and flowed largely in an inverse relationship with the strength of royal rule in England. A strong king like Henry II was able to impose himself, though with a vast empire to attend Wales could only be a peripheral concern and he happily accepted feudal submissions made by the Welsh rulers. Before he was overwhelmed by troubles in England in 1256, Henry III went far to establish English dominance over all Wales, laying the groundwork for his son Edward I. But during periods of disorder, under King Stephen, or during the later years of King John or Henry III, the Welsh states were able to revive dramatically and to kick against English control.

When Edward I came to the throne in 1272, the Prince of Wales, Llewelyn ap Gruffydd, provoked the king by refusing to do homage and by planning to marry Eleanor, Edward's first cousin, and the daughter of Simon de Montfort – the rebel baron who had waged war against Edward's father. In 1276 began the first of Edward's Welsh wars which would eventually see the country entirely conquered, with English administration imposed upon the population and enforced by a chain of magnificent castles.

walled town with an enormous new castle which Edward intended as his administrative centre in Gwynedd. It had remained substantially incomplete and was now a scene of utter destruction.

Soon after the rebellion had broken out the previous September, a force of Welsh partisans had infiltrated the town on market day and gone on the rampage, setting fire to many buildings, destroying English government records and massacring settlers. While some escaped, those captured by the Welsh were shown no mercy. Many, wrote a contemporary, 'swallowed swords' that day. Singled out for special attention was the king's favourite,

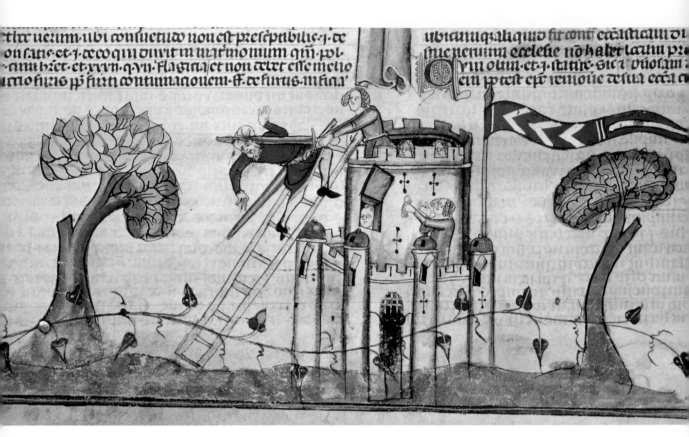

ABOVE *The perils of attempting to scale a castle's walls by siege ladder are made clear in this vivid fourteenth-century illumination*

RIGHT *The lower ward of Caernarfon Castle (foreground) leading to the upper ward. Both Conwy and Caernarfon were designed with two connecting sections, rather than concentric rings of walls*

Roger of Pulesdon, the man Edward had made his first sheriff of Anglesey, who was widely loathed by the Welsh as an extortioner. He had been tasked with collecting recently-imposed English taxes in the region, a certain route to unpopularity, and in the eyes of the Welsh had abused his position. From a family of 'marcher' lords in the border county of Shropshire, he was hanged from the eaves of his own house in the town. The Welsh quickly turned their attention to the adjacent castle. Its north wall facing onto the town was still under construction. Nevertheless, it was already more than four metres high from the bottom of the adjacent ditch. The rebels probably used siege ladders to scale the wall which, since it was unfinished, did not yet have the machicolations and other defences which would help a garrison to prevent large numbers climbing up. (A finished castle was difficult to attack in this way because of the

MADOG AP LLYWELYN

Frustratingly little is known about the personal history of the man most associated with the Welsh rising of 1294–95 – Madog ap Llywelyn. He seems to have been distantly related to the former royal dynasty of Gwynedd, members of which had used and been accorded the title Prince of Wales. His direct ancestors were from a side branch of the family who ruled over the small region of Meirionnydd.

He was not the sole leader of the rebellion. To the south, another former princeling deprived by the English, Morgan ap Maredudd, took the lead. But Madog quickly became the primary figurehead, perhaps because of his family link to the great rulers of Gwynedd who had held clear ascendancy in Wales. He dusted off for himself the title they had used of 'Prince of Wales', by which he is referred in a number of contemporary sources, English as well as Welsh.

The resentment Madog was able to exploit in 1294 was bitter and widespread. English rule in the north-west was only a decade old and the imposition of a harsh new tax on a poor population unused to such exactions fomented unrest. The final straw seems to have been Edward's attempt to conscript Welshmen to serve in his war in France – a war which at the same time significantly reduced the English military presence in Wales, creating an opportunity the rebels were quick to exploit.

Subjugated for a decade by a common enemy, the Welsh had come to feel an increased sense of national unity, allowing Madog to put himself at the head of what has been called 'a classic anti-colonial revolt'.

After the comprehensive defeat of his forces at Maes Moydog on 5 March 1295, Madog retreated to his family heartland of Meirionnydd and went into hiding. In July, after the rebellion had been comprehensively quashed and Edward had returned to England, he turned himself in and, though his life was spared, saw out his days imprisoned in the Tower of London, dying on 2 January 1313.

difficulty of getting enough men up past the arrows and missiles aimed at them by the defenders above.) Once inside, the Welsh burned timber buildings and slaughtered the garrison and royal officials. Nearly five months later, Caernarfon was still under their control and its castle, on whose construction Edward had already lavished a fortune, now stood in ruins.

With only a small force, however, Edward soon realised that he risked being overwhelmed in a disordered and hostile territory. Any doubt was erased when Welsh rebels attacked and captured most of his baggage train, forcing him to return in haste to the security of Conwy Castle. English control – so recently imposed – now hung by a thread, across the old territory of Gwynedd and in Wales

more generally. Apart from this castle and the walled town that lay below it, and a handful of other castles and towns dotted around the fringes of the mountains, the whole region was now under the control of Edward's enemies.

Sheltering in Conwy Castle from the Welsh bands and the battering storm, with only the stone walls and an under-sized army to protect him, the king knew he had no immediate prospect of re-taking Caernarfon. However, he knew that if he could hold out until the weather improved, the main army would be able to rejoin him, and he would then be in a position to re-impose his authority on the turbulent Welsh. Meanwhile, the Welsh were equally aware that they faced a race against time. If they were to gain access to Conwy Castle, it would have to be soon, while the appalling weather prevented Edward from making use of his substantial reinforcements. The outcome, as both sides knew, was in the hands of the heavens.

STAGES OF CONQUEST: THE ENGLISH CASTLES OF NORTH WALES

The king's isolation in Conwy Castle was made more poignant by the fact that the fortress was never meant to operate alone. In 1295 there were six other royal castles that the king himself had founded

ABOVE Caernarfon Castle from the western bank of the River Seiont, dominated by the triple-turreted Eagle Tower. Caernarfon means 'castle in Arfon' ('opposite Anglesey')

across north Wales (though, as in the case of Caernarfon, not all were complete). There were also four others that Edward had garrisoned after capturing them from the Welsh, as well as a number of other, smaller castles held by important English barons closer to the Cheshire border. Those English who had responded to Edward's call to settle in Wales must have believed that their presence in the territory was secure. Across north Wales, only the island of Anglesey was without an English castle.

The new castles had been founded in waves, reflecting the specific objectives of previous English operations in Wales. Edward's first war, in 1276–77, had been intended to limit the authority and territory of Llywelyn ap Gruffydd, the man who called himself 'prince of Wales and lord of Snowdon', but not to eliminate him. This campaign was not obviously what we would now consider a national struggle. Llywelyn was not widely supported outside Gwynedd; some 9,000 Welsh troops made up the bulk of Edward's army. In 1277 Llywelyn was forced to concede the Treaty of Aberconwy, which acknowledged his rule only in Gwynedd, west of the line traced by the River Conwy. The four new English castles begun during this war (Flint, Rhuddlan, Aberystwyth and Builth) were sited in north-east, south-west and in mid-Wales to cement English military gains there, but involved no encroachment into the territories still left to the prince, in Snowdonia, Anglesey and Meirionnydd.

By the time Edward launched a second offensive against Wales in 1282, his objectives had become more radical. Llywelyn and his younger brother Dafydd had attacked the English garrisons left after the first war. Attempts to impose English law on much of Wales had by this time

THE NEW CASTLES HAD BEEN FOUNDED IN WAVES, REFLECTING THE SPECIFIC OBJECTIVES OF PREVIOUS ENGLISH OPERATIONS IN WALES

provoked a genuinely national response and widespread rebellions, which inflicted serious reverses on English forces. Edward launched what was now a full-blooded war of conquest intended to remove the prince (achieved when Llywelyn was isolated and killed in mid-Wales) and to bring the whole of Wales under English dominion. Determined to establish a permanent English presence which would deter any further unrest, he brought with him an army of skilled masons, carpenters and diggers from all over his kingdom. From Northumberland to Somerset they came, willing or unwilling. An order survives for 'carpenters and diggers to be distrained [impressed] by constables'. In 1282, 1000 diggers, 345 carpenters and 50 masons congregated at Bristol and Chester prior to being sent on to Wales to begin work on the new castles. Many more would follow. In July 1286, it is recorded, 227 masons were among the huge workforce at Harlech alone.

ABOVE *The castle of Harlech, or 'fair rock', is named after the mound on which it was built*

The castles Edward founded or re-established during this period were located either on the edges of the highlands of Snowdonia or in the heart of the mountains. At the centre of his plans were three massive and entirely new English fortresses. These were based at Harlech on the Merioneth coast to the south-west of Snowdonia, on the north coast at Caernarfon, facing the western approach into the Menai Strait that divided Anglesey from the mainland, and at Conwy (formerly called Aberconwy), providing an English emplacement on the Welsh shore of the River Conwy on the eastern fringe of the mountains. The sites were chosen for their psychological as well as strategic impact. Caernarfon had long associations with the Welsh princes, and the Cistercian monastery

BELOW *Four turrets rise from the nearest of Conwy's eight towers, marking out the area enclosed by the inner ward where the royal apartments were situated*

CHAPTER FOUR

of Aberconwy – forcibly moved eight miles to make way for Edward's castle – was the hallowed burial site of Llywelyn the Great, an earlier, revered Prince of Gwynedd.

Several of the castles were accompanied by new planned towns, their defences being built by the same masons as were constructing the castles. The walls around the new town of Conwy contained twenty-one towers and three gatehouses, a work nearly as formidable as the castle itself. While trading privileges were given for the English to settle in these towns, after the rebellion the Welsh were banned from living there. It appears that this rule might have been ignored, for Welsh names appear consistently among the listed inhabitants.

With the exception of Builth, all these castles and towns were sited on the coast. The king's soldiers also now occupied a number of older Welsh castles in the mountainous interior, as bases to control important passes through the highlands. Both shipping and land traffic were afforded some degree of protection. Garrisons were positioned to launch sorties into the hinterlands whenever necessary. Edward must have thought he had done enough to secure the English presence in all parts of Wales. The 1284 Statute of Rhuddlan formally annexed the 'principality' of Wales proclaimed by Llywelyn to the English Crown. The future Edward

II – the man who would be proclaimed the first English Prince of Wales – was born while his father was in Caernarfon. Five new counties following the English model were created, and the writ of English law and government ran throughout Wales.

CONWY CASTLE: MASTERPIECE OF DESIGN

At the beginning of the thirteenth century, a chronicler monk, shocked by the ferocity with which King Edward's grandfather, King John, besieged and captured Rochester Castle in 1215, had exclaimed that 'few people now put their trust in castles'. Conwy and the other royal castles of north Wales showed how wrong this judgement had proved to be. Edward would spend some £15,000 on Conwy alone – scarcely an investment he would have made without confidence in its impact.

In fact, the thirteenth century had seen the construction of numerous castles, such as the fine baronial examples belonging to the powerful Earl of Gloucester, as well as the expansion of colossal royal fortresses, like Dover, Windsor and the Tower of London. Edward's great castles in north Wales represented the culmination of these thirteenth-century developments in design and military technology.

In the second half of the century, many English noblemen and Edward himself had gained practical experience of the use of castles in war. A vicious civil war was fought between the forces of his father, King Henry III, and a group of rebel barons led by Earl Simon de Montfort of Leicester. During this conflict, Edward had taken a leading role in the siege of Kenilworth Castle, which had lasted 172 days between June and December 1266 – the longest siege in English history to that date. In 1271, Edward found himself besieged in the fortified city of Acre, during what was the last significant medieval Crusade to the Holy Land. Such first-hand knowledge, combined with his undoubted military prowess, equipped him to make an important contribution to the design of his new castles in north Wales.

Credit for the design of the extraordinary masterpieces of Conwy, Harlech and Caernarfon has generally been granted to a man whose origins lay not in England but in the county of Savoy (straddling the borders of modern France, Italy and Switzerland), where he designed castles for Count Philip, Edward's cousin. The English financial accounts for the Welsh wars are preserved in the National Archives. They show that from 1278 onwards a Master James of Saint George oversaw the building works in north Wales. With him came numerous Savoyard masons and other craftsmen:

BELOW *The semi-circular arch entrance to Harlech's main gate is said to be of Savoyard influence*

men like Adam Boynard – or 'Adam, king of the rascals' – John Francis, William Seysel and Gilot de Chalons. They joined craftsmen and labourers recruited from all over England, divided and sent to the sites of each of Edward's new castles. There were perhaps 1,500 men working at Conwy at the height of construction work in the summer of 1285, with thousands of others working simultaneously at Harlech and Caernarfon.

Dr Arnold Taylor, the great twentieth-century scholar of Edward's castles in north Wales, identified at Conwy, Harlech and Rhuddlan design and constructional features familiar in Savoy but rarely seen in contemporary buildings in England and Wales. These included fully semi-circular arches (unusual in an age of Gothic pointed arches), windows under 'segmental' arches, pinnacles on

the copings of battlements, two types of latrine outlet projecting from the castle wall and, most distinctive of all, a form of scaffold with sloping ramps rather than horizontal platforms.

In terms of the success of a castle's design, however, these are minor details. The most significant features of the north Wales castles – the concentric walls, the massive gatehouses, the regularly-spaced towers and the water defences – can be identified in English castles long before Master James was first sent to Wales. Most of the Savoyard castles he worked on are tiny by comparison with the great castles of Edward I, and lack some of the latter's central design elements and brilliant overall planning. Probably Edward recruited James as someone with the experience to manage large workforces and to organise the supply of materials to several large

ABOVE *Winding putlog holes around one of the towers in Conwy's town wall. Computer graphics illustrate what this Savoyard feature may have looked like*

building sites at once. Early in his commission, he would have been executing designs whose general form he copied from other castles of the English Crown and baronage, such as Dover, the Tower of London, Kenilworth or Caerphilly, or which had been given to him by someone else. If there was someone else, his identity must remain an intriguing mystery, but it is a strong possibility that at least some of the ideas behind the castles came from King Edward himself.

It was by now standard practice for a castle to have more than one line of defence, but the means of achieving this varied. In general the plans of the castles took one of two forms. They either had several enclosures (also called 'wards' or 'baileys') standing one inside the other, often called the 'concentric' plan, or they had separate adjacent enclosures. Edward I's castles are most famous for the first, concentric plan, this design being seen at Rhuddlan and Aberystwyth (founded during the first war, though much altered and expanded later) and at Harlech, the great castle begun in April 1283 during the second war. The concentric design would perhaps find its definitive expression in the eighth castle in the group: that which Edward built at the end of the rebellion at Beaumaris on Anglesey, where the recently-flourishing Welsh settlement of Llanfaes was brutally levelled and removed to make way for another English borough defended by a formidable fortress.

The essential principle of having two lines of curtain wall, one inside the other and both capable of being defended independently, had been a feature of castles for over a century. Henry II had built an outer curtain wall around part of Dover Castle in the 1180s (see Chapter 1), and in the following decade, his son Richard had applied the same idea to the new Château Gaillard in Normandy (see Chapter 2). But during the thirteenth century, an improved understanding of the potential of the crossbow, shot at a low trajectory, had caused the concept to be refined, in particular by making the outer wall comparatively low and piercing it with loops. By this means, the outer and inner curtain walls might be used in conjunction by crossbowmen, rather than simply providing

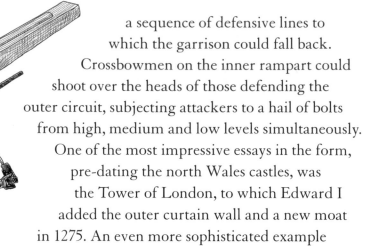

a sequence of defensive lines to which the garrison could fall back. Crossbowmen on the inner rampart could shoot over the heads of those defending the outer circuit, subjecting attackers to a hail of bolts from high, medium and low levels simultaneously. One of the most impressive essays in the form, pre-dating the north Wales castles, was the Tower of London, to which Edward I added the outer curtain wall and a new moat in 1275. An even more sophisticated example was Caerphilly in south Wales, a castle belonging to the Earl of Gloucester which he began to expand in 1277. In both cases, the outer curtain received additional protection from a water-filled moat, which had the double advantage of preventing miners from attacking the foundations of the stone wall, while also keeping attackers away from the 'dead ground' at the foot of the wall, where defenders could not see them.

ABOVE A crossbow – cocked and loaded with a bolt. Unlike the longbow, mastering this weapon did not require powerful upper body muscle

Conwy, however, conformed to the other kind of plan, with two baileys standing side-by-side. In part at least, this was dictated by the castle's site: a high, but relatively narrow ridge of sandstone overlooking the confluence of the wide River Conwy with a smaller tributary which offered no real scope for enclosing one ward within another. The castle did make a nod towards the concentric principle, however: at either end a barbican, with walls much lower than those of the main curtain and thin, low turrets, offered additional protection.

These barbicans were dwarfed by the main body of the castle, which formed a rectangle of walls, over 50 feet high in places, punctuated by massive round towers, four on each side. On the south side, facing the Gyffin stream, the curtain wall bowed out slightly, to follow the contours of the rock on which the castle was built. Otherwise the castle's plan was entirely regular, even down to the details. Each segment of the north curtain wall overlooking

RIGHT The adjacent wards of the castle. In the event that the outer ward fell, the inner ward (foreground) could be sealed off to protect the defenders within

ABOVE The south side of the castle, which bends to follow the contours of the rock. All of the castle's eight towers are topped with arrow-loops at alternating heights and crenellations

the town of Conwy, for example, was pierced by two tall arrow-loops, while each stretch of the parapet running between the towers was topped with seven merlons. On the top of each tower the merlons contained an arrow-loop, alternating between 'high' and 'low' positions, permitting defenders on the tower tops to shoot either straight out or on a plunging trajectory to ground level.

Since most of the internal layout of the castle was hidden to the outside observer, only someone familiar with the building might realise the significance of the four small turrets which rose above the four towers closest to the River Conwy. These towers overlooked the inner ward of the castle, furthest from the main entrance – these contained the apartments built for Edward I and his queen. The turrets served a dual purpose. They provided an additional element of security, by improving the view for look-outs. From these uppermost perches of the castle, which itself rose up from a great rock 15 metres above the surrounding landscape, views stretched for miles around. Soldiers could look inland for an attack coming on foot, or for the more welcome sight of a supply ship sailing into the Conwy estuary. The turrets were almost

certainly also intended for display, acting as 'banner towers' from which the royal standard could be flown when the king was in residence at the castle.

The most effective defensive principle of Conwy Castle was also the most obvious: it was, to any would-be assailant surveying it even briefly, imposing and well-designed. It was as likely to deter an attack in the first place as to hold one off. The sheer physical mass of the castle, the close spacing of its towers, the height of its curtain wall, and the visible emplacements for crossbowmen and archers would cause all but the most determined assailants to think twice.

A closer look would show that the castle offered little scope for miners. To the south and east rivers acted as a moat, while on the north and western flanks a deep ditch had been cut from the rock on which the castle stood, creating steep sides of sharp and jagged rocks which would be perilous to climb at any time, let alone under fire from the numerous arrow-slits above. Even so, Master James took no chances. He covered the potentially vulnerable garderobe-outlets on the northern side with stone caps, and on the southern side, overlooking the Gyffin stream, he kept the outlets at a high level, with a long drop over the rocks.

ABOVE *The four turrets of the inner ward. Seven hundred years ago the lions of England would have flown from these turrets*

ABOVE *Conwy Castle's outer ward, which contained the Great Hall (left) and domestic buildings, such as the kitchen (now reduced to wall-footings on the right of the ward)*

RIGHT *The Gyffin stream at low tide, on the south side of the castle. Access to water is one of the key defensive features associated with Edward's castles in Wales*

There were only two approaches into the castle. The main entrance, at the north-west corner, was by means of a high stone ramp, running up towards a pivoting drawbridge under the miniature turrets of a small gateway into the west barbican. The ditch at this point was fully 28-feet deep from the drawbridge to the bottom. A second entrance at the eastern end was a much more private affair. It was largely destroyed during the construction of bridges in the nineteenth and twentieth centuries, but an early seventeenth-century drawing shows a narrow and probably dangerous path spiralling around the rock to a stair which rose steeply up into the castle's eastern barbican. At the base was a dock where the royal barge or, more routinely, vessels bringing supplies, could moor, under the eye of the barbican from which crossbowmen could give friendly boats their protection.

At the top of the stair, the path ran through a small garden in this eastern barbican, appropriately placed beneath the windows of the royal lodgings. Both entrances to the castle proper were defended by a feature more spectacular than anything built to date in an English castle: a line of machicolations – slots at parapet level – which allowed defenders to drop large stones or other projectiles directly onto the heads of anyone attacking the main gates below them.

Only once inside the castle could a visitor appreciate that the interior was divided into two distinct parts, an outer and an inner ward; a castle within a castle. Since most would enter on foot from the western end, the entrance from the town, the eastern water-gate being reserved for the royal party and those delivering goods, the western bailey constituted the outer ward. This was used by the main body of the garrison, and as such was larger than the

BELOW *A reconstruction of Conwy Castle and its town in the late thirteenth century. Unlike the castle we see today, the walls were white-washed and the water-gate (bottom right, leading from the barbican to the wooden dock) was intact*

inner ward, to which only the most trusted and distinguished were granted access. The great hall – scene of large-scale banquets and entertainments – thus stood in the outer ward, along with the main chapel of the castle. The hall would also have been used for judicial sessions, held by either the constable of the castle (who was also the mayor of the town) or the justiciar of north Wales (the king's chief minister in the region). Conveniently next door, in the basement of a tower opening from the hall, was the prison, where those awaiting trial or those found guilty might be interred. There were also ancillary buildings: a kitchen, a brewhouse, two bakehouses, as well as the common latrine. All these buildings made use of the castle well in the outer ward, 91-feet deep and fed from a natural spring. Overlooking the outer ward were six of the castle's massive round towers, each containing two storeys of large rooms – heated and with two-light windows – over a basement. It was no doubt in these towers that the bulk of the castle's garrison lodged.

At the eastern end of the outer ward, a further series of internal defences controlled access to the inner ward beyond. A deep rock-cut ditch ran across the width of the castle at this point,

ABOVE, TOP *Stone machicolations line the parapet (centre) above the eastern entrance to the inner ward. Through them, projectiles such as heavy objects or boiling oil could be dropped on attackers*

ABOVE, BOTTOM *The menacing sight of the stone machicolations would have greeted any who climbed the steps from Conwy's water-gate*

MACHICOLATIONS

A machicolation is an elevated floor opening, created by a parapet projecting outwards from the top of a castle wall, allowing stones or other objects to be dropped onto enemy soldiers doing their worst at the foot of the wall. The word is suitably descriptive, deriving from the old French *mâcher*, to crush, and *col*, neck.

Early castles used wooden hoardings, often quickly constructed in case of a siege, which likewise provided some protection for defenders leaning over to drop missiles. Stone structures, however, were both stronger and resistant to fire. It has been speculated that the innovation derived from the Middle East, and was brought back to Western Europe by Crusaders returning from the Holy Land.

Machicolations were more common in French than in English castles, Conwy being the first to incorporate them as a permanent stone feature. Here the machicolations jutted boldly forward above six courses of rounded corbel-stones, a device both practical and flamboyant that must have impressed and intimidated anyone passing under them.

A variant of the external machicolation was employed in the interior of castles to allow defenders to attack any intruders who succeeded in getting past the outer walls. Holes in the roof of entrance passages through which rocks and other missiles could be dropped or thrown on people passing below were aptly known as 'murder-holes'.

RIGHT *The chambers on the left of the inner ward housed some of the royal apartments in which the king and queen would have stayed when in residence*

bridged by a stone causeway, with a drawbridge spanning the last few feet. On the far side of the ditch rose a stone wall, as high as the external curtain wall, pierced only by a single small door which was protected by a turret. Only once admitted through this wall did the visitor find himself in a much smaller courtyard, with two-storeyed ranges on two sides and a high tower behind the buildings at each corner of the enclosure. This was the inner ward, built under the direction of Master James as a private area for the use of King Edward, his queen, Eleanor of Castile, and their immediate household. Heated and well-lit chambers on the first floor, with a private chapel, were set over storage rooms and a kitchen at ground level.

ABOVE, LEFT *The Queen's Chamber in the inner ward. Edward's wife, Queen Eleanor, never lived to see the castle completed*

ABOVE, RIGHT *The Prison Tower on the outer ward's south side. Located beside the Great Hall, captives were left to consider their fate just metres from where the castle's feasts took place*

RIGHT, TOP *Conwy's outer ward. The foundation stones (on the left) mark out the area which enclosed the kitchen*

These were buildings of the highest quality, built for a monarch and his consort, though they were very little here. Eleanor saw Conwy when it was under construction but never returned, having died in 1290, four years before the crisis which would force Edward back. Though ruined, the rooms survive better in their original layout here than those of any other castle in England and Wales. The traceried windows that lit the royal lodgings at Conwy were works of architecture as fine as those of contemporary abbeys and cathedrals. They serve as a reminder that no mere military functionality would suffice for the apartments of a king, however willing he might be *in extremis* to share the deprivations of his men. Interestingly, a few telling errors suggest the speed with which the exterior curtain walls and towers of the castle were raised (to create quickly a defensible enclosure in an unsettled land) before a definite plan had been made for the buildings that would sit within them. Thus the internal walls of the royal lodgings cut across external features such as the embrasure of a crossbow-loop. Evidently the outside walls were well advanced before the building season of 1285, when the royal lodgings were begun. The speed of the work here remains astonishing.

In one respect, Conwy Castle was rather unusual. At other castles that he built for Edward in north Wales, including his masterpieces at Harlech and later Beaumaris, James adopted a design feature that had been used to great effect in English castles since the late twelfth century. At these, the towers that flanked the main gate were incorporated into a much larger composite structure, with residential accommodation on the upper floors, that modern scholars have labelled a 'keep-gatehouse'. This turned the gate-passage into a long tunnel which could be defended by a sequence of devices: two or three portcullises; a succession of wooden gates; loops in the side walls allowing defenders to shoot into the carriageway; or 'murder-holes' in the ceilings above, through which rocks could be dropped onto attackers trapped by the portcullises. The fact that some of these devices needed to be operated from above might have made life inside the gatehouse a

ABOVE *The well next to the middle gate in the outer ward. A drawbridge led from here to the inner ward*

PREVIOUS PAGE
The middle gate led to the inner ward (centre left). Royal apartments (far left) are overlooked by the Stockhouse Tower (top right)

FAR LEFT *The private chapel of the inner ward, for use by the king and his consort. The intricately carved sandstone is in an excellent state of preservation*

LEFT *The remnants of ornate traceried windows can still be seen in the royal apartments of the inner ward*

little awkward: at Harlech, the two front portcullises could only be raised and lowered from inside the chapel. Conwy Castle, however, did not possess a proper 'gatehouse' (see Gatehouse box, p.223). The entrance to the outer ward was no more than an arch in the curtain wall, closed by timber bars, a single portcullis and a set of wooden gates (the grooves through which the portcullis ran remain visible). Inside the arch there was an adjacent timber-framed building, with an upper room containing the mechanism for the portcullis and porters' lodges at ground level, but this was a largely self-contained structure, only communicating at ground level with the two western towers of the castle.

In addition to the practical aspects of defence, a consideration of equal importance was the psychological impact the castles would have on the population of north Wales. In this context, one key aspect of Conwy Castle's remarkable appearance in its landscape is not obvious today, except on very close inspection. The walls of the castle, like those of Harlech, were entirely covered with white lime render. This served a practical function in protecting the rough

BELOW *Murder-holes in the vaulting of the King's Gate at Caernarfon Castle. Death would rain down on any enemies passing beneath in the form of projectiles*

IT WAS CERTAINLY THE MOST VISUAL STATEMENT IMAGINABLE OF THE NEW REALITY OF ENGLISH POWER

stonework from the elements. But it also made this extraordinary structure stand out from its surroundings in a manner that must have stunned those seeing it for the first time. It appeared, perhaps, as a 'tower of ivory' – an image from the biblical Song of Songs – and was certainly the most visual statement imaginable of the new reality of English power.

Similar visual statements were made at Edward's other Welsh castles. Another verse from the same book of the Bible may have underpinned the display of wooden shields painted with the royal arms which hung from the battlements of Rhuddlan Castle and probably others too. The most ostentatious treatment of all, meanwhile, was reserved for Caernarfon Castle, conceived in 1283 as the centrepiece of the English architectural programme, at a new town intended as the regional centre of English administration. Mindful of the legendary (and accurate) associations of the place with an ancient Roman fortress, Edward I and Master James incorporated explicit references to Imperial Roman architecture into the design of their new castle – associating Edward's rule with the power and longevity of Rome. Thus, the towers at Caernarfon Castle were octagons, decagons or other polygons, rather than round or D-shaped as at the other Welsh castles – a deliberate echo of Roman buildings such as the Multangular Tower in the city wall at York, or the pharos at Dover Castle. The walls at Caernarfon were faced with dressed-stone blocks, most of which were locally-quarried limestone, but which incorporated four horizontal bands of yellow and red sandstones, imitating the distinctive courses of bricks or tiles that characterised Roman walling. Several of the towers were topped with elaborate sculptures (added during the reign of Edward's successor, but probably intended in the 1280s) of human heads and eagles, giving the largest of the towers the name 'Eagle Tower' – a claim, easily

GATEHOUSE

Entrances to castles were often the most vulnerable point. Castle builders tried to ensure they were sufficiently provided with defences to deter and, if needs be, thwart attackers. But defences could not be so elaborate that they restricted the ease with which people, horses and carts could come and go on a daily basis.

Early stone gateways consisted of a single square-bottomed tower with an entrance incorporated into the design. By the end of the twelfth century, however, we begin to see entrances flanked by two towers – like those built by Henry II at Dover Castle. The advantage of the two-towered over the single-towered design was that it was potentially possible for more of the garrison to guard the entrance and to shoot projectiles from either side of the gate at attackers (known today as 'flanking fire').

Gateways were fitted with a range of features to maximise their effectiveness to the point where they often became the strongest part of a castle's defences. Drawbridges and portcullises, for example, were standard. It was not uncommon in the Middle Ages for castle entrances to be bolstered with outer works (such as those which famously fell to the French during Prince Louis's siege of Dover 1216 – see Outer Works box, p.165). Similarly, entrances could be fortified from within, as the 'Great Ramp' at Krak des Chevaliers was (Chapter 3).

The thirteenth century saw the emergence of the 'gatehouse'. This gateway structure had the dual purpose of providing high-standard accommodation – often for the constable of the castle – as well as strong defensive features.

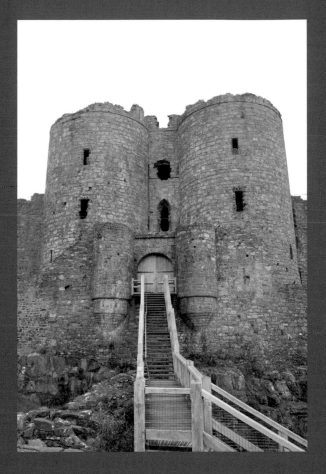

This era witnessed some formidable gateway architecture. The gatehouses which Edward I built into some of his castles in North Wales, Harlech and Caernarfon for example, are equipped with many protective layers and are amongst the strongest in the world. The gatehouse at Caernarfon was not wholly completed, but would have involved no fewer than five doors and six portcullises, as well as a drawbridge, murder-holes, arrow-loops and a right-angled turn.

ABOVE, LEFT *The Eagle Tower at Caernarfon Castle is so named for the stone eagles which perch on its crenellations, which deliberately recall the prestige of Imperial Rome*

ABOVE, RIGHT *The decorative bands of lighter sandstone in Caernarfon's walls indicate that, unlike Conwy, the castle would not have been white-washed*

understood by the Welsh, to the strength and immortality possessed by the King of the Gods with which this bird was associated in ancient Rome.

THE PRACTICALITIES OF DEFENDING CONWY CASTLE

In normal circumstances, without the royal household and army in attendance, the garrison that defended Conwy Castle was not particularly large. In October 1284, when the castle walls were still far from complete, the king issued a number of writs appointing several of his knights as constables of the new castles. He entrusted Conwy to a knight of Burgundian origin, Sir William de Cicon, who had probably been introduced to Edward by the Savoyard Sir Otto de Grandson, one of the king's closest friends. Cicon had served the king in both his first and second Welsh wars, becoming constable of Rhuddlan in 1282, and taking an important role in provisioning the forces in north Wales during the invasion of Snowdonia.

As constable of Conwy, a post he held until his death in 1311, he oversaw the completion of the castle; at the same time,

by his appointment as mayor of the new town of Conwy, he also supervised the construction of the town and its defences – a magnificent battlemented stone wall with 3 gates and 21 towers – as well as the arrival of its first settlers. The king's initial writ to Sir William concerning Conwy Castle set out the constable's responsibilities in only general terms, but contained more detail about the resources at his disposal:

ABOVE *The view from Caernarfon's walls across the Menai Strait to the Isle of Anglesey, a significant seat of Welsh opposition to English rule in the late thirteenth century*

> *The king has entrusted to his beloved and faithful William de Cicon his castle of Aberconwy, together with its weapons and everything else in the castle for its defence, to be held as long as it pleases the king. He has granted him 190 pounds yearly for keeping the said castle ... Besides himself and his own household, he is to maintain at his own cost thirty fighting men for the defence of the castle; fifteen of these are to be crossbowmen, and also a chaplain, an artiller, a carpenter, a mason and a smith, and from the remainder there shall be gate-keepers, watchmen and other officers needed for the castle.*

The basic garrison of thirty fighting men was similar to those installed in the other north Wales castles. Harlech had a complement of exactly the same size, while the much larger Caernarfon had ten more, as did the small Castell-y-Bere, a castle in Merioneth captured from the Welsh. Accounts compiled in several castles during Madog's rebellion show that while numbers occasionally fluctuated, most of the castles did contain a garrison of the size that Edward had stipulated, and with named officers filling the posts of smith, chaplain and the others that the king had prescribed. The garrisons generally made no provision for cavalry, which would have been scant use given the mountainous terrain, though the constable himself and perhaps one or two other dignitaries would be horsemen. The location of any stabling inside the castles has never been identified. The emphasis on crossbowmen (*balistarii* in the original Latin wording) is no surprise, for the crossbow was the key weapon used in castles of the period.

Conwy Castle also contained a few items of heavier weaponry. In the 1280s, the constable accounted for two 'engines'. These were of an undisclosed type, sadly, but clearly expensive and complicated pieces of carpentry. Later documents mention more than one *springald*, a type of large crossbow mounted on a frame or a pivot, sometimes deployed on wall-walks or on the tops of towers. Edward was a passionate advocate of siege machines and in his wars with Scotland he later created the largest stone-throwing catapult ever built, a contraption named the 'warwolf'.

Some of the other castles in north Wales were certainly equipped with powerful siege-engines including trebuchets, hurling rounded balls provided by the castles' stonemasons. In the early fourteenth century Beaumaris Castle, for example, had a trebuchet small enough to be mounted on top of a wall. Most of the other items listed in these inventories of the castles' armouries were items of body armour, both metal and leather.

None of these indications of the peacetime garrison at Conwy, of course, are any guide to the force present during the emergency of

THE BLACKSMITH

Smiths were not necessarily popular figures in medieval society. Houses in towns were made largely of wood, and air quality was already poor, so few wanted to live next to a forge, with sparks flying from its chimney along with thick smoke from its fire. They were greatly respected nonetheless. In Anglo-Saxon society the smith was a high-ranking officer. Over time their work proliferated, and by the medieval period small-scale forges all over the country turned out simple but essential items from horseshoes and stirrups to weapons, armour and all-purpose knives. All occupations were dependent to some degree on the work of the smith.

The process of building and garrisoning a major castle was no exception. Construction teams relied on spades, pickaxes, wedges and nails. In an area like Wales, which the English Crown had long been attempting to subdue and fortify, demand was particularly high. A document of the early thirteenth century records a delivery to Wales from an ironworks in Durham of 1,260 shovels, 160 picks and 100 hatchets. Though iron ore was common all over the country, sources in Northumberland, Durham and Cumbria, among other places, were particularly well-exploited in medieval times.

Once the castle was built, a smith would need to be on-hand to produce and maintain weapons in the armoury – helping to ensure a plentiful supply of arrows for the archers, for instance – as well as providing equipment for essential repairs. The official garrison record for Conwy Castle for 1284 gives us a detailed breakdown of those who lived and worked there on a regular basis. Under the leadership of one William Sikun were thirty fighting men as well as 'a chaplain, an engineer, a carpenter, a mason and a smith'.

1294–95 when Edward I himself was besieged within the castle. The army that the English king then led into Wales was vast, including something in the region of 35,000 foot-soldiers. If large numbers remained in north-east Wales to mop up resistance there after Edward's initial advance, perhaps 20,000 forged on with the king and drew up along the river Conwy at the end of the year. Clearly very few of these men could have crossed the water with the king to celebrate Christmas in the castle, and the scale of the floods in January kept the bulk of the army on the English bank. Nevertheless, Edward had with him sufficient soldiers to undertake his sortie westward, however rash this might have been. Clearly many more than the usual complement of thirty men were squeezed into the castle towers.

It is very likely that the numbers in the castle were supplemented further by untrained personnel gathered from among the inhabitants of the adjacent town. Garrison lists from the castles of Harlech and Criccieth made during the same crisis included the names of men from the towns there, as well as the numbers of women and children, inside the castle for protection. We know from documents relating to a later emergency, in the early years of the fifteenth century, that townspeople were organised into a civilian militia to defend the town and to supplement the castle garrison, and the same probably took place in 1294. It is possible that the bows and arrows listed in the inventories of the castle armouries were weapons to be handed out to any such civilian conscripts rather than for the full-time soldiers.

THE CASTLES IN THE CRISIS

The chronicler Walter of Guisborough tells us that in January 1295, the main body of Edward's army was prevented from crossing the Conwy river by flooding, which must have turned the estuarial river into a lethal, fast-moving sheet of water. It was then, he says, that the king himself, holed up in the castle with his much smaller force, 'came under siege for a certain time'. We do not know what happened in any detail, but presumably the Welsh hoped to follow up their destructive triumph at Caernarfon with a similar move against another of Edward's recently-built castles which so painfully symbolised for the Welsh their subjection to English rule.

Unlike Caernarfon, however, the castle at Conwy was complete. Having plundered Edward's baggage train earlier in the month, the rebels may have possessed some additional weaponry. Nevertheless, they certainly lacked the heavy siege engines which might have inflicted serious damage on Conwy's formidable walls – and Edward must have felt reasonably secure within them. The Welsh, no doubt, hoped to make an impact as they had elsewhere by catching the English off their guard – and to the extent that sufficient supplies had not been brought into the castle to feed a force many times the size of the normal garrison, they had succeeded. For the English residents of the town of Conwy, moreover, this must have been a terrifying time. Word must have reached them of the fate of Caernarfon, and the ruthless slaughter of its English population after a Welsh force gained access. Now, in January 1295, Conwy potentially faced the same fate. Bands of marauding Welsh soldiers not only cut off supplies and looked for any opportunity to penetrate the town or castle walls, but also assaulted other settlements in the surrounding countryside. Several mills in the Conwy valley were burnt at this time. However secure he was against direct attack, for as long as the Welsh were raiding unhindered they posed a serious problem for Edward's castles, in restricting or interrupting their supply lines. The anecdote about

BELOW *Conwy Castle from the eastern riverbank where the majority of Edward's army was forced to encamp*

BEER WAS THEN A BASIC NECESSITY OF LIFE BECAUSE, UNLIKE THE WATER SUPPLY, IT COULD BE TRUSTED NOT TO CAUSE DISEASE

Edward sharing the last barrel of wine with his men might not be true. It is certainly the sort of story that would have had obvious propaganda appeal to a chronicler and his English readers. But it accords with ample evidence in the English Exchequer accounts that great efforts were needed to keep the castles provisioned. At a time when Wales was battling against English occupation, this must have been increasingly true. Writs were sent by the king back to England commanding the brewing of beer, to be dispatched quickly to north Wales. Beer was then a basic necessity of life because, unlike the water supply, it could be trusted not to cause disease.

The greatest concern, particularly since the loss of Caernarfon, was for the castles furthest from England: Criccieth, Harlech and Aberystwyth, all standing on the coast of the Irish Sea. These three were far from Chester and north-west England, but could be reached by sea from Bristol and from Irish ports. As early as October 1294, as the Welsh rebellion gained momentum, the treasurer of the Dublin Exchequer was organising the transport of corn and other foodstuffs. From January 1295, one of the king's clerks, Richard of Havering, was stationed in Ireland organising shipping to Harlech and Criccieth. Havering's record of materials he sent by the *Goodyear* across the Irish Sea still survives. The ship was accompanied by an armed escort, and carried wheat, barley, oats, herrings, salt fish, salt, canvas (for sacking), crossbow quarrels (for the new castle at Beaumaris), iron, coal, bowstrings, wax, tallow, cups and plates, shoes and sandals.

The fact that these castles managed to hold out during the rebellion showed the great intelligence with which Edward I and his agents had chosen their locations, realising that making them accessible to supply ships might prove their salvation. At one of the

castles, a huge effort had been needed to contrive this. Rhuddlan Castle stood on a hill, beside the site of an old Norman castle, two miles inland. To remedy this, a workforce of over 70 diggers worked for three years to cut a straight channel for the meandering river Clwyd, so that ships could reach the foot of the castle hill. At Caernarfon, Conwy and Harlech, a fortified dock and water-gate were important elements of the castles' design from the beginning. This lesson was remembered for years to come: after the rebellion, the inhabitants of Conwy listed merchants from Dublin and Drogheda as their most valued trading partners.

THE END OF THE REBELLION AND ITS AFTERMATH

King Edward remained in Conwy until the beginning of April 1295. After the crisis at the end of January, his circumstances had steadily improved. Critically, early in February the weather picked

ONCE EDWARD'S VAST ARMY WAS FINALLY ABLE TO CROSS THE RIVER, THE WELSH REBELS WHO HAD BEEN TERRORISING THE DISTRICT MELTED AWAY

up and the floods abated. Once Edward's vast army was finally able to cross the river and move west, the Welsh rebels who had been terrorising the district melted away, moving, perhaps, up into the mountains where they would be difficult for the English to track. Certainly things were soon stable enough for the newly-elected archbishop of Canterbury, Robert Winchelsea, to visit the king at Conwy Castle to receive royal confirmation of his election. In general, supplies were now more secure, although in March the stores of ale began to fall short again. Edward seems to have used Conwy as his base, from which he planned a campaign to teach the Welsh a lesson. Since February his principal architect, James of St George, had been on the Wirral Peninsula supervising the construction of pontoon bridges for the king's army to use in making a large-scale crossing to Anglesey. On 4 March orders were given for them to be transported to Conwy. Here, repair and fitting work was being carried out on barges and ships to be lashed together as part of the bridge.

Closer to hand, the unrest did not immediately pass. One chronicle, produced at Hagnaby Abbey in Lincolnshire, mentions a sortie made from the castle by Edward's frustrated troops in mid-March, during which 500 Welshmen were killed. Plate and utensils were recovered, it is said, which had been seized from the King's baggage train two months previously. Elsewhere in Wales, English forces had gained a decisive advantage as winter neared its end. In early March, the Earl of Warwick, in the borderlands of Shropshire and Powys, received intelligence that Madog ap Llywelyn had led a large force of Welshmen south into the region. Marching his men through the night, the earl succeeded in surprising Madog's army

RIGHT *Looking back at the castle from the top of the town walls, which include no fewer than 21 towers to guard the population*

at Maes Moydog near the township of Llanfair Caereinion. With a combination of cavalry and crossbowmen he inflicted on Madog a heavy defeat, while a second English column captured the Welsh baggage train. The Welsh leader himself managed to escape the battlefield, but from this point an English victory was assured.

In early April, the king was ready to launch his second, more considered advance westward to Bangor, along the route of his earlier, ill-fated sortie. By the beginning of June, the English were once again in secure possession of Caernarfon. Madog himself evaded capture until late July, moving around his home territory of Meirionnydd. This had once been a kingdom, then a fief of Gwynedd to the north, but of late – since the Statute of Rhuddlan

MONASTIC CHRONICLES

In England history writing as we know it began in monasteries. From single line descriptions of annual events on calendars recording the dates of notable church festivals – particularly Easter – to thorough-going histories like Bede's eighth-century *Ecclesiastical History of the English People*, it was monks living and working at abbeys who wrote some of the most important accounts of events used by historians today.

Often the monks had practical motives. Abbeys had interests and privileges to defend. In their foundation and daily life they often had aristocratic or even royal connections. They were often situated in or near important cities or routes of trade and information and thus had access to news and reason to record significant events taking place in their region. In general in England a culture of record-keeping developed during the medieval period. Abbeys became repositories of information which central and local government could consult on significant issues. Kings like Edward I might specifically request, for example, material pertaining to England's historical relationship with the neighbouring realm of Scotland.

But often also individual monks relished for its own sake the task of keeping vivid histories of their times. As monastic chronicling reached its height during the thirteenth and fourteenth centuries, chronicles became popular reading matter among clergy and laity alike. Even in a pre-printing age, numerous copies circulated of chronicles that dealt with national as well as local events.

The chronicle of Walter of Guisborough, for instance – important for the later years of Edward I's reign in particular – was written about 1305 by a canon at an Augustinian Priory in Yorkshire. (Not surprisingly, it is particularly detailed and reliable regarding events in the north of England and Anglo-Scottish relations.) He traced his chronicle back to the Norman Conquest of 1066, using earlier histories written by monks like William of Newburgh, before preparing an account from about 1290 in which he used personal information and preserved original documents. It was written with a story-teller's eye – and the fact that it survives in ten manuscripts suggests that it circulated widely.

– it had become an English-style county. Finally, with English armies converging on him, Madog was forced to give himself up to the justiciar of north Wales. Uncharacteristically, Edward granted Madog his life, but sent him as a prisoner to the Tower of London, where he remained in captivity for many years. His name appeared on a list of Welsh captives there during the reign of Edward's son, receiving four pence halfpenny per day for his keep, a fairly comfortable regime. The constable of the Tower finally recorded Madog's death on 2 January 1313.

RECONSTRUCTION AND INNOVATION

Even before the conflict was over, the king had begun to address the few deficiencies in his fortification of north Wales which the rebellion had highlighted (or caused). Most importantly, reconstruction began quickly at Caernarfon, the only one of the royal castles and fortified towns to fall to the rebels. Critically, in September 1294 the castle had remained incomplete, particularly on its northern side, where it adjoined the town – and the additional protection of a wooden palisade could not prevent the rebels scaling the wall. When work at Caernarfon resumed in June 1295, it was these northern defences of the castle and the damaged stone wall around the town that provided the focus of the new work. When completed, the north wall stood as high as the southern stretch, while its towers – of the same polygonal shape – followed the pattern set in the 1280s. The ostentatious coloured banding of the south side, however, was not continued in the new work.

There was evidence of continued innovation at a military level. On the north side, as at Conwy and other castles, crossbow loops and other defensive features were incorporated inside several of the buildings overlooking the town. The builders added an ingenious new device whereby several of the loop-holes opened internally into three separate embrasures, allowing three crossbowmen to shoot, at different angles, in rapid succession. The castle's north gate – the main entrance from the town – was designed with a drawbridge, at

least six portcullises, and murder-holes in the vault above (although in the event it was never finished). The fine hall on the top floor was suitable for feasting and entertainment, but could also play a role in defending the castle, having more of the triple crossbow loops as well as access to a murder-hole which opened into the gate-passage below. Edward's post-rebellion castle architecture expressed military caution as well as ostentation and a desire for impact that befitted these seats of English royal government in Wales.

BEAUMARIS, THE EIGHTH WELSH CASTLE

There was still one major outstanding task. This was the creation of a new English castle in the one area where none existed – the island of Anglesey. It was here that Madog's rebellion had grown into a movement which gravely threatened the stability of Edward's Welsh domain. When Edward's army crossed the Menai Strait, they seem not to have encountered the fierce resistance for which they had prepared. Edward stayed at Llanfaes, which had been an early focus of Madog's rebellion. Edward's son later suggested that a savage reprisal took place. 'After the last war of

ABOVE *Beaumaris, the last of Edward's castles to be built in Wales, was laid out on flat ground, which made its architectural symmetry possible*

the lord Edward our father against Madog ap Llywelyn', he wrote, 'our said father utterly destroyed the said manor and town of Llanfaes'. Some historians, though, have suggested that the Welsh themselves had earlier done the burning. Either way, Edward moved quickly to stamp his authority. Only seven days after his arrival, his Exchequer recorded the first payments for the construction of a new castle, sited not in Llanfaes itself, but about half a mile to the south, beside the old mooring place for a ferry across the Menai Strait: a place called 'the Beautiful Marsh', or in Old French, '*Beaumarreis*'.

This new castle of Beaumaris was to be the largest of all the king's Welsh fortresses, and a compilation of their finest design features. It had three concentric lines of defence: a water-filled moat (connected to the sea but also fed by a fresh-water spring), an outer curtain wall with twelve towers and two gatehouses, and – 50 feet further in – a taller inner curtain, with six mural towers and two gigantic gatehouses, controlling access to the inner enclosure. The plan of the castle was near-symmetrical, a square enclosure within an almost regular octagon, with a tower marking each angle and the mid-point of each line of wall. But Beaumaris was more than merely a well-organised work of architecture: its outer circuit and the battlements of the inner ward contained some 300 loops for crossbowmen. Anticipating that an enemy might blockade the castle by land, Master James added a dock on the south side, opening directly from the Menai Strait, which would allow a laden forty-ton vessel to sail right up to the castle gate. The lessons of the rebellion had been well learned.

These ambitious projects in Wales came with a vast price tag, and they occupied men who could otherwise have assisted Edward elsewhere. In the spring of 1296 the workforce at Beaumaris numbered more than 3,000 men and would have cost £250 per week (well over £100,000 in modern money). The beginnings were auspicious, the pace of construction in the first year breakneck, but soon there were other calls on the king's attention and on his financial resources. Master James had foreseen that the rumoured war on two fronts, against both the French and the Scots, would jeopardise the supplies of money and materials to north Wales. Soon, the payment of workmen and soldiers guarding the building site, already in arrears, fell further behind. By the end of the century, merchants from the new towns in north Wales and elsewhere in north-west England were complaining that the keepers of the works were impounding goods without paying for them. Unpaid for months, the soldiers at Caernarfon Castle had pawned their weapons. The focus in London was elsewhere: the wars in Scotland, against Andrew Moray, John Comyn, William Wallace and finally Robert Bruce, would last the rest of Edward's life and would bring disaster to his son. The castles at Beaumaris and Caernarfon remained unfinished, and apart from one further castle at Queenborough

THIS NEW CASTLE OF BEAUMARIS WAS TO BE THE LARGEST OF THE KING'S WELSH FORTRESSES, AND A COMPILATION OF THEIR FINEST DESIGN FEATURES

in Kent, for the remainder of the Middle Ages the royal works organisation never again mustered the resources to build a concentric castle from scratch.

LATER HISTORY

In the long term, Edward I's ambitions in Wales were fulfilled with a remarkable degree of success. North Wales remained under English government, and several of the new English boroughs that he established beside his castles grew and prospered. The towns of Conwy, Beaumaris and Caernarfon remain important regional centres today, and Aberystwyth is one of the largest and most vibrant towns in mid-Wales. There were risings in other parts of the country, but after 1295, the English government in the north saw no serious challenge for over a century, and Edward's extraordinary castles must provide at least part of the explanation for this.

This is not to say that English rule went unchallenged or was popular. The documentary record left by the fourteenth-century English administration is patchy, but occasional hints of unrest do emerge. In 1313, for example, an account mentions in passing that a royal agent had been sent to Conwy to recover the castle and town from certain 'disobedient' men who were holding them against the king. A number of panicky injunctions had been issued soon after Madog's rebellion, banning the Welsh from living and trading near the royal castles. Within a generation of the conquest, the new towns, planned as exclusively English enclaves, did contain Welsh men and women. Occasional scares, such as the murder in 1343 of an important royal official, set back the process of accommodation between English and Welsh.

What was soon evident was that these Welsh castles, built on a colossal scale and far from the centre of English government in London, would be difficult for the king's works organisation to maintain. Surveys carried out in 1321 and 1343 revealed worrying structural defects at all of them, as well as stocks of unusable weapons in the armouries, and rotting food, soured wine and mead in the cellars. In fact, of course, this was a good sign: the castle garrisons had been able to provision themselves from local markets in the towns, and had not needed to put their armaments to the test. Nevertheless, in 1332 the chancery of Edward III – Edward I's grandson – acknowledged that the castles were not fit for the king to stay in, should he travel to north Wales; and in 1399, when *his* grandson, Richard II, was forced to take up residence in Beaumaris, Caernarfon and Conwy, there was little sign of improvement.

When the first serious challenge to the castles after Madog ap Llywelyn emerged at the beginning of the fifteenth century, many of them were found grievously wanting. The story of Conwy was perhaps most ignominious of all. On 1 April 1401 – Good Friday – a carpenter, arriving for work as usual, turned on the watchmen at the gate and murdered them, allowing a party of Welsh rebels to occupy the castle almost without opposition. Their leaders were the brothers Gwilym and Rhys ap Tudur, kinsmen of Owain Glyn Dŵr, the charismatic, self-styled 'prince of Wales'. Theirs was the family that would produce a dynasty which would restore Welsh rule over Wales, and England besides. Gwilym and Rhys held the castle against the English for several months, a source of profound embarrassment to the government of the new king Henry IV – and an inspiration to Owain and his compatriots to rise in rebellion across the whole of Wales. In the years that followed, Owain's men sacked several castles, including Criccieth and Aberystwyth, and captured others. Harlech became an important centre of government for Owain's fledgling Welsh state, the seat

BUILT ON A COLOSSAL SCALE AND FAR FROM THE CENTRE OF ENGLISH GOVERNMENT IN LONDON, THE WELSH CASTLES WERE DIFFICULT TO MAINTAIN

of a parliament and a princely residence for himself and his family, though a strategy of economic blockade gradually reclaimed this and other castles for the English. In the end, Owain died a hunted though uncaptured outlaw.

During the Wars of the Roses, in the fifteenth century, the remoteness of the Welsh castles from south-east England, as well as their security against attack, made operations there unusually protracted. The Lancastrian garrison at Harlech held out against the Yorkists from 1461–1468, after the rest of the country had been won by Edward IV. 'Kyng Edward', wrote a chronicler, 'was possessed of alle Englonde, excepte a castelle in Northe Wales called Harlake'. The final Yorkist siege is believed to have inspired the famous song, 'Men of Harlech'. In the seventeenth-century Civil Wars, similar factors produced a drawn-out conflict in Wales between Royalists and Parliamentarians. Little had been done to upgrade the castles' defences since the Middle Ages. Some gun-platforms had been mounted on top of the buildings, but there were no gunports in the walls, or earth-filled bastions to protect the outer walls. As a consequence – a fortunate one for modern historians – the Parliamentarians found it unnecessary to inflict a radical 'slighting' on the masonry. A certain man from Beaumaris was employed to 'take down one or two castles', but from the evidence of Conwy and the others, he seems to have done relatively little beyond make a hole in the wall of the Bakehouse Tower at Conwy and perhaps remove crenellations at some others. Thus today they survive very substantially intact, as fine a testament to medieval castle-building as exists anywhere in Europe.

THUS TODAY THEY SURVIVE VERY SUBSTANTIALLY INTACT, AS FINE A TESTAMENT TO MEDIEVAL CASTLE-BUILDING AS EXISTS ANYWHERE IN EUROPE

RIGHT *Below the north-west tower, steps lead down the rock of Harlech, which was lapped by the sea during Edward's reign. Harlech was central to the revolt of Owain Glyn Dŵr in the early fifteenth century*

CASTLES OF THE TEUTONIC KNIGHTS:

MALBORK CASTLE

HEADQUARTERS OF THE TEUTONIC KNIGHTS

ABOVE *In this early twentieth-century painting by Peter Janssen, the Teutonic Knights are depicted in their distinctive white surcoats at the outset of the Prussian Crusade in 1236*

O n 18 July 1410, Heinrich von Plauen arrived in haste at Malbork Castle, located on a branch of the River Vistula, 25 miles from the Baltic Sea. This was the principal base of the Order of Teutonic Knights, and the administrative centre of the Baltic state these warrior monks had carved out while pursuing the conversion of the pagan tribes of north-east Europe. Word had reached von Plauen of a terrible battle in which the grand master of the Order and other leading knights had been slain. Acting leader, he had travelled as fast as he could, with the two thousand soldiers he had held back at his own castle of Schwetz, upriver to the south-west. He put the interest of the Order first, leaving Schwetz at the mercy of the invading Polish-Lithuanian army in a desperate bid to secure Malbork. At around the same time, the garrison at Malbork was further reinforced by nearly 1,500 survivors of the battle; a small complement of the force which had suffered such losses. These men were in a desperate state. All were weary and many displayed wounds sustained in the fighting three days earlier. They relayed blood-curdling accounts – which did nothing to cheer the already despondent garrison – of one of the largest and most murderous battles fought anywhere in medieval Europe.

In fields near the village of Tannenberg, among the streams of the Mazurian marshes, the Teutonic Knights had suffered a catastrophic defeat at the hands of the Polish king. Some 8,000 of their soldiers had been killed, another 14,000 taken captive, and hundreds of their most important members did not rise from the battlefield. If spirits were not low enough at Malbork, as news of the disaster travelled north with the bedraggled survivors, a wagon arrived at the castle gates. In it were the bodies of the Order's highest-ranking officials, the men who had led the Teutonic Knights only days earlier on the fateful march east to

LEFT *Encompassing an area of some 52 acres, Malbork is one of the largest castles in the world*

cover the movements of the vast enemy army. Among them were Grand Master Ulrich von Jungingen, Grand Marshal Friedrich von Wallenrode, and Grand Treasurer Thomas von Merheim – wrapped in clean white sheets and dressed in purple robes in preparation for a dignified burial at Malbork.

The task now faced by von Plauen was a daunting one. For some time it had been clear that the huge invading army of the Polish-Lithuanian alliance was not interested in half measures. They sought nothing less than a comprehensive victory over the Teutonic Order. To achieve this, victory on the battlefield was only the first step. They knew they had to capture and destroy the heavily fortified castle at Malbork, the aim being the end of the state the Order had ruled for nearly two centuries along the shore of the Baltic Sea.

Such was the scale of the allied triumph at Tannenberg that their momentum seemed unstoppable. With Teutonic castles surrendering left and right to the forces of King Władysław II of Poland and Grand-Duke Vytautas of Lithuania – Olsztyn, Morag, Preussmarkt and Dzierzgoń among numerous others – many among the garrison at Malbork were resigned to defeat and ready to give up the castle without a fight. At this point, von Plauen took it upon himself to turn things around, to motivate the substantial garrison he now commanded to hold onto the great castle for the sake of the Teutonic Order he had vowed to defend.

WARRIOR MONKS

The year 1099 saw the success of the First Crusade by European Christians to recover Jerusalem and the Holy Land from Muslim control. It established a precedent, and an ambition, which would persist for the next two hundred years – and a militant approach to conquering and converting the 'heathen' which would last longer than that.

Shortly after this initial Crusade, two religious orders formed which sought to protect the increasing number of pilgrims now

THE TEUTONIC KNIGHTS

The Order of St Mary of the German House (the Virgin Mary was their patroness and spiritual guardian) remained a purely German movement. The role of these 'Teutonic Knights', as they were more commonly known, was initially to transport German Crusaders across the sea to the Holy Land and to tend them there. The German merchants who founded the movement nursed their wounded countrymen at the first siege of Acre (1189–91). Once that city had been conquered, the Pope approved the Order's founding of a hospital following the precedent of the Knights Templar.

Crusading momentum in the Holy Land was on the wane, and competition from the other Orders hindered expansion. The loss of Acre – the last major Christian stronghold in the region – a century after its first siege saw the Order redirect its attention. After a false start in Transylvania, it was invited by a Polish ruler to confront and convert heathen Prussians causing turmoil on his northern border. (It was only by conquest and assimilation of this Baltic people that the German state of Prussia later acquired its name.) The Knights were granted the frontier territory around Chelmno, north of Torún, as a base from which to operate.

From here they established a substantial territory in the pagan Baltic region east of Germany. This broad but ill-defined area extended from the river Oder, encompassing the northern part of present-day Poland and sweeping in a broad arc to Königsberg in present-day Russia. They recruited a steady stream of new 'brothers' from the German heartlands, who took a lifelong vow to the Order and its strict moral code as they would to a monastery. They promised to tend the sick, offer hospitality to pilgrims and guests, and

take God's fight to the enemies of the faith. They renounced personal possessions and donned the Order's distinctive garb of a white tunic (worn over chainmail) to which was stitched a black cross.

On the battlefield the Knights were distinguished by their armoured cavalry and quality crossbowmen who were recruited from the rich German heartlands – one of the leading production centres in Europe for iron and steel body-armour and for crossbows. Their specialist castle-builders allowed them to consolidate their gains in difficult terrain in which they were significantly outnumbered by the indigenous population.

flocking to the Holy Land. Known as the 'Knights Hospitaller' and the 'Knights Templar', they combined the aggressive fighting skills needed to provide military protection, with a spiritual and ascetic life becoming to those in holy orders. Then, at the point when they were losing their initial impetus, they were joined by a third organisation. In 1190, the Order of Teutonic Knights was created, not by clerics, but by the German merchants of Bremen and Lubeck.

Redirecting their focus from the Holy Land to the pagan lands of the Baltic, the Knights launched a 'northern Crusade'. This would become an outlet for the zeal of Christian warriors now that the Levant – the hinterland of the eastern Mediterranean shore – seemed lost. This campaign received wide support in Christendom, and chimed with the ethos of the medieval German Church, which encompassed a militant element. The Holy Roman Emperor authorised the conquest of Prussia as part of the Empire's policy against heathen nations. And the Pope issued a bill granting the Order rights of conquest over land won.

The Knights quickly overran the lower reaches of the River Vistula, building their first castles during the 1230s, of timber and earth banks. In a land of rivers, swamp and forest, a scanty supply of good building stone meant it was used only for foundations. Over the following decades they expanded their control along the Baltic coast. The Order's close ties with German merchants ensured a steady stream of colonists who were attracted by privileges; the influx fostered an attitude to the non-German population which was increasingly ruthless. Towns were established and castles built, or rebuilt, from brick. The business of constant warfare and hospitality

THE KNIGHTS COMBINED THE AGGRESSIVE FIGHTING SKILLS NEEDED TO PROVIDE MILITARY PROTECTION WITH A SPIRITUAL AND ASCETIC LIFE

demanded a regular source of income so that the Knights became deeply involved in the economy of the lands they occupied, trading particularly in wheat, wool and amber. In 1283, the Order established its own state, which became the dominant political and economic force in the region.

Aggressive expansion motivated the Knights even when religious conversion was not a justification. During the fourteenth century, at their height, Pomerania to the west was targeted in a bid to link the Teutonic state with the German lands. In 1308 the important Baltic port of Gdańsk was captured. Then, to counter papal criticism by proving their crusading role was paramount, the Knights turned eastwards to the vast state of Lithuania, which covered much of present-day Russia from the Baltic to the Ukraine.

The harsh Baltic winters meant campaigns differed from those elsewhere in Europe. Cavalry had to ride in single file, through trenches cut deep in the snow. But in the dense forests of Lithuania, where most campaigning took place during the fourteenth century,

BELOW *A map showing the location of Malbork in Poland*

winter was often preferred for raids because visibility was clearer after the deciduous leaves had fallen. Frozen rivers became 'winter roads', facilitating deep penetration into the pagan lands. Later in the year forest undergrowth hampered movement, while melt-water swelled the rivers, turning their banks to mud and taking a heavy toll on horses.

The Crusade lasted nearly a century, bringing bloodshed as well as much valuable booty for the knights. They overwhelmed the lands of pagan communities up to the River Dnieper and almost as far as Moscow, launching campaign after campaign deep into the dense forests of Lithuania. They were assisted by a steady flow of Crusaders from Western Europe. With Christendom defeated in the Holy Land, knights from France, Spain and England travelled east to support the work of the Teutonic Order. Henry Bolingbroke, later Henry IV, was present with three hundred men at the siege of Vilnius in 1390, and numerous other Englishmen had joined this northern Crusade during the fourteenth century. Visiting knights were

BELOW *A reconstruction of how Malbork may have appeared in the early fifteenth century. The Order's religious headquarters tower over the Middle and Lower Castles*

entertained generously at a rapidly-growing network of over 120 castles, of which Malbork, having moved to the centre from the state's western edge as its territory expanded, became the principal. They were distinguished from most medieval castles in Europe by two characteristics: they were as much monastic as military structures, and they were largely built not of stone but of red brick.

For all the Order's attempts to claim a divine purpose, however, it was clear that evangelical objectives were no longer foremost. Territorial domination and economic control of the Baltic lands took precedence over the enforced conversion of pagans to Christianity – and, inevitably, the Knights' policy of aggressive expansion had led to confrontation with Poland, their most powerful neighbour; a country which longed for access to the Baltic Sea.

Polish rulers, based in their capital at Kraków, became bitterly hostile to the expansionist Teutonic state, but their military campaigns against it were intermittent and unsuccessful. In 1386, however, the situation changed. The grand duke of Lithuania accepted the crown of Poland as Władysław II, having converted to Christianity himself and married that country's queen. Together they united the two states of Poland and Lithuania against the common enemy sandwiched in between. At the same time, divisions grew within the Teutonic state between the monastic knights and the German settlers, creating an opportunity for its enemies. In 1410, an attempt would be made to halt the Order's expansion once and for all.

THE CONSTRUCTION OF MALBORK CASTLE

For centuries conquest has been consolidated by military construction, and this was certainly the case in Teutonic Prussia, where a network of castles was created denser than anywhere else in Europe (each within a day's march of another to ensure that relief was at hand). In the late thirteenth century – as Edward I built Conwy and other great castles to tighten his grip on Wales –

THE BRICK-MAKER

In certain regions, such as the Netherlands or the Baltic, good-quality building stone was scarce and expensive. At castles of the Teutonic Knights like Malbork it was used only for decorative elements – in the entrances to the church and chapter house, for instance, or the façades of the grand master's Palace. While early fortresses were made from wood, later castles were built primarily using red brick. (Teutonic castles at Gniew and Radzyn, for example, were also brick-built.) Brick had the advantage over stone of being a relatively flexible material that could absorb impact shocks from trebuchets or cannon. (The difficulty of transporting heavy siege weapons in a region devoid of good roads meant they were not as regular a feature of warfare as elsewhere in Europe, but cannon were made and used, not least by the German knights themselves, who exploited the casting skills of the Order's bell-founders.

Entirely German in its make-up and origin, the Teutonic Order had its castles designed and built by German master-masons, with the necessary skilled craftsmen brought from the German lands, including brick-makers and layers as well as carpenters, glaziers and blacksmiths. Only basic labourers were available locally.

The bricks used to build a castle like Malbork were made on site – initially in the original outer court. During the second half of the fourteenth century they were fired in kilns on the opposite bank of the river. They varied in size, but were usually about 15cm by 28–30cm by 9cm, with dark headers (burnt bricks) used as a decorative feature of the fortress from its inception. The limestone needed to make the mortar which bound the bricks together was imported from Gotland, the Swedish island which was an important Hanseatic trading centre and was briefly conquered by the Teutonic Knights at the end of the fourteenth century.

at Malbork, work began to assert the authority of the Teutonic Knights over their expanding state.

Tracing its history, however, is difficult. Whereas there are royal records detailing the construction of the castles at Conwy and Harlech and the earlier English royal castle at Dover, no documents survive to illuminate the building of Malbork. Historians are forced to rely on architectural detailing in an effort to understand the construction phases of this vast castle. Nevertheless, much can be deduced.

When the first part of Malbork to be built – the 'Upper' castle – was begun in 1276, the region lay on the western extremity of

Teutonic Prussia. Under the German commander Heinrich von Wilnowe, work began on a fortified religious settlement which could consolidate the rule of the Order in an area which had recently witnessed a failed uprising by the local population. Unlike many earlier castles of the Order, which depended on locally-available resources, this was not to be built from wood. Skilled craftsmen were brought from Germany – brick-makers and layers, glaziers, carpenters, blacksmiths – while basic labourers were commandeered locally. Brick walls were constructed on foundations of hard rock that rendered mining very difficult. At Malbork – on the banks of the River Nogat, flowing north-east from the Vistula into the Vistula Lagoon – the first 4 to 7 feet of walling was built on massive boulders taken from the bed of the adjacent river, in-filled with smaller stones.

The castle was finished by about 1300. Its first phase took the form of four wings with three storeys, high pitched roofs – steeply

HOSPITALITY AS WELL AS WORSHIP AND DEFENSIBILITY WAS AT THE CORE OF THE CASTLE'S PURPOSE

angled to cast off the snow – and built around a square cloistered courtyard. A fortified quadrangle of this sort constituted a recurring design among Teutonic castles. It encompassed a church, chapter house, dining hall, kitchen and dormitories. This combination of elements was not found together in Western Europe: a holy cloister within a formidable military enclosure, a monastery within a castle. The style was austere, in keeping with the Order's code which eschewed frippery in favour of a hard life of prayer and military rigour. In their hall the brothers ate communally: simple fare, consumed in silence or in contemplation of a lesson read aloud, unless the presence of visiting Crusaders justified an exemption. Hospitality as well as worship and defensibility was at the core of the castle's purpose.

An outer court accommodated support staff and services, protected by a moat and a curtain wall. The ground floor rooms, massively vaulted, were used for storage of food, drink, weapons and other materials, all necessary for the lifestyle of the knights. A prison was built conveniently adjacent to the guard room, perhaps intended for high-status prisoners. The kitchen vault was supported on a line of circular columns, with the principal hearth served by a flue that rose above the roofline of the castle. The serving areas were placed on one side, with a dumb-waiter on the other to transfer food to the second-floor dining hall with its seven windows and central columns supporting painted vaulting.

Of the four wings, two had dormitories on the first floor which slept some sixty people, while another twenty or so officials and dignitaries slept in smaller rooms in a third wing. From the mid-fourteenth century they were served by a detached lavatory tower, the dansk tower, linked to the castle by a first-floor corridor. This was originally built of wood and later rebuilt in brick on an arcaded

PREVIOUS PAGE
The knights dined in several halls, depending on the occasion and time of year. The Great Refectory was the largest of these and would have been used for the Order's key feasts

RIGHT *Much of the castle has been over-restored, but the pointed arches and fan vaulting of this cloister are good examples of the gothic architecture with which the Order is strongly associated*

The dansk tower appears to be a formidable defensive structure, but its primary purpose was to house the castle latrines

support in the late nineteenth century. It was probably also intended as a final resort during a siege; towers with this dual function were a recurring feature in Teutonic castles. Another survives at Toruń, while the communal lavatory tower at Kwidzyn, with its arcaded corridor to the fortress, is another remarkable example.

On the fourth side of the courtyard lay the chapter house and the great church – always the most important structure for this monastic order, and especially so here, where it would become the Order's primary church in Prussia. Its entrance is striking, with a line of five recessing columns and capitals and figured arches set in a vaulted bay. Richly painted, and decorated with glazed clay tiles of animals, this lavish portal illustrates the Last Judgement and has been known since at least the fourteenth century as the 'Golden Gate'. The church is divided into two parts – the nave of the 1280s, and an apse extension of the early 1330s. Vaulting runs over both nave and apse (and

also in the chapter house) dating from 1331–44: the earliest ribbed vault in the Baltic coastal region, influenced perhaps by the recent development of English chapter houses like York and Wells.

The remodelled church became the growing organisation's spiritual centre – surmounted now by a slender bell tower. Outside stood the patroness of the Order: a 26-foot stucco relief of the Virgin Mary with the child Jesus, richly-coloured and clad in elaborate Venetian mosaic work. Marienburg, as Malbork was then known, means 'the fortress of Mary', and the life of the warrior monks was organised around the festivals associated with the Virgin. In the early fourteenth century the grand master commanded every member to recite a *Salve Regina* or an *Ave Maria* every hour of the day, while other Teutonic castles – Marienwerder, Frauenburg – also invoked her protection. Below the apse is the ground floor chapel of St Anne which was set aside for the

ABOVE, LEFT *Bright colours and intricate carvings are typical of Malbork's decoration, and remind us that the castle also functioned as a palace*

ABOVE, RIGHT *The Virgin Mary, patroness of the Teutonic Order, lent her name to the castle which was originally called Marienburg, or 'Mary's fortress'*

tombs of the grand masters. Thirteen were buried here from 1341 – including Ulrich von Jungingen, slain on the fields near Tannenberg.

The continued expansion of the Teutonic state meant that what was initially an outpost relatively near the border had quickly moved towards the heartland. In 1308, less than a decade after Malbork's first incarnation was completed, the Knights conquered the port city of Gdańsk and the adjacent region of Pomerania. They massacred many of the local inhabitants and imported large numbers of German settlers. Shortly after this, the headquarters of the Teutonic Order was moved from Elblag (Elbing to German-speakers) 15 miles south to the more secure town of Malbork. A year later this shift was confirmed when the grand master of the Order also transferred his base to Malbork from Venice – the latter location, convenient when shipping men to the Holy Land had been the Knights' primary purpose, was less useful now that the Baltic was their principal theatre.

This move by the head of the Teutonic Order was accompanied by a rise in the number of knights visiting Malbork en route to or from attacks against the Order's enemies. Further expansion

LEFT *The buildings and courtyard of the Middle Castle (left) alongside the outer buildings of the Lower Castle (right). Flat terrain enabled the Knights to replicate their fundamental design throughout the land*

RIGHT *The burning of the Templars. The Teutonic grand master moved his headquarters to the Baltic where it wielded greater power at a time when another Order was being persecuted*

was required if the castle was to provide enough accommodation of suitable quality for these visitors. From 1310, the Upper Castle was extended by a Middle Castle, with an imposing gatehouse and three wings surrounding a much larger courtyard. This was major work that would continue into the second half of the fourteenth century. The new building included a sequence of rooms for visiting knights and honoured guests, and a great hall for their meals and entertainment. A new outer castle was also developed to the east, with stables, barns, granaries, a bakery, foundry and workshops, spread across a vast courtyard. This covered almost the same area as the town of Malbork on the other side of the Upper Castle. At the same time a permanent bridge, flanked by towers, was built across the river.

RIGHT *The grand master's apartments in the Middle Castle. Malbork was the Knights' headquarters, a military stronghold, the principal religious centre of the Order and a luxurious palace for the head of state*

The new Knights' Hall could hold some four hundred guests, and was one of the great secular apartments of medieval Europe – its fine painted walls lit by large windows and crowned by a complex vaulted roof. Leading up a stair from the hall, as in any great medieval residence, were the private apartments of the lord, in this case the grand master. Developed in three stages as the Teutonic Order grew in importance during the fourteenth century, from a relatively modest lodging it became one of medieval Europe's outstanding palaces – no less so for being set within a highly defensive complex. This is particularly apparent from the riverside, where an elaborate frontage rises through four storeys to a wall-walk crowned by a high pitched roof. It is decorated with arcading, traceried windows, six-sided turrets and panelled battlements in stone and brick, a stark contrast to the military façades of the Upper Castle and the relative simplicity of the Knights' Hall nearby. Having the grand master's private palace here in the Middle rather than the Upper Castle, meant he could more easily entertain his guests and preserve, in the Upper Castle, a serenity in keeping with its quasi-monastic function.

FROM A RELATIVELY MODEST LODGING IT BECAME ONE OF MEDIEVAL EUROPE'S OUTSTANDING PALACES

From the high end of the Knights' Hall a stair opens into an ante-chamber, leading onto the richly decorated reception room, the Master's private chapel, and then his bedchamber. Late in the fourteenth century, this suite was enhanced by a lavish new wing, built facing the river to provide further reception rooms and two additional dining rooms or refectories. Used in summer and winter respectively, the latter were used primarily as audience chambers for receiving envoys and honoured guests. The Summer Refectory used expensive stone brought from Sweden, with a single pillar supporting the ribs of a complex radiating vault that rests on corbels

LEFT *The Summer Refectory was a communal dining area for the Knights during the summer months. The many windows allow more light to flood in here than in the nearby Winter Refectory*

between the large windows. The Winter Refectory had heating vents in the floor and a lower ceiling, but was similarly vaulted from a central granite column. Its walls were painted with wreaths of flowers, and figurative or heraldic motifs. This new building was one of the architectural glories of medieval Europe, at odds with the wholly military character of the earlier castle, and it marks the zenith of the Order's power and authority.

Beneath the grand master's private residence additional rooms were created in which the administrative functions of the Order were carried out – a fundamental concern now that Malbork had become the Knights' primary seat – and a chancellery responsible for the financial well-being of the Order was located in offices below the two dining rooms.

By the early fifteenth century Malbork stood much as it is seen today, with the walled and gated town adding further protection to the castle. Developed over more than a century, Malbork was now among the largest fortresses in the world – covering more than twice the area of the town that protects its western flank. The various stages of building had produced not one castle but three, within a single gigantic enclosure – a fitting seat of power for the ambitious Teutonic state.

RIGHT *Covered walkways over the castle battlements protected the garrison from the elements but also from enemy projectiles in the event of a siege*

FAR RIGHT *Successive walls increase in height so that each can be protected by the one behind. The castle's southernmost tip, seen here, would have been a familiar sight to those living in the town*

For all its emphasis on devotion and splendour, the builders never lost sight of the fact that this was a castle for knights who were not native to the region and who were always under threat from the surrounding population and from external invasion. These men relied on networks of such castles as bases from which to shelter, and mount sorties to quell unrest. From the time that it became the Order's primary seat of power, Malbork, in particular, needed to be thoroughly secure.

Approached from outside it is obvious that this was a defensive fortress as well as a palace. The entrance to the castle from the town was joined by a second from across the river. This bridge has since gone, but the two pyramid-capped gate-towers which commanded this approach from the mid-fourteenth century still stand. All three

RIGHT *The entrance to the Middle Castle was secured with multiple barriers, including iron doors and a portcullis – which meant that this vulnerable gap in the walls was virtually impenetrable*

castles – High, Middle and Outer – were surrounded by moats. The entire fortress was ringed with concentric walls capable of being isolated and defended independently. Most of the corners were protected by square or rectangular towers, some high enough to serve as watch-towers or defensive posts. All gates and passages were protected by drawbridges, portcullises, iron-clad doors, shooting galleries and machicolations (see Machicolations box, p.214). By the second half of the fourteenth century the castle was among the most impregnable in Europe, and as such was the obvious target for any army that wished to strike at the heart of the Teutonic state. But it was not long before it would face the greatest threat in its history.

In the mid-summer of 1410 the knights assembled a substantial army in the Outer Castle, in readiness to defend the Order, according to their oaths. The combined armies of Poland and Lithuania had crossed its borders seeking a decisive confrontation. It was a daunting prospect, but confidence remained high: the Knights had known few permanent setbacks during the previous century and a half, and were instilled with the conviction that – with God's and the Virgin's help – their righteous cause would triumph.

The knights left Malbork on horseback, attired in their traditional uniform – a white mantle, emblazoned with a black cross, over body armour of iron or steel, with plates covering the front and back, which in turn covered a chain-mail hauberk extending over the body, arms and legs. By their sides they bore swords which, from the early fourteenth century, had been enhanced with an extended grip and double-edged blade to help overcome the increasing weight and robustness of armour. As they rode they unfurled banners which they believed were God's as well as their own. They went now to face a man who, though born a pagan, had fervently embraced the same Christian God. The strength that each side derived from their faith would only add to the brutality of the confrontation.

THE BATTLE OF TANNENBERG

The knights' troubles began with an event they might have been expected to welcome: the conversion to Catholic Christianity of the pagan grand duke of Lithuania. In 1386, Jogaila married Queen Jadwiga of Poland and was baptised in Kraków as Władisław Jagieło. Subsequently crowned king of Poland, his marriage united the two states of Poland and Lithuania. The king took his new-found Christian values extremely seriously, converting Lithuania with unprecedented vigour.

While the knights' supposed mission on their eastern flank was suddenly and dramatically advanced, in reality Lithuania's mass conversion was a crisis for the Order. Their Crusading purpose, it suddenly seemed, was no longer justified. When they refused to

accept this (protesting that Władisław's conversion was a fraud), the newly strengthened Polish state had the justification it needed to turn against its long-standing enemy.

The alliance followed a precisely determined plan. The combined Polish and Lithuanian armies would take the initiative, ensuring that all military operations took place on the knights' territory. The culmination of the assault would be the killer blow: the seizure of the great castle at Malbork, headquarters of the Teutonic state. If the heart of the Order could be captured, the entire body-politic would surely collapse.

The campaign that followed involved three armies: that of the kingdom of Poland, allied to that of the grand duchy of Lithuania,

ABOVE The Battle of
Grunwald *(1878) by Jan
Matejko. Grand Master
Ulrich von Jungingen
is overwhelmed by the
Polish-Lithuanian forces as
Grand-Duke Vytautas of
Lithuania rides triumphant
in the centre*

fighting the Teutonic Order. It began in mid-June 1410, with a
series of skilful Polish diversionary raids which concealed their
true objective. Then, at the beginning of July, the Polish army
was joined by that from Lithuania at Czerwińsk on the Vistula.
This combined force marched northwards across the border of
the Teutonic state to Kurzetnik, which they reached on 10 July,
expecting to face the Knights in battle.

The Knights meanwhile marched to a position on the other
side of the river where they held a strong castle, leaving the enemy
to confront a perilous river crossing if they wanted to engage. But
King Władysław had other ideas. Despite his advantageous position
on the banks of the River Drweca, he opted to avoid the crossing
which would be necessary if he was to face the enemy at this point.
Instead he swept eastwards to take up a better position on the
open land near the village of Tannenberg. The Knights shadowed
the Polish-Lithuanian armies, the two forces marching almost in
parallel, with the Knights edging gradually closer to their enemy.
About sixty miles south-east of Malbork, a battle was finally joined
that would prove to be one of the most devastating and decisive
military encounters of the Middle Ages.

The sheer scale was staggering. The Teutonic Knights had
amassed a force comprising an estimated 21,000 cavalry and 6,000
infantry. The Polish army was made up of 18,000 cavalry and 9,000
infantry, along with a large number of armed servants. This was
joined by a Lithuanian force of some 15,000 soldiers. The Knights
therefore faced an army almost twice as large as their own – but also
one which was far less well-organised.

On the morning of 15 July 1410 the grand master, Ulrich von
Jungingen, together with his army, left their camp at Grunwald
to confront their enemy on the low ground between the villages of
Tannenberg and Łodwigowo. He positioned his artillery in the front
line, but the cannon in the centre were concealed by the infantry
flanking them on each side. He opted not to take the initiative,
however, waiting for his enemy to make the first move.

THE CROSSBOW

The crossbow was a vital weapon for medieval armies. Whereas the longbow was held vertically and drawn by hand, the crossbow was mounted horizontally on a block of wood called a stock. It was drawn mechanically, or with a foot stirrup so as to use the greater power of the leg muscles. It was then locked in place before being aimed and fired using a trigger mechanism like a gun. Unlike the longbow which, with its greater draw length, fired a long, thin arrow, the bow of a crossbow was much shorter and shot a short, stubby 'bolt'. This bolt was thicker and heavier than an arrow and could penetrate chainmail.

Where battles for castles were concerned, the crossbow was a standard weapon for besieged and besieging forces alike. Evidence survives of a workshop at Malbork in 1409 at which there were enough materials to make over a thousand

new crossbows. In the surviving inventories of arms stored at Conwy and Edward I's other Welsh castles, crossbows predominate. Most were of the type primed by placing a foot in the stirrup and hooking the string to the crossbowman's belt, though a few were more elaborate and powerful weapons fitted with cranks to draw the string. The fact that during a siege both sides depended on the crossbow meant that its shooting range often determined the distance between them. The distance varied, but a crossbow could certainly shoot enemy soldiers from over 200 yards.

Using the weapon from within castle fortifications overcame its chief disadvantage – its relatively slow rate of fire (as soldiers took time to reload). But the crossbow also had a huge advantage. Unlike the longbow, which required great strength and skill so that only well-practised archers could use it, crossbows were relatively easy to operate, meaning soldiers could be armed with them after only brief training. Since the weight of the drawstring was held by the trigger it could be carefully aimed and so was very accurate.

Not everyone approved of the fact that an inexperienced foot-soldier could use a crossbow to kill a fully-armoured and well-trained knight. Such was the weapon's deadly efficiency that in 1139 the church even tried to ban its use except for the purposes of crusading against Muslims. This didn't work of course, and the crossbow claimed many prominent victims. Among them was King Richard I of England, who died from an infected wound after being shot in the shoulder while attacking a castle at Châlus-Chabrol in March 1199. Under Richard's brother and heir, King John, civil war broke out in England and foreign mercenaries flooded into the country to fight for the highest bidder. So unpopular was this that John was forced to grant a clause in the Magna Carta which attempted to banish foreign crossbowmen – though this too had little effect.

For his part, King Władysław spent the early hours of the day fervently at prayer (to the Christian God he had now accepted), to the consternation of his cousin and second-in-command – the grand duke of Lithuania – who was anxious to pursue military rather than spiritual preparations. Suddenly there was a commotion. Two messengers from the Teutonic grand master rode up to where the king was praying. With them they bore unsheathed swords which they thrust into the ground at Władysław's feet, challenging the king to use these, if need be, to engage the Knights in battle. It was a challenge Władysław was happy to accept. He had no need, he informed the messengers, for other men's swords. He had plenty of his own, and God was behind him. Nonetheless he would accept those sent to him by an enemy who craved his blood.

The king had already deployed the Polish army on the left wing of the battlefield, while the Lithuanians took the right and he himself kept in safety to the rear. At 9 a.m. the battle began. When his enemy failed to attack, the grand master ordered his cannon to be fired, but rain had dampened the gunpowder, minimising the damage they could cause. In response, the Lithuanians charged the Order's left wing. As the armies engaged, according to the vivid account of the Polish chronicler Jan Długosz, the roar of battle was 'as loud as a rockfall'. The noise of lances breaking and swords striking armour drifted for miles on the wind, like 'clanging hammers in a blacksmith's forge'. For an hour the fierce fighting was evenly-poised. Then the Order's archers, their crossbows unaffected by the rain, forced the Lithuanians into a hasty retreat. Scenting an early victory, bands of knights – including a number of visiting Crusaders – pursued the Lithuanians for several miles, seizing booty and prisoners, before rejoining the main fray.

The grand master now launched an attack against the body of the Polish army, but a substantial number of the Lithuanian forces had recovered, and he was caught in an encircling move and was killed on the battlefield. His death was the turning point of the battle. Suddenly the Knights were rudderless, and began to flee –

many of them attacked as they did so by the same mercenary forces who had been paid to support the Teutonic cause. King Władysław followed his advancing army until he reached the grand master's headquarters, which was promptly looted, its barrels of wine drained by elated and battle-weary Polish soldiers. Seven standards belonging to the Knights, tattered and torn, were found hanging forlornly in a thicket of trees and borne in triumph to the king.

From the higher ground of the Knights' camp, Długosz suggests, the king could see the infantry and cavalry of the Teutonic Order spread across the skyline in flight, the rays of the evening sun glinting on their armour. They were pursued until darkness fell, with some 14,000 taken prisoner. Many thousands, meanwhile, lay dead or dying on the battlefield. While the dead were being buried, looting was rife. The Polish king insisted, however, on respect to senior members of the Order. The body of the Teutonic grand master was found and shown to him, mortal wounds on the chest and forehead. This, and the corpses of other dignitaries of the Order, Władysław ordered to be ceremonially dressed and placed in a wagon so that they could be returned in honour to Malbork Castle for burial.

The Teutonic Knights had lost the battle partly, no doubt, because they faced numerically superior forces. But it is also clear that the military operations of the Polish-Lithuanian army were carried out to a well co-ordinated plan by King Władysław who, unlike the grand master, took no direct part in the fighting – a deliberate strategy by a commander who was entirely new in military operations. After this devastating defeat for its large army, and the deaths of its grand master and numerous other leading Knights, the capture and destruction of the Order's headquarters at Malbork Castle seemed inevitable.

THE SIEGE OF MALBORK

The invaders had set out with an ambitious goal: they sought not merely to inflict a decisive defeat on the Teutonic Knights in battle, but to capture their great castle. If they achieved this, they would be

free to take over the Prussian State and destroy entirely this Germanic thorn in their side. Now the first part of their mission had been accomplished: at Tannenberg, the Knights and their army had been decisively defeated. Such had been the scale of this defeat that most of the surviving Knights, as well as the Polish-Lithuanian leaders, assumed the loss of Malbork was a formality. As the victorious armies gathered themselves together on the battlefield, word travelled quickly with the fleeing remnants of the Teutonic army. When reports reached the garrison at Malbork, both of the devastating defeat their members had suffered and of the impending arrival of the Polish and Lithuanian armies, most greeted the appalling news with despair. The reaction of many was to want to flee the castle before the enemy appeared outside the walls.

In fact, though, it wasn't only the Knights who had problems. The Polish and Lithuanian armies had suffered profoundly themselves during the great battle. They were exhausted and depleted, having lost 9,000 men, with a further 8,000 wounded, and could make only slow progress on the 60-mile journey north-

BELOW *A mural which represents a later siege of Malbork in 1457. The Upper Castle is perhaps the most realistic rendering in the depiction*

west to Malbork. For two days after the battle the armies attempted to recuperate, in spite of voices among the king's advisers who beseeched their leader to move fast. The whole army was gathered around the royal chapel tent to hear Mass, while the captured banners of the Knights fluttered in the breeze; and a messenger was sent home to order services of Thanksgiving in every church in Poland. When they did finally set off, with a reduced though still formidable force of about 12,000 Lithuanians and 15,000 Poles, they could manage no more than about nine miles per day.

The time this gave the garrison at Malbork was critical. As the grand master and other leading Knights fell on the field of Tannenberg, their castle was left undermanned and weakly-defended; easy prey, it seemed, for the victorious Polish king. But Heinrich von Plauen, waiting at his castle of Schwetz, heard the ill-tidings and rushed with his small army to rally Malbork's defence, arriving on 18 July, three days after the battle.

The castle garrison was reinforced by some 1,500 survivors of Tannenberg, 200 seamen from Gdańsk, and the garrisons of nearby forts and castles. They came to help defend the Order's principal stronghold – responding to the rallying cries which sped throughout the Teutonic state – and the garrison rallied under von Plauen's determined leadership. Thought of surrender was put aside, and everything was done to prepare the castle to hold out against the enemy force. Fortunately they had plentiful supplies both of food and armaments, as the Teutonic castles were generally kept lavishly supplied. Cannon, increasingly important in siege situations for attackers and defenders alike, were wheeled into position to bombard a besieging army.

Even at this late hour von Plauen sought to avoid a siege. On 24 July he despatched messengers to King Władysław with a request for his peace delegation to be granted safe passage. But the king of Poland and Lithuania, fresh from a comprehensive victory on the battlefield, was in no mood to negotiate. As he made his way north, outlying castles belonging to the Knights had rushed to

HEINRICH VON PLAUEN

Heinrich von Plauen the Elder (as he is called to distinguish him from relatives of the same name) was born about 1370 in the 'Vogtland', a hilly, wooded region in the German-Slav borderland, around Saxony and Thuringia. Plauen was a town in the region.

Many of those who joined the Teutonic Knights originated from this area of south-eastern Germany. More than 40 per cent of brothers came from Thuringia. The German knightly class in general was deeply infused with militant Christianity and as a young man in 1391 von Plauen travelled east on Crusade – a period when the Knights were trying to capitalise on civil war in Lithuania between Jogaila and his cousin Vytautas. Initially von Plauen, like many young aristocrats, did not join the Order but served as a Crusading guest. Though they made use of auxiliaries from both the indigenous and settler communities of the Teutonic state – and increasingly paid for mercenaries – the Crusading tradition nevertheless provided the Knights with an important stream of fully armed and mounted fighting men from Germany and beyond. Geoffrey Chaucer's fictional knight – 'in Lithuania he had ridden, and Russia' – was one such.

Some time later von Plauen joined the Order fully: a lifelong commitment. As a Brother he vowed to abide by the Order's strict rules which included chastity, the renunciation of property, obedience to God, the Virgin and the Master of the Order. Though brethren did not have to come from aristocratic backgrounds, increasingly it helped in terms of advancement. In 1402 he was made Komtur (Commander) of the district of Nessau and five years later was promoted to Komtur of the town and castle of Schwetz, the position he held when the Polish and Lithuanian armies invaded in 1410.

Having taken the initiative in defending the Order's main stronghold at Malbork – and with so many of the leading Knights killed on the battlefield at Tannenberg – von Plauen was dramatically chosen as the 27th grand master of the Order in November of the same year. He faced a formidable rebuilding task: literally, for numerous fortresses had been damaged or destroyed; and figuratively, for the reputation of the Order throughout Europe had been gravely affected by their defeat. By the Peace of Thorn (Torún) in 1411, he salvaged the Knights' core lands, and worked to raise the war indemnity and ransom for prisoners imposed by an international commission. His bid to wage another war with Poland in 1413 caused major divisions within the Order, however, and von Plauen was removed from office that October, briefly imprisoned, and later given a lesser position near Königsberg, where he died in 1429.

surrender without a fight. He sent word back to Malbork that he would be arriving at the castle the following day, and could deal with any exchange of paperwork then. His implication was clear, and von Plauen did not mistake it.

Assessing the castle's defences, its new commander was concerned that the narrow streets and houses of the town outside the walls would allow the besieging army to take cover, preventing the garrison from returning fire. He took decisive action, sending soldiers through the town to clear out all the residents, allowing them to take refuge within the castle, before setting the town alight.

The next day, lookouts on the walls of Malbork watched as the vanguard of the enemy army began to arrive outside the castle and take up important strategic positions. Minor skirmishes took place throughout the day, with Lithuanian and Polish soldiers fighting with the garrison troops for possession of the now abandoned and burned-out town. On 26 July the size of the besieging force continued to swell. Crucially, however, von Plauen had succeeded in restoring morale among his garrison, and the Polish-Lithuanian alliance soon found, to its surprise, that it would not take this crucial Teutonic stronghold without a struggle.

The defenders who lined the castle's walls were obviously prepared to fight and the Knights even made a bold effort to keep control of the ruined town beneath their walls. That evening, sporadic fighting continued amid the narrow streets and charred buildings, but the castle garrison was heavily outnumbered by Polish soldiers. Many of those who came out to engage the enemy were killed, and those who were not soon retreated within the castle walls, ceding the town to the enemy. Some of the Poles

THE POLISH–
LITHUANIAN
ALLIANCE SOON
FOUND, TO ITS
SUPRISE, THAT IT
WOULD NOT TAKE
THIS CRUCIAL
TEUTONIC
STRONGHOLD
WITHOUT A
STRUGGLE

in the main army took this as a sign of impending victory. With frenzied shouts and couched lances, they charged through the town as far as the church near the castle wall. According to Długosz, a major chance was spurned by the Poles: a breach had opened in the castle wall which might have allowed access had the king sent in large numbers of troops immediately. He failed to capitalise on this, however, leaving the Knights to work frantically through the night to patch the breach using vast oak beams ripped from within the castle.

In an effort to increase their security the garrison also set fire to the main bridge across the river, a tactic which seems to have been a help as well as a hindrance to their enemy, which was now able to graze horses freely in the fields across the river without fear they might be targeted by troops from the castle. After night had fallen, King Władysław had his cannon brought forward within range of the castle ramparts – some in the sector controlled by his Lithuanian soldiers, others by the charred timbers of the bridge. From these positions they were able to begin a steady bombardment of the castle, focusing their attacks particularly on the south-eastern side of the outer wall. Although not yet the all-conquering weapons they would become, cannon were nevertheless of growing importance in warfare all across Europe – as much for their psychological impact as the physical damage they inflicted.

Morale among the besieging armies remained high: the submission of the garrison seemed only a matter of time. As the siege was underway, Władysław gave his attention to the division of the spoils: allocating captured Prussian castles to his Polish commanders, and even allocating castles to the north of the Teutonic state which were as yet uncaptured. Most of the important individuals in the state made the same assumption. Largely, no doubt, in an effort to avoid reprisals and the seizure of their land and wealth, a steady train of knights, nobles and bishops travelled to the outskirts of Malbork to offer their submission to the Polish king.

Infused with von Plauen's determination, however, the garrison refused to give up. In an effort to halt the relentless cannon fire

GUNPOWDER ARTILLERY

Mechanical engines of war which hurled projectiles date from ancient times. In the trebuchets of the medieval period they reached a state of such lethal efficiency that stone fortifications were unable to resist a protracted assault. A new revolution began, however, with the harnessing of chemical explosives, of which gunpowder was the first effective example.

Invented in China, rudimentary forms of gunpowder artillery were in use in Europe by the thirteenth century, though it would take another century for them to become widespread or particularly effective. In the 1350s Petrarch observed that weapons very rare a few years previously, 'viewed with greatest astonishment and admiration', had become common: 'so quick and ingenious are the minds of men in learning the most pernicious arts'. Across Christendom craftsmen were familiar with the techniques required to cast cannon in bronze or iron because they were used to making church bells. Bell-founders were put to work at Malbork producing cannon for the Teutonic Order.

Early cannon were only powerful enough to damage weak points like wooden gates or roofs. By the early fifteenth century, however, great bombards were being fashioned which could target castle masonry – hence the terms 'bomb' and 'bombardment'. They reloaded very slowly, were unreliable and were too heavy to be useful in open warfare; but they were helpful in a static siege situation. The great walls of Constantinople were famously subjected to a forty-day barrage by the guns of the Ottoman Sultan when the city was taken in 1453. Sometimes the psychological impact of the noise and smoke was as important as the physical impact of the cannonballs. Over time the quality of gunpowder improved significantly, and lighter cannon were developed. These cannon were known in Spain as *ribadiquines*, and were used by attackers to damage the protruding barrels of the defenders' guns – until gun placements were redesigned in response.

Though efforts were made to adapt existing castle fortifications to the use of cannon – reducing towers to create platforms and altering wall openings to allow their use – in truth it was the perfection of cannon which ultimately dealt the final blow to the medieval castle. The balance of advantage in a siege, already shifted by the trebuchet, moved further from the garrison sheltering within the walls to the besieging army. Another long-term effect of the cannon was to shift the balance of power within states towards the centre, with well-equipped royal armies increasingly dominant over regional nobilities whose castles no longer provided an effective resort for local retinues.

a bold sortie was launched from the castle, a group of Knights charging out in full armour, hoping to catch the besiegers by surprise. Such a sally had been anticipated, however, and Długosz reported that the attack was halted at the river: 'fierce fighting ensues and in this most of the enemy (i.e. the Teutonic Knights) are killed, the rest retreat towards the castle, pursued by the Poles as far as the round tower'. At this point luck turned against the rampaging Poles: a castle wall that had been seriously destabilised by the incessant pounding it had taken from the surrounding guns suddenly collapsed just as the Polish soldiers passed through. Many were wounded by the falling masonry, and others were struck by arrows shot down at them from above by members of the garrison. The helmet of one Polish knight, recorded Długosz, was so disfigured by a falling stone that only the help of a blacksmith's hammer would allow it to be removed.

As the siege ground on into August, a second foray by the Knights had a greater impact. The force rushed quickly from the castle gate and succeeded in capturing the commander of the Polish siege train, in wounding a number of his men and in damaging several of the cannon which tormented the Malbork garrison day and night. Nevertheless, even von Plauen was beginning to accept that for him and his Knights, there was ultimately no way out. At some point in August a brief truce allowed him to meet with King Władysław outside his castle walls to discuss terms. Von Plauen argued that the Teutonic Order had been practically destroyed, and suggested that the Polish-Lithuanian alliance could hold onto all the lands they now considered rightfully theirs in return for sparing its remnants. But Władysław sensed the increasing desperation within the garrison and saw no reason to agree to these terms.

Even now, however, all was not hopeless for von Plauen and his men. Relief, it seemed just possible, might yet arrive from afar. The Battle of Tannenberg sent ricochets throughout Europe, for so many of the continent's knights had ridden to join this northern Crusade. When news of the confrontation reached Sigismund

MANY WERE WOUNDED BY THE FALLING MASONRY, AND OTHERS WERE STRUCK BY ARROWS SHOT DOWN AT THEM FROM ABOVE

ABOVE *The castle from the river's western bank. Any besiegers here would have to contend with the barbican, river, moats and several layers of wall before reaching the Upper Castle*

of Hungary, the latter promptly wrote a message encouraging all Prussian peoples to aid the Teutonic Order. Morale among the garrison received a massive boost, and von Plauen responded by approaching Sigismund's brother, King Wenceslaus, the German King who ruled in Bohemia. Wenceslaus responded immediately, sending a loan for von Plauen to use in hiring mercenaries. He also promised an army to relieve Malbork which would arrive by the end of September. It was folly, Długosz lamented, to allow the Order to communicate so freely with its allies. In August an elderly priest managed to smuggle 30,000 Hungarian ducats out of the castle with which to buy mercenaries in Gdańsk.

As the days passed and the castle garrison refused to give way, morale and confidence among the besieging forces fell away dramatically. As ever, many of them had other things on their minds. Harvest time was approaching – a time when few during the medieval period could afford to be away from their estates. King Władysław had learned, moreover, of the plans being made by Sigismund and Wenceslaus, and feared an assault from the rear by a large army. Unrest was increasing among his mercenaries, who had not been paid, and could not be because Władysław had banked on access to the huge wealth contained within the castle. His gunners were worryingly short of ammunition. Distrust developed between the Lithuanian and Polish leadership. And to add to all of this, that perennial threat to encamped medieval armies, sickness, had infiltrated the Lithuanian camp in the form of a dysentery epidemic. It could only be a matter of time before it spread to the Poles. Finally, on the 18 September the siege was abandoned by the Lithuanian forces, and by the Polish forces the following day.

What had seemed a formality after the overwhelming victory on the fields of Tannenberg had failed to become a reality. This was a tribute to the strength of Malbork Castle as well as to the spirit and bravery of von Plauen and his garrison – and was also an indictment on the tactics of Władysław, who failed to cement what had seemed a decisive triumph over his enemy. He would return home, as the Polish chronicle admitted, 'more as one defeated, than as a conqueror'.

Von Plauen, meanwhile, had saved the Teutonic Order from annihilation, and was duly elected as its next grand master. But there was no doubt that the Order had been dealt a massive blow. Its perception of itself as invincible had been shattered. With the conversion of Lithuania and its association with Poland, it had lost its ideological justification for further expansion eastwards. For the Polish state, meanwhile, its great victory at Tannenberg had seemingly secured the country from the danger of Teutonic attack. The possibility of defeating the Knights once-and-for-all and of gaining access to the Baltic Sea – so vital to the economic life of a Poland that was still land-locked – had become very real. With the failure to take Malbork, it would remain an ambition which would take more than fifty years to achieve.

END OF THE TEUTONIC STATE

For nearly two centuries, the presence of the Teutonic Order blocking the way to the Baltic coast had helped to bind together the disparate parts of the Polish state against this common enemy – while the process of integration in turn, during the fourteenth century in particular, fostered Polish patriotism and resistance. Earlier defeats in battle – by the Tartars from Russia and then by the Germans – had not lessened Polish resolve but rather had strengthened their patriotism. The German chronicler, Widukind of Corvey, explained the obstinacy of the Poles against the Germans by the fact that Poles 'would endure all poverty for freedom'. The convincing victory at Tannenberg in 1410 electrified the Poles into furthering their war against the Teutonic Order. Offensives launched in 1422, and again in 1433, resulted in the seizure of several more castles.

The Order had not resigned itself to final defeat, however. For their part, failure on the battlefield heralded a new resolve to go back on the offensive, and to partition the burgeoning Polish State between themselves and their long-standing ally, the Holy Roman Empire. Von Plauen himself was at the forefront of those who wanted to launch an immediate counter-attack – but was stripped of his leading position in consequence. What the Order had not anticipated, however, was the economic disaster which would follow the military one.

Poland was primarily a grain producer, while the Teutonic Knights who controlled the Baltic coast had made the lower reaches of the Vistula the grain chamber of Europe. The river provided transport to Gdańsk, where the grain was shipped by vessels of the German Hanse to Flanders, France and England. During the early fifteenth century, however, wheat prices fell while wages increased. The burgeoning towns on the Vistula, including Gdańsk, Toruń and Elbing rose against the aggressive rental increases imposed by the Teutonic Order. A 'Prussian Union' was formed by representatives of the major towns to wage war from within on the government of the Teutonic Knights, encouraged by the local nobles who in 1454 appealed for help from the Polish king.

Increasingly forced to employ mercenaries, meeting their payments crippled the Order financially, while failure to pay caused serious discipline problems. The Knights were forced to give up their castle at Toruń and by the spring of 1454 had lost control of all their castles except for Malbork and Sztum. Later that year the start of a thirteen-year war between Poland and the Teutonic Knights led to the fall of Sztum, and to Malbork coming briefly under siege once more. A defeat for the Polish army on the battlefield led to a Teutonic revival, associated with Heinrich Reuss von Plauen, a later grand master distantly related to his famous namesake.

FINDING MERCENARIES REMAINED PROBLEMATIC, AND THE EXTRAORDINARY STEP WAS TAKEN OF PAWNING MALBORK

Funding mercenaries remained problematic, however, and the following year the extraordinary step was taken of pawning Malbork, along with other towns and castles which still belonged or had returned to the Order. At the castle of Gniew near Malbork the Knights were bound, and suffered the indignity of having their characteristic beards shaved off. Unusual among knights of the time, this facial feature had earned them the nickname 'bearded ones'. At Malbork itself a group of Bohemian mercenaries mutinied, sacrilegiously upturning a crucifix in the chapel before negotiating a sale of the Order's principal castle to the Polish king. The holy castle of the Teutonic Knights passed finally into enemy hands not after a brutal siege but after a piece of squalid double-dealing by a group of disenchanted mercenaries.

Remarkably, under Reuss von Plauen the town of Malbork held out for several years, but the end was inevitable and the Order succumbed. By the Treaty of Toruń, West Prussia, Pomerania and the port of Gdańsk were transferred to Poland. The Teutonic Order retained their hold over East Prussia – transferring their capital to Königsberg – though they pledged allegiance to the

Polish king. The final blow came in 1525, when the grand master recognised the Reformation, declared East Prussia a secular duchy, and persuaded the Order to adopt the Lutheran faith. Though the Order survived in name, its original ethos and purpose disappeared, as did the distinctive uniform of these northern Crusaders: the black cross-stitched onto the white tunic.

DESTRUCTION AND RECONSTRUCTION

In 1626 Malbork was taken over by the invading Swedish army, who demolished much of the Outer Castle to prevent it being used militarily. By this time military technology – artillery and firearms in particular – had developed dramatically, leaving the old Teutonic castles hopelessly outmoded and largely ignored during campaigns. The remaining castle did subsequently serve as an army barracks, and then became a military storehouse. During the eighteenth century, under Frederick the Great's expanding Prussia, a textile factory was installed in the grand master's Palace.

It was not until the early nineteenth century, with its rising tide of German nationalism, that the castle's historical importance was appreciated, and its preservation ordered by the King of Prussia. Much restoration work was undertaken towards the end of that century: capably achieved, though some of the replacement work was determined by comparison with other Teutonic castles rather than on the basis of structural or archaeological evidence at the site. The courtyard of the Upper Castle, for instance, is largely today as it was rebuilt between 1880 and 1902: the work based on the cloister arcades in comparable Teutonic castles in the region. It is likely that the original wings round the courtyard were far more forbidding – as they are at the relatively complete and less restored castle at Gniew. Kaiser Wilhelm II himself attended a pageant to celebrate Malbork's restoration, in which men paraded before him dressed as Teutonic Knights.

Both the fortress and town of Malbork, as much else in Poland, suffered horrendous damage during the Second World War,

culminating in the explosion of an ammunition dump in the castle in
1945. The church, the chapel under it, and the bell tower were almost
completely destroyed, while much of the eastern ranges of the High
and Middle castles were left in a parlous condition. When the war
ended a few months later, nearly half the castle had been devastated.

Ever since, restoration has been in progress. From 1945 to
1970 the damaged structures were rebuilt and re-roofed, while
subsequently conservation work was carried out in the interiors.
Though advanced, this continues to this day.

The castle's history, however, has made it problematic for
modern Poland. To some Poles, this imposing structure, like other
Teutonic castles, has been a symbol of German oppression: built by
Germans to help them hold down territory they had conquered.
As a result it is not always seen as part of the native culture of the
Polish state, whose spiritual and secular heart is considered to
have been Wawel Cathedral and the castle at Kraków in southern
Poland. Increasingly, though, the legacy of the spectacular castle
at Malbork has been reclaimed by Poles, and the story of its heroic
resistance to the besieging forces in 1410 retold and admired.

ABOVE *Such was the
extent of the damage
inflicted on the castle
during the Second World
War that restoration is still
ongoing today*

THE RECONQVEST OF SPAIN:

GIBRALFARO CASTLE

THE EMIRATE OF GRANADA AND THE PORT OF MÁLAGA

During the early months of 1487, the inhabitants of the Muslim port city of Málaga, mid-way along Spain's southern coast, followed events with growing unease as large Christian armies moved relentlessly nearer. The hostile forces were those of Ferdinand, king of the expanding state of Aragon, united with the neighbouring state of Castile by Ferdinand's marriage to Queen Isabella (see Ferdinand and Isabella box, p.312) Together the two states would form the core of what later became modern Spain. For some time Málaga's population had been growing, and its conditions of life deteriorating, as refugees fled further inland from the towns and villages which had fallen into Christian hands. If surrender was considered by Málaga's military garrison, it was firmly rejected. Last-minute repairs were carried out on the massive city walls, on the Alcazaba, the great citadel within the town, and on Gibralfaro, the huge castle which dominated the hill above.

It would be a pivotal confrontation: Málaga had formidable defences and was garrisoned now by battle-hardened Berber troops from North Africa, reinforced by similar soldiers falling back from areas which had recently passed into Christian hands. As the religious antagonism between Christian and Muslim had escalated, the Berber garrison grew increasingly vehement in its determination to defy the infidel – in contrast to some of the longer-term residents of the city who preferred to surrender on advantageous terms. But the momentum was with the advancing Christian armies, which could call upon supplies and expertise from all over northern and central Spain as well as from European countries to the north.

After more than 750 years, the future of the emirate of Granada, the last Muslim-ruled region in Spain, hung in the balance. If Málaga and its great castles fell, independent Muslim

LEFT *Málaga's mighty fortifications stand today as a reminder of the Islamic rule in the Iberian Peninsula which lasted for over seven hundred years*

rule in Western Europe would quickly disappear. Neither the Muslim Emir nor the Christian rulers were in any doubt about what was at stake. A few years previously, as he planned his campaign, Ferdinand had been approached by an old royal adviser who impressed upon him the central importance of capturing this vital port and sea link to the Islamic world of North Africa if a reconquest was to be achieved. 'With Málaga taken', he wrote to the Christian king, 'Granada is yours'.

Málaga's castle of Gibralfaro was part of a complex set of castles, watchtowers and walls intended to defend the state and its population from Christian Spanish attack, by land or sea, as well as from enemies in the Muslim world. This conflict would be the ultimate test.

THE CONSTRUCTION OF GIBRALFARO

From about 1250, the gradual but relentless Christian reconquest polarized religious communities and pushed Muslims from elsewhere in Spain to migrate to the shrinking regions still under

MUSLIM CONQUEST AND CHRISTIAN RECONQUEST

The confrontation between Christian and Muslim in the Iberian peninsula began in 711, when a small army of Arabs and Berbers slipped across the straits which separated North Africa and Europe, invading the Christian Visigothic kingdom of Spain. The Visigothic state rapidly collapsed. From a new capital at Córdoba, most of modern Spain and Portugal was ruled as Al-Andalus (instead of the Roman Hispania) – initially under the wider Muslim caliphate based in Syria, but later by independent rulers who called themselves caliphs. Until the tenth century it remained religiously diverse: the majority of the population still Christian, with a significant Jewish presence.

In the north, however, in Galicia and the mountains of Asturias, Cantabria and the Basque Country, small groupings of Christians retained their independence. Though divided in most things apart from their religion, they would prove the springboard for a long process of reconquest – in Spanish, *reconquista* – which led centuries later to the siege of Málaga and Gibralfaro.

Unitary rule from Córdoba did not disguise serious religious and ethnic divisions in Al-Andalus. In 1031 a great *fitna*, or break-up, took place as a result of which the caliphate of Córdoba split into multiple small kingdoms. By this time, the Christian statelets of the north, seeds of the later medieval kingdoms of León, Portugal, Castile and Aragon, had descended from the northern mountains into the central Spanish plain. After 1031, with their Muslim opponents often fighting each other, the Christians began to move south on a much larger scale. In 1085 the former capital, Toledo, was restored to Christian hands. Between 1230 and 1250 a major push conquered Córdoba itself and Seville. Christian settlers arrived as Muslims fled to those cities such as Málaga, Granada and Almería which remained under Muslim rule.

For many decades a period of relative stability ensued. The Nasrid Emirs of Granada established a Muslim State which defied the Christian kingdoms to the north and retained links with the rest of the Islamic world. Cross-border trade went on, despite the Church's prohibition. Individuals moved across to start a new life. Sporadic raids in both directions damaged crops and property and took prisoners. Light cavalry riders, hunched forward like modern racing jockeys, struck fast and then retreated; watchtowers were built along the frontier to provide early warning. But the 'reconquest' was not a systematic or continuous process.

Nevertheless, Christian ballads evoked an eternal conflict between Christian and Muslim, and with the accession of Isabella I to the Castilian throne in 1474, and her husband Ferdinand to that of neighbouring Aragon in 1479, the final act commenced.

Islamic rule. The emirate of Granada became the only part of the Iberian peninsula to have been an Islamic state, as opposed to a mixed community under Muslim rule, though even here there were always small Jewish and Christian minorities, mainly engaged in trade. Nevertheless, substantial religious uniformity did not prevent Granada having serious political divisions of its own, which led at

times to outright military conflict. The great castle of Gibralfaro was
originally built as much to exercise control over the local population
of Málaga as to defend the town from sea or land attack.

Málaga's location, surrounded by high mountains to the
north, east and west, and by the sea to the south, provided it with
considerable natural protection as well as direct access to the trade
and culture of the Mediterranean. These advantages had attracted
settlers at least as far back as the Phoenicians more than 750 years
before Christ. Allied to these natural defences was a citadel built
on a hill within the town which dates to its earliest years. The
citadel or 'Alcazaba' built by the rulers of Granada in the eleventh
century, still standing in central Málaga today, contains traces of
earlier structures which stood in Phoenician and Roman times. It
was in the eleventh century that Málaga and its fertile hinterland,
the Axarquía, first became part of the emirate of Granada, after the
fracturing of Muslim rule in Al-Andalus – and they remained key

to Granada's survival when Ferdinand and Isabella undertook their campaigns in the 1480s.

It was always obvious to governors of Málaga, however, that for all its advantages the site has a crucial weakness: a high ridge to the east, rising more than 130 metres above the neighbouring sea, which overlooks the town and its citadel. Occupying this vantage point any hostile army would be in a commanding elevated position. The obvious solution was for the Málagans themselves to dominate this high ground with a fortification of their own. A fortress was built here as early as the eighth century, by Abderrahman I (756–788), the Emir of Córdoba, and there had been Roman, and probably Phoenician, defences there long before. The purpose of Abderrahman's fortress (as, no doubt, of its predecessors) was to protect the fortification at the heart of Málaga.

Then, in the early fourteenth century, Emir Yusuf I – a cultured man determined to stand up to the Christian King of Castile, Alfonso XI, who had taken up the *reconquista* with vigour – began to rebuild this elevated bastion, creating the Gibralfaro castle which still stands today. The name is a combination of *jabal*, the Arabic word for rock, which led also to Gibraltar, Tariq's Rock, and *pharos*, the Greek word for lighthouse. This elevated position above the Mediterranean at Málaga held an ancient beacon to assist vessels arriving at the port. Yusuf fully recognized the importance of Málaga to Granada, which depended on the sea access it provided, both for trade and for military reinforcement from Islamic North Africa. On a narrow strip of land between the Baetic mountains and the Mediterranean, the city also served as a crucial gateway between the east and west of the emirate.

The ridge on which Gibralfaro was built is rocky and highly uneven – conditions which were bound to influence the construction of the

THE NAME IS A COMBINATION OF *JABAL*, THE ARABIC WORD FOR ROCK, AND *PHAROS*, THE GREEK WORD FOR LIGHTHOUSE

RIGHT *'La Puerta de los Cuartos de Granada' – the Gate of the Granada Quarters – leads into the Alcazaba through the inner wall with its alternating bands of brick and rough-hewn rock* (mampostería).

castle. Both the main walls and the linked subsidiary defensive walls had to zig-zag to follow the uneven terrain, and both the principal gateway and the turrets were built at an angle. Access past the outer gates was by 'labyrinthine' paths with high walls and towers; an attacking force would be obliged to double back on itself before it could attempt to enter the main enclosure, giving defenders more time to counter-attack from the towers above. Entrances which turned in this way became a common feature of Muslim fortifications in Spain at this time; often at each turn an enforced gateway would provide an additional layer of defence.

Like the Alcazaba below, Gibralfaro was constructed largely using a technique known in Spanish as *mampostería*: a method of combining stones, barely worked, and bricks which was common to Christian and Muslim castle building in Spain. This is still used in the region today, but usually in combination with cement.

Perhaps the most striking and unusual feature of Gibralfaro was the forbidding double wall known as the *Coracha* – a fortified and steeply inclining corridor some 600 metres long and 14 metres wide, which linked the castle to the Alcazaba below. This passage incorporated five sharp turns which provided archers posted on the tops of the walls with a clear range of fire (rather than the restricted one available from a straight wall). This type of work did occur elsewhere in southern Spain – at Maros in Jaén province, for example – but tended to link the external wall of a castle with an outlying tower which commonly protected a well. Its purpose, in other words,

in the parched landscape of southern Spain, was often to protect the garrison's water supply, though in the spectacular Málaga case it provided a relatively safe passage between the city's two fortresses.

Water supply was a vital consideration for any castle builder, and in a climate like that of Andalusia, with limited rainfall for much of the year, it was of overwhelming importance. In the Muslim world, it should be remembered, water

was deemed important not only for drinking, but also for other purposes, such as ritual washing. The management of water for agriculture as well as drinking and washing was famously sophisticated in Andalusia and other Muslim regions. Beneath Gibralfaro was built a complex system of wells (some of which still survive) so extensive that perhaps as many as 5,000 men could have been garrisoned there at a moment of great crisis such as occurred in 1487. Examples of this expertise can be seen elsewhere, such as the cisterns at Cáceres.

One external threat in particular that confronted those manning the castle from the mid-fourteenth century had not been envisaged by those designing earlier fortifications on the site, and it was this above all which impelled Yusuf to rebuild Gibralfaro. In the early decades of the fourteenth century, a fundamental change had begun to take place in the nature of warfare in Europe, driven by a technological development which in the long term would help give European states an edge even over the great empires of Asia: the gunpowder revolution (see Firearms box, p.315).

Whereas Muslim powers elsewhere in the world were to varying degrees insulated from these developments, the surviving Muslim-ruled state in Spain, the emirate of Granada, was familiar with technology which influenced the ongoing rivalry between the Spanish states. Muslim rulers in Spain, like their Christian counterparts, made use of artillery both in offensive and defensive operations. The Emirs of Granada, indeed, had acquired early expertise in the use of gunpowder – perhaps because, unusually in Europe, Spain had natural deposits of potassium nitrate (commonly known as saltpetre).

In response, builders of fortifications on both sides of the Andalusian frontier in the fourteenth century had already begun to adapt to the threat and use of gunpowder and artillery. Yusuf rebuilt Gibralfaro in the knowledge that fortifications were needed at his vital port of Málaga which could withstand sustained artillery fire – a perfectly feasible undertaking given the limitations of the cannon of his day.

As it happened it was not until after his time, in the later fifteenth century, that Málaga came under large-scale assault by Christian armies – but throughout this period of sustained tension on the Castilian–Granadan frontier the garrison had to maintain a state of readiness. In such conditions, it was never likely that castles in Andalusia would follow the trend of some in countries further north, as the fifteenth century wore on, of evolving into domestic residences with comfortable apartments and glazing. Of the surviving features in the great castle at Gibralfaro it is perhaps the Muslim gunpowder store which tells us most about the characteristics of late medieval warfare as it was experienced there in 1487.

The impact of firearms is seen also in the outer fabric of Gibralfaro. Arrow-slits, which were an essential part of outer fortifications while archery remained the main method of defence, were adapted into gun embrasures known as *troneras* – though initially these remained narrow and cross-shaped. Increasingly, however, in the 1460s and 1470s, square, splayed gun ports were built, as became standard in such fortifications in subsequent centuries. At Gibralfaro in 1487, artillery would be used both by defenders and attackers – for the first time in the Granada war – and the defensive guns were placed in embrasures, which were often situated in thick defensive walls at ground level.

WALLS

In general, the thicker a castle wall, the more resistant it was to bombardment or undermining. Time was critical during a siege: the longer defenders were able to hold out, the greater the chance of relief forces arriving or the attackers giving up. But building thick walls was expensive and time-consuming, and for this reason masons often dressed large stones for the outward faces of a wall, placing rubble infill between them. Henry II well understood the defensive merits and intimidating effect of thick walls when he built those of Dover Castle's keep over 6 metres thick in places (see Chapter 1).

Whether a castle was made of stone or brick, a lime mortar was used to bind the building blocks together, which takes decades to set to its full strength. As a result castles were at their weakest when first built.

Walls erected to provide another layer of defence to the castle's nucleus are known as curtain walls. The frequent use of multiple layers of these walls in a castle is called a concentric design (as seen, for instance, at Dover, Château Gaillard or Krak des Chevaliers). One might assume that walls should always be as tall as possible, but concentric defences were most effective when the outer walls were lower than the inner, so that soldiers on the inner wall could shoot downwards over the outer wall.

Three principal features were frequently applied to walls by castle builders to increase their defensive potential: arrowloops, battlements and hoardings.

Arrowloops are narrow gaps or slits – usually vertical – through which crossbowmen or archers could shoot. In the wall behind them were embrasures: breaks in the masonry large enough for a man to get into, which indicate whether the loop was meant for crossbowmen or archers. Small embrasures where a man would clearly

need to be crouching were for crossbowmen; archers needed more space to accommodate their longbows. Arrowloops in the form of a cross allowed either weapon to be used (the arc of a crossbow being horizontal). With the advent of firearms, gunloops began to be built, which from a distance look like thermometers – with long vertical slits and a round hole at the bottom to accommodate the gun itself.

Battlements, or crenellations, consist of blocks of masonry on the tops of walls which alternate regularly with gaps of a similar size. They allowed members of the garrison to shoot through the gaps and to take cover behind the masonry.

Hoardings were structures which were built onto the outward faces of walls and towers to allow defenders to drop objects on any attackers at the bases of the walls without being directly exposed to attack. Initially they were made of wood, but later stone structures were integrated into the walls, known as machicolations.

THE FINAL WAR

In the last days of 1481, Muslim forces launched a surprise attack on the Christian-held frontier town of Zahara, capturing both the fortress and the town itself. It was quickly apparent that this was not merely another border incident in the zone of friction between the Christian and Muslim states. For one thing, it was unusual for such assaults to occur in winter. More significantly, the Muslim troops were commanded not by a regional commander but by the Emir of Granada, Abu'l Hasan Ali, in person.

The response came from a similarly high level. Such incidents on the frontier were normally dealt with on the Christian side by local magnates and their retinues. But this time the Castilian Monarchs themselves, who were wintering in Valencia, on the east coast of Spain, decided to react personally and in strength. The Granadans had established themselves powerfully in the town, so that regional forces, under the command first of Rodrigo Ponce de Léon, Marquis of Cádiz, and then of King Ferdinand himself, proved unable to eject them quickly. As a result, troops and war material were brought in from other parts of Spain, as far away as the north coast, to supplement the local Andalusian forces. Between the spring of 1482 and 1484, the Christians' military objectives expanded: from punitive raids they put their minds to the long-term conquest of Muslim regions and came to target much of the western half of the emirate of Granada. There were raids and more systematic attacks on the fortified town of Loja as well as on the main town of the region, Ronda, which was defended by a formidable gorge as well as walls, towers and a castle.

The practice of winter campaigning continued in 1484–85. The more or less continuous presence of Ferdinand and Isabella, at the front or in the region, meant this remained a 'total' war rather than reverting to the sort of frontier sniping which had gone on for decades. To add to the Granadans' problems, the state faced an internal political crisis, which shifted the balance in favour of the Christians. On 21 April 1483 Boabdil, who as Muhammed

XII would be the last Muslim ruler of Granada, fought and lost a battle in Christian territory, at Lucena, south of Córdoba. To escape imprisonment he consented to become a vassal of the Christian monarchs. His own son and eldest brother were handed over as hostages to encourage him to honour the agreement, but even so, the move was clearly unacceptable to many in the Granadan political class, and it led to debilitating internal conflict that seriously weakened the Muslim war effort. In addition, the Christian rulers combined their growing military activity with an economic blockade of the land and sea boundaries of the Muslim state which depended heavily on imports for its survival. As the noose tightened, the years between 1485 and 1487 would be the crucial years of the war – and the decisive culmination of this period came at Málaga.

ASSAULT ON MÁLAGA

In April 1487, Ferdinand's army began an assault on the town of Vélez-Málaga, a few miles inland to the east of Málaga itself. At the time, the Málagans – many of whom supported Boabdil, Ferdinand's vassal – were giving practical support to the Christians by allowing supplies for them into their port, and Ferdinand and his commanders expected both towns to negotiate a peaceful surrender. The stakes could not have been higher. It had long been clear that, if Málaga fell, the emirate would effectively be cut in half, and that it would then only be a matter of time before the capital Granada would also be in Christian hands. While in May Vélez-Málaga duly surrendered, it was not clear that Málaga would follow suit, and Ferdinand ordered both his artillery and maritime forces to move to the area in case he needed to besiege this principal port. Although the momentum was firmly with the Christian forces, the emirate of Granada was no pushover. It still controlled sizeable forces: an important regional garrison like that at Málaga would have numbered some 10,000 men, even before being reinforced by soldiers from elsewhere, while the great palace-fortress of the Alhambra at

Granada might be manned in a crisis by some 40,000 soldiers. Camped in the village of Vexmillana, a few miles from the city, Ferdinand sent emissaries to meet its authorities, to urge them to negotiate on the grounds that Muhammad Al-Zagal, Boabdil's uncle who then ruled in Granada, had failed to save Vélez-Málaga and that they would surely suffer a similar fate.

For the ensuing events we rely heavily on Christian records, but the narrative seems clear. One major source is the official royal chronicler, Hernando del Pulgar, who was present in the Castilian camp thoughout. Established at Gibralfaro, and in the Alcazaba below, was the Granadan garrison of hardened Berber troops from North Africa. They were known to the Christian Castilians as *gomeres*, and had a reputation as fierce fighters. Some of them, including the leader El Zegri, had experienced defeat at Ronda and were determined to exact revenge. The Málagan forces were commanded by a man called Hamete Zeli, which may be the Spanish rendering of Ahmad al-Thagri: a man described as 'a doughty old warrior'. Also within the city walls were families of Muslim refugees who had fled from outlying towns, villages and farms which were now in Christian hands. Among them were also Jews who had converted to Christianity, but had then fled the Inquisition, which had established itself in Seville in 1480 and Córdoba in 1482, and threatened to accuse them of 'judaizing', or reverting to their old faith. As the Christian forces advanced on their city, one would think that things looked bleak for Málaga's citizens. However, the contemporary Christian writers record that the population remained confident that this threat would be snuffed out. They had faith in their massive fortifications and in the North African

IT STILL CONTROLLED SIZEABLE FORCES: AN IMPORTANT REGIONAL GARRISON LIKE THAT AT MÁLAGA WOULD HAVE NUMBERED SOME 10,000 MEN

garrison. They also expected supplies and perhaps reinforcements from Muslim states around the Mediterranean.

Hamete Zeli was certainly one who still felt confident. He abruptly informed Ferdinand's messenger, that he had not been entrusted with this great city in order to surrender it. According to two royal chroniclers, the Castilian envoys were badly treated, contrary to normal diplomatic practice. When they returned to his camp, the king summoned a council of commanders to discuss the next move; opinion was divided and a tense debate ensued. Some argued that since Vélez-Málaga had surrendered, and all the other significant places around Málaga had also been captured, a land and sea blockade would be sufficient to bring about the city's surrender, without the need for a violent siege. Others disagreed. Since the king had now positioned his camp for a siege, they claimed, a surrender would be induced more quickly if he ordered it to be carried out. They were backed by others who feared that without a siege, even with the blockade in place, Muslim reinforcements (of men and supplies) might get into the city through the port, significantly lengthening the war. Ferdinand listened to his advisers and weighed his options, then made up his mind: he issued orders for his camp to be positioned for a siege, and for his land and maritime forces to move into place for action.

Even after their recent success, the Christian commanders were under no illusion about the challenge that faced them. Pulgar stresses the respect among Ferdinand's armies for the formidable strength of the Alcazaba, for the city walls and for the fortified naval base upon which Málaga's great importance rested. The walls were made harder still to penetrate when the Muslim commander Hamete Zeli responded to the arrival of the Christian land and naval forces by ordering the burning of houses close to the city walls – ensuring that any attackers would be exposed and vulnerable to counter-attack. Most significantly of all, however, it was the great castle of Gibralfaro high above the city which daunted the attacking forces. The castle was recognized by Ferdinand and his

commanders as vital to their prospects in taking the city as a whole: only by seizing this great bastion could victory be theirs. And yet it seemed, Pulgar remarks, simply 'untakeable'. What followed – beginning with the attempted capture of Gibralfaro Castle – was both the bloodiest and the most crucial military action of the entire Granada war.

Facing Gibralfaro, at the back and top of the town, was another hill of equal height which Pulgar estimated was about the length of two crossbow shots from the castle itself. It was steep, rocky terrain – difficult for fighting – but a significant strategic location which the Christians were keen to occupy. It was here that the first action took place, when the Muslim defenders burst forth to engage the Christian troops massing outside their city. An entire day was spent in hand-to-hand fighting whose savagery showed all too clearly how much was at stake, the bitter hatred and desire for revenge which existed, and the fervent religious dimension – fighting whose capacity to injure and kill had only been heightened by the development of genuinely portable handguns which were now used side by side with the more traditional technology of sword and crossbow:

*[The Muslim defenders] seemed to have a greater desire to kill
Christians than to preserve their own lives. The fighting went
on for six hours, and the sounds of the trumpets, the shooting,
the cries of warning, the clash of weapons, the noise of the
handguns and of the crossbows on both sides were so loud that
the hillsides re-echoed....So great was the desire for vengeance
that it predominated over the desire for gain, and no one made
any attempt to take prisoners, only to kill and maim.*

Ultimately Christian troops did manage to take the hill, having to
walk, exhausted, over the bodies of their dead comrades, while the
surviving Muslim troops withdrew behind the castle walls. Having
secured a key position, Ferdinand's small army of craftsmen set to
work to build, facing the defences, a temporary fort of timber and
earthworks surrounded by ditches, which they called an *estança*
(see The Carpenter box, p.82). It was one of the most remarkable
technical achievements of the entire war; opposite Gibralfaro this
makeshift structure rose up to the same height as the castle
battlements themselves. All around the besieged city they
constructed an extraordinary chain of similar fortifications –
equipped with artillery, with temporary field workshops to service
both men and guns, and garrisoned by no fewer than 2,500 cavalry
and 14,000 infantry, under the command of the Marquis of Cádiz.
At regular intervals along this encircling encampment were
stationed units of crossbowmen and hand-gunners to target any
defenders who dared raise their heads above the walls.

Once the Christians had dug themselves in, a static battle
began, in which both sides used their artillery to devastating effect.
The technology might have been developed in the Christian nations
of Europe, but in Spain Muslims had not been slow to learn from
an enemy that was always so close at hand. As Pulgar observed:

*The Moors were provided with many bombards and other
cannon, and had skilled gunners and all things necessary for*

defence and attack. When they saw that the King's tent was pitched there [opposite Gibralfaro], they shot at it with so many cannons and field-guns that it was necessary to move the tent to a safe position behind a hill.

If quality of artillery was not an issue, quantity certainly was. Within a short space of time the Christians were able to bring into action many more guns than were possessed by the Muslim defenders. Back in 1482, at the outbreak of the fighting in the emirate of Granada, Diego de Valera had written a memorandum to King Ferdinand in which he advocated an attack on Málaga as the most effective way of bringing the Nasrid emirate to a quick end. An historian and political commentator as well as a military man, Valera advocated the extensive use of artillery batteries, both on land and mounted on barges off the coast. Events in May and June 1487 around Gibralfaro and the city itself soon confirmed to

BELOW *The* Coracha's *north-western wall, which connects the Alcazaba to the Gibralfaro above. The walls appear stepped so that they remain at a broadly consistent height from the ground as they ascend the hill*

Ferdinand the wisdom of Valera's advice. The Castilian king was persuaded that it was reinforcements to his artillery in particular that were needed, and additional guns and expertise arrived in a steady stream from all over Spain and beyond. One such consignment of guns was brought all the way from Flanders, on a fleet commanded by Ladrón de Guevara.

Continuous bombardment from this massive Castilian arsenal, however, made enormous demands on the supplies both of ammunition and gunpowder. Though forged iron cannonballs were now available, gunners were forced at times to fall back on old-fashioned stone ammunition and King Ferdinand resorted to ordering that old, discarded stone cannonballs be collected and brought from Algeciras, to the west, where they had been left scattered after the capture of the town by Alfonso XI of Castile nearly a century and a half earlier. While cannonballs might also be returned by the defender's guns, powder was not and the continuous artillery fire put a serious strain on supplies. Desperate that the barrage not be broken, Ferdinand's agents scoured Europe for more powder.

In spite of the superiority of the Christian forces in terms of modern weaponry, within a few weeks a threat emerged against which fifteenth-century technology offered no response. In addition to the casualties caused by the daily fighting and the incessant barrage, sickness – that great terror of armies closely massed for a long siege – descended in the form of the bubonic plague. Word of its spread among neighbouring communities, allied to an ongoing shortage of food supplies, caused serious discontent among the Castilian forces which was not glossed over in Pulgar's account:

> *In some places near Málaga, there was plague, and the men of the army feared that it would reach the camp. When ships or the trains of pack animals were delayed, food shortages arose. And as so often happens in large armies, some men began to complain. Some bad Christians, men with light heads imbued*

FERDINAND AND ISABELLA

From completing the 'reconquest' of Moorish Spain and laying the basis for the modern Spanish State to sponsoring the first transatlantic voyage by Christopher Columbus, the achievements of King Ferdinand and Queen Isabella have secured them a pivotal position in European history.

Isabella inherited the throne of Castile from her half-brother in 1474, having to fight off numerous plots and rebellions by those who objected to her succession. Despite a series of betrothals organised by her half-brother — many of them rejected by Isabella herself — she married in secret the man to whom she had first become engaged: Ferdinand. He had inherited the throne of Aragon in 1479; they were second cousins, but secured a papal dispensation which waived the usual laws of consanguinity.

From the outset they agreed to rule in partnership. Isabella was monarch in her own right, Ferdinand King of Castile only by right of his wife. Their motto was '*Tanto monta, monta tanto*', which can be rendered as: 'as much as one is worth, so much is the other'. By their marriage a unified entity known as 'España' was forged for the first time since the eighth century — though provinces like Castile and Aragon long remained in reality distinct administrative entities.

Accorded the title 'Catholic Monarchs' by the Pope, both Ferdinand and Isabella were profoundly and dogmatically religious. Ferdinand helped to establish and promote the Inquisition in Spain. Together they not only completed the *reconquista* by defeating Granada but in the same year forced all Jews to convert or face expulsion.

They had five children together, the last of whom was Catherine of Aragon, first wife of King Henry VIII of England.

with corrupt desires, thought that for these reasons the King
would be forced to abandon his campaign. Incurring great
harm to their souls, and peril to their bodies, they crossed over
to the Moors [inside the city] and told them what was
happening, even exaggerating, and saying that the soldiers were
discontented, and every day some slipped away, without
permission from the King and his officers.

He did not exaggerate. Desertions from the besieging force were
an enormous boost to the morale of those holding out within
Gibralfaro and within the city below: with the defences holding
out, tales of hardship and disquiet among their enemies appeared
to justify the confidence of the Muslim garrison that they could
hold out successfully. As the stalemate continued, Queen Isabella
herself, then in Córdoba with her court, became worried that the
losses were becoming too great to bear, with still no reason to think
that the mighty bastion of Gibralfaro would fall.

Sensitive to her concerns, Ferdinand decided to adopt an
approach which served him well throughout the war, when morale
in the field was flagging: he summoned his wife and her female
entourage to the royal camp to provide welcome distraction for
his beleaguered troops. Fully aware of the dire conditions which
prevailed, on this occasion Isabella took some persuading before
she would agree, but eventually she and her retinue did set out for
Málaga during June. Their arrival served a dual purpose. Not only
did it raise morale among the besiegers, but it also made it clear to
the defenders that, whatever they might have been told by Christian
deserters, the Castilian armies had no intention of going away.

If it averted a serious mutiny among the besieging forces,
however, the experienced and sharp-eyed men in the royal camp
were well aware that Hamete Zeli and his men were unlikely to
be overawed by a display of pomp and chivalry. They knew all
too well that the Muslims remained in control of the port, which
forced the Christians to land their men and materials on the

ABOVE *The view down to the Alcazaba and city of Málaga from the Gibralfaro, which guards the high ground*

adjacent beaches. They knew too, from hard experience over the preceding weeks, that even when their large guns did manage to make breaches in the massive walls, defenders were well-practised at responding. The Muslim garrison used up-to-date techniques of hand-gun and light artillery cross-fire to cause serious casualties among any force that tried to penetrate the breach, and were thus able to prevent Christian troops from making incursions. Although there is no surviving Muslim account of events, it is clear, even from the Christian sources, that in spite of several weeks of siege, morale in the city remained high. Pulgar was full of admiration:

> *Although they had no food supplies inside, and could hope for none from outside [because of the blockade], although they saw their companions fall dead and wounded in the fighting, it was worthy of note how bold this barbarous [sic] people was in battle, how obedient to their commanders, how hard-working as they repaired the fortifications, how astute in the ruses of war, how constant in the pursuit of their objectives.*

As the weeks of the hot Andalusian summer went by, and Gibralfaro and the city of Málaga continued to hold out against the encircling Christians, there were further debates on tactics and strategy between Ferdinand and his commanders. Some urged that they should risk all in a full, frontal assault on the defences, from Gibralfaro on the heights down to the seashore, so as to avoid a siege that might drag on into the winter. Respect for the castle's defences, however, and for the prowess and commitment of its garrison, made Ferdinand reluctant to adopt this approach. Instead it was decided that mining and sapping would be used, with the aim of bringing down enough of the walls to force a surrender.

A notable feature of the entire Granada war was the ability displayed by the King and Queen, as well as the nobility and other institutions, such as city and town councils and the military religious orders, including Santiago, Calatrava and Alcántara, to mobilize

FIREARMS

Early cannon which exploited the explosive power of gunpowder were heavy and cumbersome. They were a threat in static siege situations, where they might be used by besiegers to attack and to try to break down weaker fortifications, and by defenders to damage or destroy siege weapons and camps. But they were of no value in fast-moving open warfare or as an addition to the weaponry of individual troops.

Already by the late fourteenth century, experiments had been made with smaller hand-held cannon. One Arab treatise of the time describes a weapon which seems to have been a hand firearm attached to a long stick. By the late fifteenth-century, light, hand-held firearms were increasingly available, and were used to devastating effect. Contemporary sources for Isabella and Ferdinand's Granada campaigns frequently refer to these weapons, generally calling them *espingardas*.

Such lighter guns – the ancestors of arquebuses and muskets – allowed attackers to target defenders in person. If big guns could not pierce fortress walls and other outward defences, the small ones could drive defenders from the battlements, thus opening the way for besieging infantry.

It was about this time that 'matchlock' devices emerged which avoided the need for a soldier to push a lit match down the muzzle of his gun while simultaneously attempting to aim it. A pulled lever, precursor to the trigger, dropped a match held clamped into the flashpan.

So effective were these weapons against personnel that the former chronicler of the Christian monarchs in Spain, Alfonso de Palencia, who saw them in action in the Granada war, thought them instruments for making war on the human race itself. Armies, including those of Palencia's king and queen, Ferdinand and Isabella, deployed them ever more extensively.

immense resources of men and material. The attempted mining of the walls of Gibralfaro and Málaga was a case in point. Experts were brought from the far north of Spain and set to work. The Muslims, however, quickly took counter-measures and succeeded in preventing the attackers from undermining the city's defences. As the chronicler Pulgar vividly describes, participants on both sides were confronted with the nightmare scenario of fighting at once on three levels: in the air, on the ground, and now under the ground as well.

SUICIDE ATTACKS

For the armies of Ferdinand and Isabella, as for many besieging forces, there were threats from the rear as well as from the city under attack. Word reached them from their Muslim ally in Granada, Boabdil, that his uncle, Al-Zagal, had dispatched a column to relieve the siege of Málaga. They were, the Christian leaders were told, suicide fighters, determined either to liberate the city threatened by infidel forces, or to die in the attempt, for which they would be richly rewarded in paradise. But Boabdil proved a loyal vassal to Ferdinand and Isabella, his new master and mistress. He ordered that Al-Zagal's column be intercepted by his own troops, in an action which led to many deaths and the flight of the survivors to Guadix. The Spanish monarchs were understandably grateful to Boabdil for this, and showered yet more gifts and honours upon him. Yet this added threat posed by the mounting religious antagonism between the opposing sides did not disappear. An even more spectacular threat was about to arrive in the royal camp outside Málaga.

In spite of the setbacks he had suffered, Boabdil's uncle Al-Zagal remained determined to do all he could to prevent the Christians conquering the rest of the emirate. In the territory still under his control, a charismatic Muslim leader volunteered to make another attempt to relieve the beleaguered port of Málaga. He was Ibrahim al-Jarbi, apparently from Jerba in Tunisia, but then living near Guadix. He came up with the idea not just of another relief expedition but also with a plot to assassinate Ferdinand and Isabella themselves. As Pulgar put it:

> *This Moor proclaimed that he was a holy man, and that God [Allah] had revealed to him, through an angel, what was going to happen. In this way he knew that the Moors were going to be saved, and Málaga would be victorious against the Christians [who] were besieging it.*

Al-Zagal was clearly willing to support this attempt to do God's work. Ibrahim managed to enlist about four hundred men, some of whom were North African Berbers and the rest native Granadans. It was made clear to all that, as in Al-Zagal's earlier abortive expedition, they were to kill as many Christians as possible. This was before they either freed their fellow Muslims in Málaga, or else died in the attempt and went directly to paradise. Travelling mostly at night across open country they managed to surprise the Christian forces in one of the *estanças*, on the seashore to the east of the city. They attacked at dawn, and while about half of them were killed in the fighting, the rest managed to rush the Christian lines, some swimming round the fort and others clambering over the defences, which they could do because they far outnumbered the garrison on duty at the time.

Unfortunately, there is no surviving Muslim account of what followed, but according to Christian writers, Ibrahim al-Jarbi, known as Abraén in the Christian chronicles, took no part in the attack and made no attempt to get into the *estança*. Instead, he remained at some distance, in a hollow, dressed in the robe of a sheikh or imam, and with his arms raised, apparently in prayer. Some troops who were clearing the battlefield spotted him, and took him to their commander, the Marquis of Cádiz, Rodrigo Ponce de León. During his interrogation, Ibrahim told the Marquis that he had received a divine revelation. Don Rodrigo was sceptical, but nonetheless asked for more details, which the Muslim refused to provide, saying that he could only reveal what he had been told to the king and queen in person.

His supposed religious status was evidently respected, and he was taken to the royal tent, amazingly with his dagger still in his belt. The rumour that he was a holy man quickly spread around the camp, and people crowded to gaze at him. When he arrived, though, Ferdinand was taking a siesta, to sleep off a large lunch, and the Queen ordered that he should not be disturbed. Ibrahim was sent to wait in another tent nearby, occupied by some of Isabella's ladies, and it was there that problems arose. It seems that the supposed holy man had no Spanish, nor any knowledge of who

THEY WERE SUICIDE FIGHTERS, DETERMINED EITHER TO LIBERATE THE CITY OR TO DIE IN THE ATTEMPT

ABOVE *This coin was minted with New World gold. The heraldic symbols of the monarchs' principal dominions are shown (right)*

he was with. The immediate entourage of the Catholic ruler, and particularly the ladies, were elaborately dressed, while the attendant men, no doubt taking a break from the fighting, were probably also wearing their rich, courtly attire. In any case, anxious to achieve his mission quickly, and still in possession of his weapon, Ibrahim attacked a couple whom he thought to be the king and queen. In fact, they were a Portuguese nobleman of royal blood: Alvaro de Portugal, son of the Duke of Braganza, and his wife Felipa. He gave Alvaro a serious head-wound, almost enough to kill him, then lunged at Felipa, though he missed her. At that moment, a Castilian treasury official, Ruy López de Toledo, rushed in and grappled the assailant to the ground. What followed would affect the outcome of the siege itself, but also future relations between Christians and Muslims, inside Spain and out.

The noise of the misdirected assassination attempt attracted a frenzied crowd. Ibrahim was seized, and instead of being arrested for trial, was cut to pieces on the spot. Then someone (the Christian sources do not record his identity) suggested catapulting the dismembered remains over the city wall. In response, the Muslims of Málaga carefully collected up the pieces, sewed them together to make a recognizable human form, washed and perfumed the corpse, and gave it a full Islamic funeral. Pulgar conveys the religious fervour and the anti-Christian fury of the occasion, and records that things then deteriorated further. The Málagans decided to respond in kind to this atrocity which infringed conventions of war in Europe, even in the case of a siege, where indiscriminate military action was conventionally permitted. A prominent Christian prisoner was seized and executed. Placed in a seated position on an ass, his corpse was then dispatched towards the Christian lines, in grim parody of Jesus' entry to Jerusalem on Palm Sunday.

STARVATION AND SURRENDER

After this, the action at Gibralfaro and Málaga took an even more brutal turn. Conditions among the besieged garrison and population had begun to decline alarmingly owing to the lack of food. The starving scavenged in desperation for anything that might keep them alive but deaths due to deprivation multiplied, sapping the will to resist of even the hardiest of the defenders. A rare and anonymous Arabic source, the *Nubdhat al-'Asr* ('Fragments of the time'), states that when food supplies ran out inside the defences:

> *They had to eat whatever was edible: horses, asses, donkeys, dogs, hides, the leaves from the trees, and when even these things ran out, the pangs of hunger were indeed terrible. Many of the finest of those who had sustained the siege died, and at that point many gave up and sought peace.*

All this is fully, and quite sympathetically, confirmed by the Christian chronicler, Pulgar. The initial Málagan reaction to the terms first offered by Isabella and Ferdinand, before Hamete Zeli and his Berbers insisted on rejection and resistance, had been to accept them, in the hope that, as in all previous cases, Muslim life would be able to go on under Christian rule. Now, though, after the expenditure of so much blood and treasure, and in the new conditions of bitter religious hatred which had developed between the two sides, it would be much harder to secure peace terms, rather than unconditional surrender. Two leading citizens of

ABOVE *Watchtowers, such as this one near Málaga, were built by the Granadans as beacons so that news of attack could be communicated across vast distances*

Málaga, Ali Durdush and Amar Benamar, led the peace party, with spiritual support from an Islamic scholar, Ibrahim ben Harith. Once again, though, Hamete Zeli and his North Africans insisted on resistance, if necessary to the death.

It was clearly a decision with which some Málagans, lacking the aggressive fervour of the Berber garrison, were unhappy. As the violent stalemate continued, the deprivation and suffering in Málaga worsened. The Christians, meanwhile, received supplies from the rest of Spain, from other parts of Europe and even from Muslim North Africa. Finally, Ali Durdush and Amar Benamar plucked up the courage to cross the lines, offering to become subjects of Isabella and Ferdinand. Perhaps unsurprisingly, given the strength and duration of the resistance, they were told that normal terms involving religious and social rights were no longer available. Now they were faced with a grim choice: death or captivity. When this harsh ultimatum was reported back to Málaga, the citizens, no doubt encouraged by Hamete Zeli, declared that far from surrendering they would hang all the Christian prisoners from the battlements, and burn the entire city if necessary to ensure it would never be Christian. The Spanish rulers responded in kind, announcing that if a single Christian prisoner was harmed every Malagan would be killed in retaliation. In the end, Ferdinand and Isabella relented sufficiently to allow at least such peacemakers as Ali Durdush to survive, but it was in a climate of bitter hatred that the citizens surrendered the city, the garrison gave up the Alcazaba and Gibralfaro, and Spanish forces finally entered Málaga, in July 1487. What they found within the walls was shocking confirmation of the suffering the city had endured. The stench was so bad, and disease so rife, that the king and queen did not enter until the following month; not until 18 August 1487 were their royal standards raised above the Alcazaba and the castle of Gibralfaro.

Some six hundred Christian captives were found in the city by the Castilian army, and according to another chronicler of the war, Andrés Bernáldez, they were 'so weak and yellow with their great hunger that they wanted to die, all of them with the chains and fetters on their feet, and their very long hair and beards'. Soon, the fetters would be removed from them and placed on the bulk of the Muslim population, all of whom became captives of the king and queen. Royal officials were ordered to register every prisoner. About 6,000 of them were reserved to Isabella and Ferdinand, while 3,000 were distributed among the knights and nobles who had taken part in the siege, along with any property they owned. A Christian government was set up, and the Muslim population was expelled from its dwellings and corralled. They were treated as goods and chattels, a third of them being kept to form part of an exchange of prisoners with rulers in North Africa, a third were granted as slaves to those who had fought on the Christian side in the campaign, and a third were sold to defray some of the Crown's expenses in the siege. A hundred of the Berber troops were sent as a gift to the Pope, fifty young Muslim women went to the Queen of Naples, as well as thirty to the Queen of Portugal, and there were other gifts of captives as well. Most of the Muslims had forfeited all rights by conquest, but Ali Durdush did duly receive his safe-conduct, and the small Jewish community in the city, which had endured the privations of the siege along with the Muslim majority, were allowed to be ransomed by Jews elsewhere in Spain.

The surrender document specified that every single Muslim was to be ransomed, 'male and female, old and young, grown up or [infants] at the breast', as well as their Muslim slaves. They had to pay for their freedom, and the release of their property, gold, silver, pearls or silk, to the value of thirty gold doubloons per head. To ensure that full payment would be made, without any false claims of poverty, all their property was to be auctioned, with the proceeds going to the Crown. If the resulting amount was insufficient to pay at least two-thirds of

A CHRISTIAN GOVERNMENT WAS SET UP, AND THE MUSLIM POPULATION WAS EXPELLED FROM ITS DWELLINGS AND CORRALLED

their individual ransom, they were to find and pay the remainder within sixty days. The final third was to be paid, half by the end of April 1488 and half by the end of October in that year. If any Málagan Muslim left the city before his or her ransom had been fully paid, a hostage had to be left in the hands of royal agents in Seville, Córdoba, Jerez de la Frontera or Écija. None of these Muslims would ever live in Granada again.

Though Málaga had been identified as the crucial target in bringing about the end of Muslim rule in Spain, their bloody and hard-fought success at Málaga did not bring Ferdinand and Isabella immediate victory in the war. The fact that it lasted another four-and-a-half years was due in part to the skill and determination of the remaining defenders, under the command of Al-Zagal, and partly to human and economic exhaustion on the Christian side. Though Christians had the advantage, the two sides were still relatively well-matched in morale and equipment. Later steps in the campaign involved a return to negotiation as a means of resolving the conflict, in spite of Christian confidence that they would prevail in the long term.

Finally, at the beginning of January 1492, Granada surrendered after Boabdil – now the ruler in place of Al-Zagal – negotiated terms which included safe conduct, and a compromise in which he would offer to kiss the hands of the Spanish monarchs before they gracefully declined. The entire emirate became the 'kingdom' of Granada, under the jurisdiction of the Crown of Castile. Since the city of Granada itself did not resist a lengthy and violent siege, as Málaga had done, Boabdil and his government were able to negotiate terms. These appeared to guarantee Muslims religious freedom and the continuation of their traditional social and economic customs under Christian rule. In reality, however, the situation remained unstable in much of the former Nasrid emirate,

NOW THEY WERE FACED WITH A GRIM CHOICE: DEATH OR CAPTIVITY

with a large proportion of the Muslim elite departing to live in exile. The remaining population came under increasing pressure from Christian settlement and the introduction of the personnel and institutions of the Catholic Church.

THE LEGACY OF GIBRALFARO

Gibralfaro Castle, and its 1487 siege, were important in military history. They witnessed what seems to have been the first major artillery battle in modern European warfare. The siege as a whole played a major part in the deterioration in Christian-Muslim relations, both political and social, which continued into the sixteenth century. The back of Muslim resistance in the emirate of Granada was broken by the surrender of Málaga, and this collapse brought to a head other simmering tensions between those religious communities throughout Spain which had lived together, relatively

BELOW *Plate armour and cannon such as these would have been a common sight in Málaga during the summer of 1487*

peacefully, for several centuries. The distribution around Spain of Málagan captives increased tensions between established Muslim communities in Spanish towns and the Christian majority. Stories from the Christian captives who were released by the victorious troops at Málaga did nothing to soothe feelings. Isabella and Ferdinand exacerbated the mutual hostility between Christian and Muslim by having some of the Christian captives' chains attached to the outside wall of the royal Franciscan church of San Juan de los Reyes (St John of the Kings) in Toledo, the ancient Visigothic capital. There they still remain, though in a very different Spain.

In addition, there was another historical irony which arose from the siege of Gibralfaro and Málaga. Although the Jews living in the city at the time apparently played no part in the fighting, and suffered all the misery and deprivation of being besieged, after 1487 they found themselves under a darkening cloud. Spain's Jewish communities, whose history went back at least to the time of Jesus, had lived under both Muslim and Christian rule, with varying degrees of success and security. Since the late fourteenth century, they had been under increasing pressure to convert to Christianity, and many had done so. Now, as Ferdinand and Isabella approached what they saw as their triumph, in ending Muslim rule on the Iberian peninsula, the remaining Spanish Jews were told in 1492 either to convert or leave the country. Thus the fall of Granada, as well as being the logical outcome of the siege of Málaga, was accompanied by the expulsion of hundreds of Jews, who fled either to Muslim North Africa and Ottoman Turkish territory or, ironically, to the papal city of Rome.

Later still in that year, word of the achievements of another man who was present at Boabdil's final surrender of Granada began to spread through Spain and Europe beyond. 'This present year on the 2nd January', he wrote to the king and queen, 'I saw the royal banners of Your Highnesses planted by force of arms on the towers of the Alhambra'. This man was a Genoese explorer in the employment of Ferdinand and Isabella called Christopher

GIBRALFARO CASTLE

PREVIOUS PAGE *The view south-west over the port of Málaga from the castle fortifications. In 1487 the seascape was filled with the sails of the blockading Christian fleet*

RIGHT *The chains of the Christian prisoners who were released from Málaga when it capitulated in 1487 still hang today from the Monasterio de San Juan de Los Reyes in Toledo*

Columbus. He had struck land, far away across the Atlantic, that he took to be the eastern edge of Asia. Over the coming decades the growing fervour of the Spanish reconquest would be projected outwards into what, it transpired, was a new and unconverted continent, as Spaniards savagely subdued indigenous American empires in the Christian cause. The heightened religious fervor and crusading zeal which accompanied the blood-letting at Gibralfaro and in the city of Málaga in the summer of 1487 – preceding, as it did, the final ousting of Muslim rule from Spain and the expulsion of the Jews – turned out to be the precursor to developments whose impact would be felt across the globe.

The great castle of Gibralfaro, meanwhile, was reduced to a bit part. While inland castles fell into ruin, wholly redundant now the reconquest was complete, coastal fortifications did continue to play a role. The threat from Muslim states of North Africa, centred mainly on Algiers, Oran, Tunis and Tripoli, remained. During the sixteenth century the Ottoman Turks made a major effort to dominate the western Mediterranean – though pushed back by the Battle of Lepanto, off the Gulf of Corinth, in 1571. While these were threats to the Spanish coasts, rather than potential land invasions, licensed piracy undertaken by Turks and their North African allies remained a major threat until the nineteeth century. As a result, defences such as those of Málaga were maintained and garrisoned on the orders of successive Habsburg and Bourbon kings – though later conflicts like the War of Spanish Succession, the Peninsular War or the Spanish Civil War made no use of outmoded castles, and the Alcazaba and Gibralfaro would never again be subjected to the sort of military assault they suffered in 1487.

THE HEIGHTENED RELIGIOUS FERVOR AND CRUSADING ZEAL TURNED OUT TO BE THE PRECURSOR OF DEVELOPMENTS WHOSE IMPACT WOULD BE FELT ACROSS THE GLOBE

CONTRIBUTOR BIOGRAPHIES

DR JOHN GOODALL
(Dover Castle chapter)

John Goodall is a leading castellologist whose comprehensive, award-winning work, *The English Castle: 1066–1650*, is likely to remain essential reading for scholars and enthusiasts of castles for many years to come. He was formerly a Senior Properties Historian at English Heritage, authoring many guides to significant historical sites during this time. In addition to his academic pursuits, including an important study relating to the siege of Dover Castle in 1216, John has contributed to various television series over the years and is currently the Architectural Editor for *Country Life* magazine.

Select publications:
The English Castle: 1066–1650 (Yale University Press, 2011)
Portchester Castle (English Heritage, 2003)
'Dover and the Great Siege of 1216' in *Chateau Gaillard XIX: Actes du Colloque International de Graz, 1998* (Brepols Publishers, 2000)
Pevensey Castle (English Heritage, 1999)

PROFESSOR LINDY GRANT
(Château Gaillard chapter)

Lindy Grant specialises in the architecture, politics and religion of Medieval France within a European context during the eleventh to thirteenth centuries. She is currently writing a significant biography of Blanche of Castile, the wife of Prince Louis of France who captured much of south-east England during the invasion of 1216. Lindy is Professor of Medieval History at the University of Reading.

Select publications:
'Les repercussions de 1204 sur l'architecture et la sculpture normande' in *1204: La Normandie entre Plantagenets et Capetiens* (Brepols Publishers, 2007)
Architecture and Society in Normandy, 1120–1270 (Yale University Press, 2005)
'Aspects of the Architectural Patronage of the Family of the Counts of Anjou in the Twelfth Century' in *Anjou: Medieval Art, Architecture and Archaeology* (British Archaeological Association Conference Transactions XXVI, 2003)
Abbot Suger of Saint-Denis: Church and State in Early Twelfth-century France (Longman, 1998)

DR BENJAMIN MICHAUDEL
(Krak des Chevaliers chapter)

Benjamin Michaudel is an archaeologist with a particular interest in Islamic and Crusader military architecture in the Near East during the medieval period. Benjamin's work has taken him to Egypt and also to Syria, where he has led a number of castle surveys and excavations, including the important Knights Hospitaller stronghold of Margat (Marqab) in 2008. Benjamin has written and lectured extensively within his field and was a consultant for the registration of Krak des Chevaliers as a UNESCO World Heritage Site. In 2011 he took up a Postdoctoral Fellowship in the Aga Khan Program for Islamic Architecture at the Massachusetts Institute of Technology.

Select publications:
'Le Crac des Chevaliers' in *Histoires et Images Médiévales,* special issue 20, pp. 50–7 (Editions Astrolabe, 2010)
'The Development of Islamic Military Architecture during the Ayyubid and Mamluk Reconquests of Frankish Syria' in Kennedy, H., ed., *Muslim Military Architecture in Greater Syria*, pp. 106–21 (Brill, 2005)
'Le Crac des Chevaliers, quintessence de l'architecture militaire mamelouke' in *Annales Islamologiques* 38, pp. 45–77 (2004)

Dr Jeremy Ashbee
(Conwy Castle chapter)

Formerly a curator at the Tower of London and now Head Historic Properties Curator at English Heritage, Jeremy Ashbee is one of the country's foremost experts in the management and conservation of historic buildings and ancient monuments, and a specialist in medieval castles. Jeremy's research has led him to write castle guides for both English Heritage and Cadw; his thorough survey of Conwy Castle for the latter remaining an invaluable resource for the study of North Welsh castles built by Edward I of England. He is currently writing a book about the early history of the town and castle at Conwy.

Select publications:
The Impact of the Edwardian Castles in Wales, contributor (Cadw, Castle Studies Group and University of Bangor, 2009)
Conwy Castle and Town Walls (Cadw, 2007)
Dunstanburgh Castle, contributor (English Heritage, 2007)
Goodrich Castle (English Heritage, 2005)

Dr Anthony Emery
(Malbork Castle chapter)

Dr Anthony Emery is a leading authority on medieval houses. *Greater Medieval Houses of England and Wales: 1300–1500*, his analysis of over 800 houses, has been published in three volumes. Anthony is currently completing a survey of the castles and palaces developed in England and France during the Hundred Years War, 1340 to 1460. A founder commissioner of English Heritage, he has combined a successful business career in technical publishing with one in architectural history.

Select publications:
'Malbork Castle – Poland' in *The Castle Studies Group Journal* No. 21 (2007–8)

Greater Medieval Houses of England and Wales: 1300–1500 (Cambridge University Press, three volumes)
Discovering Medieval Houses (Shire Publications, 2007)

Dr John Edwards
(Gibralfaro Castle chapter)

John Edwards is an expert in fifteenth- and sixteenth-century Spanish history. He has recently written a biography of Queen Mary I for Yale Press's English Monarchs series, which significantly makes unprecedented use of Spanish source material to broaden understanding of her reign beyond its English context. John is a key authority on the reigns of Ferdinand and Isabella, Spain's most famous monarchs, and has written widely on the subject. John is currently a Research Fellow in Spanish at the University of Oxford.

Select publications:
Mary I: England's Catholic Queen (Yale University Press, 2011)
Ferdinand and Isabella (Profiles in Power) (Longman, 2004)
The Spain of the Catholic Monarchs 1474–1520 (Blackwell, 2001)
The Spanish Inquisition (Tempus, 2000)

FURTHER READING

DOVER CASTLE

Bradbury, Jim, *The Medieval Siege* (Woodbridge: Boydell Press, 2008)

Carpenter, D. A., *The Minority of Henry III* (London: Methuen, 1990)

Goodall, John, *The English Castle* (New Haven and London: Yale University Press, 2011)

Mortimer, Richard, *Angevin England 1154–1258* (Oxford: Blackwell, 1994)

Wilson, Derek, *The Plantagenets: The Kings That Made Britain* (London: Quercus, 2011)

CHÂTEAU GAILLARD

Bradbury, Jim, *Philip Augustus: King of France 1180–1223* (London: Longman, 1998)

Gillingham, John, *The Angevin Empire* (2nd ed., London: Arnold, 2001)

Gillingham, John, *Richard I* (New Haven and London: Yale University Press, 1999)

Grant, Lindy, *Architecture and Society in Normandy: 1120–1270* (New Haven and London: Yale University Press, 2005)

Powicke, F. M., *The Loss of Normandy* (2nd ed., Manchester: Manchester University Press, 1961)

Turner, Ralph V., *King John: England's Evil King?* (2nd ed., Stroud: The History Press, 2009)

Warren, W. L., *King John* (3rd ed., New Haven and London: Yale University Press, 1997)

KRAK DES CHEVALIERS

Asbridge, Thomas, *The Crusades: The War for the Holy Land* (London: Simon & Schuster, 2010)

Kennedy, Hugh, *Crusader Castles* (Cambridge: Cambridge University Press, 1994)

Nicolle, David, *Crusader Castles in the Holy Land 1192–1302* (Oxford: Osprey, 2008)

CONWY CASTLE

Ashbee, Jeremy A., *Conwy Castle and Town Walls* (Cardiff: Cadw, 2007)

Davies, R. R., *The Age of Conquest: Wales 1063–1415* (2nd ed., Oxford: Oxford University Press, 2000)

Morris, Marc, *A Great and Terrible King: Edward I and the Forging of Britain* (London: Hutchinson, 2008)

Taylor, Arnold, *The Welsh Castles of Edward I* (London: Hambledon, 1986)

Williams, Diane M., and Kenyon, John R., (eds) *The Impact of the Edwardian Castles in Wales* (Oxford: Oxbow, 2010)

Other official guidebooks to Caernarfon, Harlech, Beaumaris and Rhuddlan Castles are published by Cadw Welsh Historical Monuments

MALBORK CASTLE

Christiansen, Eric, *The Northern Crusades* (London: Penguin, 1997)

Emery, Anthony, 'Malbork Castle – Poland' in *The Castle Studies Group Journal* 21 (2007–8), pp.138–56

Nicolle, David, *Teutonic Knight 1190–1561* (Oxford: Osprey, 2007)

Turnbull, Stephen, *Crusader Castles of the Teutonic Knights: the Red-Brick Castles of Prussia 1230–1466* (Oxford: Osprey, 2003)

Urban, William, *The Teutonic Knights: A Military History* (London: Greenhill, 2003)

GIBRALFARO CASTLE

Edwards, John, *Ferdinand and Isabella* (Harlow: Pearson Longman, 2004)

Edwards, John, *The Spain of the Catholic Monarchs, 1474–1520* (Oxford: Blackwell, 2000)

Hall, Bert S., *Weapons & Warfare in Renaissance Europe* (Baltimore and London: John Hopkins University Press, 1997)

Harvey, L. P., *Islamic Spain 1250 to 1500* (Chicago and London: University of Chicago Press, 1990)

PICTURE CREDITS

P. 8: Ira Block / Getty Images; p. 11: Ingmar Wesemann / Getty Images; p. 12: Dorling Kindersley / Getty Images; p. 13: Fitzwilliam Museum, University of Cambridge / The Bridgeman Art Library; p. 14: Musée de la Tapisserie, Bayeux, France / With special authorisation of the city of Bayeux / Giraudon / The Bridgeman Art Library; p. 17: photo © Neil Holmes / The Bridgeman Art Library; p. 18: © incamerastock / Alamy; p. 21: His Grace The Duke of Norfolk, Arundel Castle / The Bridgeman Art Library; p. 23: Robert Harding World Imagery / Getty Images; p. 34: Jose Fuste Raga / Getty Images; p. 37: © Picture Contact BV / Alamy; p. 41 (both), 43, 69, 71, 97, 102, 129, 135, 148, 149, 192, 205, 235, 263: © The British Library Board; p. 42: Courtesy of the National Library of Ireland, MS 700, f. 72r.; p. 44: The National Archives, Kew. E372/10; p. 64–5, 68, 80, 84: Courtesy of Master and Fellows of Corpus Christi College, Cambridge; p. 76 and p.159 (bottom): © Photo Pierpont Morgan Library / Art Resource / Scala, Florence (detail); p. 82, 111, 134 (right), 168, 206, 227, 254, 274: © Andrew Pinder; p. 93: Imperial War Museum 3509; p. 98: Photograph of Château Gaillard (image ref #218, figure 81, preceding leaf 61). Reproduced by kind permission of the Principal, Fellows and Scholars of Jesus College, Oxford; p. 110: Reproduced courtesy of The Board of Trinity College Dublin; p. 130, 144, 272–3, 312 (top): akg-images / Erich Lessing; p. 132: Photo © Musée de Vernon; p. 133, 249: akg-images; p. 159 (top): © Eddie Gerald / Alamy; p. 180–1: Photograph of Kalaat-el-Hosn/ Krak des Chevaliers (image ref. #149, unnumbered, preceding leaf 44). Reproduced by kind permission of the Principal, Fellows and Scholars of Jesus College, Oxford; p. 186, 190, 195, 197, 200–1, 202 (right), 204, 209, 213 (bottom), 214, 216 (left), 217 (top, bottom), 220, 221 (bottom), 223, 233, 237, 238 and 243: Photographs by Alexander Sharp; p. 187: © Angelo Hornak / Alamy; p. 247: Bildarchiv Foto Marburg / The Bridgeman Art Library; p. 279: Wojtek Radwanski / AFP / Getty Images; p. 290–1, 292, 299, , 302, 307, 308, 310, 314, 320 and 324–5: Photographs by Tom McCarthy; p. 296: Bildarchiv Steffens / The Bridgeman Art Library; p. 301: akg-images / Gilles Mermet p. 312 (bottom), 327: Index / The Bridgeman Art Library; p. 318: © The Trustees of the British Museum; p. 323: © Classic Vision / age footstock. All other photographs by Tom Clifford, except where otherwise indicated.

ACKNOWLEDGEMENTS

This book, like the television series it accompanies, is a collaborative project. Working with the whole team across a couple of continents was a huge pleasure. It was an exciting intellectual ferment, but the mistakes are all my own. Without the careful shepherding of James Evans and Alexander Sharp it would not exist. Both were scrupulous, but relentlessly positive and a joy to work with. Thanks must also go to Jane Aldous, Nathan Williams, Tom McCarthy and the Parallax team in Canada, including Nicole Tomlinson, Rebecca Snow and Hugh Hardy. Thanks also to Caroline Dawnay who has been, as always, unfailingly supportive, and Arabella Pike at HarperCollins for her excellent sense and advice, brilliantly assisted by Kerry Enzor and Kate Tolley.

The chapter contributors – John Goodall, Lindy Grant, Benjamin Michaudel, Jeremy Ashbee, Anthony Emery and John Edwards, all experts on the individual castles – have provided fine scholarship to the book.

My long-suffering wife Edwina put up with lengthy absences while she was pregnant and was never anything but unfailingly supportive. Finally, no one worked harder on this project than Tom Clifford. With enormous patience, and unfailing good humour, he overcame every obstacle and deserves all the credit.